Culture and Customs of Kenya

SUDAN

ETHIOPIA

Lodwar

*Lake
Turkana*

Moyale

Marsabit

UGANDA

Wajir

SOMALIA

Eldoret

Rift
Valley

Meru

Kisumu

Nakuru

+
Mount
Kenya

Garissa

*Lake
Victoria*

NAIROBI

Machakos

Lamu

TANZANIA

Malindi

*Indian
Ocean*

0	100	200 km
0	100	200 mi

Mombasa

Culture and Customs of Kenya

∾∾

NEAL SOBANIA

Culture and Customs of Africa
Toyin Falola, Series Editor

GREENWOOD PRESS
Westport, Connecticut • London

Library of Congress Cataloging-in-Publication Data

Sobania, N. W.
 Culture and customs of Kenya / Neal Sobania.
  p. cm.—(Culture and customs of Africa, ISSN 1530–8367)
 Includes bibliographical references and index.
 ISBN 0–313–31486–1 (alk. paper)
  1. Ethnology—Kenya. 2. Kenya—Social life and customs.
 I. Title. II. Series.

GN659.K4 .S63 2003
305.8′0096762—dc21   2002035219

British Library Cataloging in Publication Data is available.

Library of Congress Catalog Card Number: 2002035219
ISBN: 0–313–31486–1
ISSN: 1530–8367

First published in 2003

Greenwood Press, 88 Post Road West, Westport, CT 06881
An imprint of Greenwood Publishing Group, Inc.
www.greenwood.com

Printed in the United States of America

The paper used in this book complies with the
Permanent Paper Standard issued by the National
Information Standards Organization (Z39.48–1984).

10 9 8 7 6 5 4 3 2 1

For Liz

Contents

Series Foreword

AFRICA is a vast continent, the second largest, after Asia. It is four times the size of the United States, excluding Alaska. It is the cradle of human civilization. A diverse continent, Africa has more than fifty countries with a population of over 700 million people who speak over 1,000 languages. Ecological and cultural differences vary from one region to another. As an old continent, Africa is one of the richest in culture and customs, and its contributions to world civilization are impressive indeed.

Africans regard culture as essential to their lives and future development. Culture embodies their philosophy, worldview, behavior patterns, arts, and institutions. The books in this series intend to capture the comprehensiveness of African culture and customs, dwelling on such important aspects as religion, worldview, literature, media, art, housing, architecture, cuisine, traditional dress, gender, marriage, family, lifestyles, social customs, music, and dance.

The uses and definitions of "culture" vary, reflecting its prestigious association with civilization and social status, its restriction to attitude and behavior, its globalization, and the debates surrounding issues of tradition, modernity, and postmodernity. The participating authors have chosen a comprehensive meaning of culture while not ignoring the alternative uses of the term.

Each volume in the series focuses on a single country, and the format is uniform. The first chapter presents a historical overview, in addition to information on geography, economy, and politics. Each volume then proceeds to examine the various aspects of culture and customs. The series highlights the mechanisms for the transmission of tradition and culture across generations:

the significance of orality, traditions, kinship rites, and family property distribution; the rise of print culture; and the impact of educational institutions. The series also explores the intersections between local, regional, national, and global bases for identity and social relations. While the volumes are organized nationally, they pay attention to ethnicity and language groups and the links between Africa and the wider world.

The books in the series capture the elements of continuity and change in culture and customs. Custom is not represented as static or as a museum artifact, but as a dynamic phenomenon. Furthermore, the authors recognize the current challenges to traditional wisdom, which include gender relations; the negotiation of local identities in relation to the state; the significance of struggles for power at national and local levels and their impact on cultural traditions and community-based forms of authority; and the tensions between agrarian and industrial/manufacturing/oil-based economic modes of production.

Africa is a continent of great changes, instigated mainly by Africans but also through influences from other continents. The rise of youth culture, the penetration of the global media, and the challenges to generational stability are some of the components of modern changes explored in the series. The ways in which traditional (non-Western and nonimitative) African cultural forms continue to survive and thrive, that is, how they have taken advantage of the market system to enhance their influence and reproductions also receive attention.

Through the books in this series, readers can see their own cultures in a different perspective, understand the habits of Africans, and educate themselves about the customs and cultures of other countries and people. The hope is that the readers will come to respect the cultures of others and see them not as inferior or superior to theirs, but merely as different. Africa has always been important to Europe and the United States, essentially as a source of labor, raw materials, and markets. Blacks are in Europe and the Americas as part of the African diaspora, a migration that took place primarily due to the slave trade. Recent African migrants increasingly swell their number and visibility. It is important to understand the history of the diaspora and the newer migrants, as well as the roots of the culture and customs of the places from where they come. It is equally important to understand others in order to be able to interact successfully in a world that keeps shrinking. The accessible nature of the books in this series will contribute to this understanding and enhance the quality of human interaction in a new millennium.

Toyin Falola
Frances Higginbothom, Nalle Centennial Professor in History
The University of Texas at Austin

Preface

KENYA is what many people think of when they hear the word "Africa." For others, Kenya is Africa—the land of safaris, wild animals, and Maasai warriors. These are a few of the preconceptions we bring with us when we hear, see, or read about Africa, whether it is in the news, on the radio, or in the multiplex. The reality, however, is quite different. Kenya is a crossroads where peoples and cultures from Africa, the Middle East, and East Asia have been meeting for hundreds of years. As a result it is a land rich in cultural and ethnic diversity, with unique and dynamic cultural traditions. There is not one Kenya, but many Kenyas, and while this is a challenge to any writer, the much greater challenges are those faced by not just the Kenyan government but governments everywhere in Africa.

For a number of reasons it is not possible to detail the culture and customs of each ethnic group in Kenya. One is the diversity of peoples. To try and detail the heritage of each one is not merely impractical; it would not make for very interesting reading. Those who want more detailed information will find the bibliographic essay at the end of this book useful. What it is possible to do here is to give a sense of the country's rich diversity.

It is also impractical to attempt in this volume to describe the cultures and customs of each group because these cultures and customs are ever changing, as they have been from time immemorial. No group ever stays exactly the same. The herding communities of northern Kenya among whom I conducted research and with whom I worked in the 1970s are both different and the same at the beginning of the twenty-first century. Like the Maasai, who are also focused on the herding of cattle, these communities have for more than one hundred years been described as "disappearing." Yet today they continue to endure, and sometimes even thrive, following customs that are old and traditional as well as some that are new and modern and that, more often than not, exist side by side.

Even within societies, there are variations in cultural practice, a situation that leads some to seek what might be described as "real" or "authentic" cul-

Location of major ethnic groups today.

ture and customs. What one needs to understand, however, is that whatever practices or customs a community follows are all real and authentic, if only because they exist. When discussing marriage customs among the Kikuyu people, does one depict practices followed at the turn of the twentieth century, describe a service in the local Presbyterian church, or portray the independent Full Gospel Church? They are each real and authentic. What I have done in this work is describe the various customs that are still followed today and put them in the context of past practice, explaining why certain traditions have been retained. To take the issues of authenticity a little further, consider the Maasai. Among all Kenyan peoples, the Maasai stand out as probably the best known. As already mentioned, they are an example of a people who are regularly described as disappearing, but who are not. In addition, however, they are also regularly presented as the most authentic of pastoralists or herding people. What makes them the most authentic other than the fact the international media and popular culture regularly depict their young men wrapped in red cloths with a spear or wooden club in one hand, a shield in the other, and wearing distinctive long hair covered in red ochre? Do some Maasai young men dress this way? Yes, they still do, but they also wear jeans and T-shirts to herd cattle, and those who work in cities and towns wear suits or uniforms depending on the nature of their job. Which is the "real" Maasai?

The presentation of the Maasai and other ethnic groups as timeless and ahistorical is not unique to Kenya. It is perhaps more widely recognized here because this perspective is reinforced by Kenya's significant tourist industry, which regularly draws millions of people from all over the world to see its wildlife, experience the African bush, and view authentic African "tribes." Today, game parks, coast hotels, and other tourist venues actively provide carefully scripted cultural "opportunities" or shows that allow tourists to gaze at and photograph the "natives" all decked out in their "tribal" finery. These are but an extension of popular culture and what the media present globally as the "real" Africa. All of this raises the interesting issue of vocabulary and how one is to describe and illuminate the critically important role that culture plays in the life of a Kenyan today. Often, people claim that their knowledge of Africa is very limited, yet most come to the subject of Africa burdened with a set of words that speaks loudly and clearly as to what they think Africa, and by extension Kenya, is all about. These words include *natives, tribes, tribalism, primitive,* and *civilized.* My experience as a teacher has taught me that along with these words come images of *natives,* not people, who live in *huts,* not homes, wear *costumes,* not traditional or national dress, and have other derogatory implications.

The word *tribe* is generally used descriptively to mean a community of people who belong to the same ethnic group. However, it also carries with it a sense of those who are primitive and representative of groups from an earlier evolutionary stage of existence, specifically, not as fully developed and civilized as "me." In the same way, traditional is seen in contrast to modern and Western. Because the words *tribe* and *tribalism* carry strong negative connotations in contemporary Kenya, and refer to serious national problems associated with ethnic divisions, I will not use them here. Similarly, I will not use the word *primitive,* nor will I use *civilized* in juxtaposition to it. These are nineteenth- and early twentieth-century words found in government and missionary records and do not serve one well when trying to come to understand the customs and cultures of contemporary Kenya. I will, however, use the word *traditional,* which I use in its most positive sense and which may be understood to be nearly interchangeable with "rural" lifestyles and practices, where cultural traditions and practices tend to be better maintained, although even here they are and have been changing. The challenge in presenting such customs and cultural heritage is to make clear that they are everywhere present—in urban and rural areas—and not confined exclusively to those in rural areas. In addition, customs, traditions, and practices may exist from different periods and historical eras but appear side by side in cultural practice.

Acknowledgments

THE OPPORTUNITY to contribute to this series came from a suggestion by my friend and colleague Elliot Fratkin to Toyin Falola that I be invited to write about Kenya's cultures and customs. I am indebted to both for their confidence in me. As Elliot well knows, this is not the first time a suggestion from him proved significant to me.

I was fortunate to have lived and worked in Kenya off and on over a period of four years in the late 1970s and more recently, on various occasions, to visit. During these times many individuals shared their knowledge and love of Kenya with me, and to them I will forever be grateful. In Kenya these include my assistants, translators, and friends, Isaac Learamo, Larian Aliaro, and Isaac Assura. Among my colleagues and friends both in and out of Kenya include Anne Beaman, John and Sharon Berntsen, Dave Anderson, Ted Bernard, the late Neville Chittick, John Gallaty, Bernd Heine, Corinne Kratz, John Lamphear, John Lonsdale, Atieno Odhiambo, Roland Oliver, Suzanne Miers-Oliver, David Phillipson, H. Jurgen Schwartz, Sabina Schwartz, Tom Spear, Paul Spencer, Reiner Vossen, Richard Waller, Tom Wolf, and more recently, Fred Johnson and Ray Silverman. Among missionaries in Kenya who provided introductions and shared their knowledge and hospitality, I want to give special mention to Paul and Betty Teasdale and Bob and Morrie Swart. Among student friends at Hope College who during the past few years shared their Kenyas with me are Gerald Ajega, Jeff Kin, Muturi Muriuki, Leecox Omollo, Nixon Omollo, Acacia Schut, James Sitati, and Jacob Sitati. A special word of gratitude is reserved for and expressed to Godfrey and Margaret

Muriuki for their many years of support, beginning with my times as a graduate student doing research to our more recent visits on "the slopes."

While writing this book, I have also been given wonderful support by David Jensen and the library staff at the VanWylen Library at Hope College, the Andrew W. Mellon Foundation of New York, and the Global Partners organizations of the Associated Colleges of the Midwest, the Associated Colleges of the South, and the Great Lakes Colleges Association for my most recent opportunity to visit Kenya, and by Wendi Schnaufer, who as acquisitions editor of this series has been most patient and encouraging. To all of these people I say thank you. In addition I extend a special word of appreciation to Justin Sobania for technical support and to my staff in the International Education Office at Hope College: Amy Otis, Benardo Dargan, Habeeb Awad, and Kendra Williams for their friendship and understanding of my sometimes-strange allocation of time needed to finish this manuscript. To former Provost Jacob E. Nyenhuis and Associate Provost Alfredo M. Gonzales, I express my gratitude for their unwavering support and commitment to my scholarly pursuits.

My greatest debt, however, is to the numerous people of Kenya who have over the years allowed me to interview them, observe them, photograph them, and record them. For their patience in explaining their ways of life, leading me to my multiyear love affair with Kenya, and ultimately giving me the opportunity to tell some of their stories, I am forever indebted.

Neal W. Sobania
Hope College, Holland, Michigan

Chronology

4 million years B.C.E.	Australopithecine hominids already live in East Africa.
1.8 million years B.C.E.	Four different hominids live in the region.
before 1000 C.E.	Bantu-speaking agriculturists move into East Africa from the west.
ca. 1000–1300	The plains of East Africa are occupied by herding communities.
613	The prophet Muhammad begins the period of public preaching revealing Islam to the people of the Arabian Peninsula.
ca. 700–800	Early Swahili towns arise, and Islam begins to spread under the influence of Arabs who actively trade and live on the East African coast.
1331	Ibn Battuta, an Arab traveler, visits and records his travels on the Swahili coast.
1415	Chinese Admiral Zheng He delivers the gift of a giraffe from ambassadors from Malindi on the Swahili coast to the Ming dynasty emperor Yong'lo.
1498	Portuguese sea captain Vasco da Gama sails around the Cape of Good Hope to Mombasa and Malindi on the Swahili coast, from where Ahmed ibn Majid, an Arab pilot, guides him to India.

1593	Portuguese begin the construction of Fort Jesus at Mombasa, from where they rule the coast.
1696	Swahili and Omani Arabs begin a 33-month siege of Fort Jesus, eventually driving the Portuguese from Mombasa.
1844	Dr. Johann Krapf begins his missionary efforts in Kenya for the Church Missionary Society.
1884–1885	At the Berlin West Africa Conference, the European powers partition Africa into spheres of influence and set out to "effectively occupy" the lands they claimed before others did.
1888	The Imperial British East Africa Company is established with a royal charter to develop the territory through trade, signaling the start of a British presence in Kenya.
1895	On July 1 the British East African Protectorate is declared when the Imperial British East Africa Company becomes insolvent.
1898	The East African Protectorate is divided into Kenya and Uganda.
1899	After three years of construction, laying 500 kilometers (310 miles) of track, the Uganda Railway reaches Nairobi; it reaches Kisumu in 1901.
early 1900s	White settlers from Great Britain follow the railway and establish farms in the fertile highlands.
1907	The Legislative Council holds its first meeting, but without a single African member.
1915	The government introduces the *kipande,* a system of registering Africans to control their movement and where they work.
1920	Kenya becomes a Crown Colony administered by a British governor; the role of Africans is limited to lower-level administrative jobs.
1921	Harry Thuku organizes the Young Kikuyu Association to oppose the appropriation of tribal lands by white settlers, to seek permission for Africans to grow coffee, and to demand the publication of laws in Kikuyu. A year later he is arrested by the government and detained for the next nine years.
1923	The British government issues the Devonshire White Paper, declaring that apart from the White Highlands, there is to be no racial segregation and that "Primarily, Kenya is an African territory."
1925	The government introduces Local Native Councils for each ethnic group. Chaired by the local district commissioner, these effectively enforce a "divide-and-rule strategy" on the African population.

1929   Protestant missionaries initiate the "circumcision crisis," leading to charges that missionaries are trying to make Africans ashamed of their traditions.

1940   A number of ethnically based associations are proscribed and their leaders arrested.

1944   The Kenyan African Union (KAU) is formed to campaign for independence, and the first African is appointed to the Legislative Council.

1946   Jomo Kenyatta, who in 1964 becomes Kenya's first president, returns from England and a year later becomes head of the KAU.

1952   The Mau Mau rebellion, a violent campaign against white settlers, renews the African people's push for independence. The governor declares a state of emergency.

1953   Kenyatta is jailed after being charged with being the leader of Mau Mau; the KAU is banned.

1956   The Mau Mau emergency is put down after thousands are killed— the vast majority African.

1959   Kenyatta is released from jail but kept under house arrest.

1960   The state of emergency ends, and Britain announces plans to move the country toward majority African rule. The Kenya African National Union (KANU) is formed by Tom Mboya and Oginga Odinga.

1961   Kenyatta is freed from house arrest and takes over as president of KANU.

1963   In May KANU wins the general election, and on December 12 at midnight the Kenyan flag is raised, marking its independence from Britain with Kenyatta as prime minister.

1964   Kenyans vote to become a republic, and Jomo Kenyatta is elected the first president, Odinga its first vice president.

1966   Odinga, who is a Luo, leaves KANU over ideological issues and founds the rival Kenya People's Union (KPU). A year later Daniel arap Moi is appointed vice president.

1969   Tom Mboya, a former trade unionist and popular government minister, is assassinated, and ethnic unrest follows. KPU is banned, Odinga is arrested, and only KANU candidates contest the election.

1975   J. M. Kariuki, a popular member of parliament, is brutally murdered, in what is widely considered to have been a government assassination.

1977	Kenya institutes a total ban on hunting and in 1989 joins a worldwide ban on trade in dead or living endangered animals, which includes ivory.
1978	President Kenyatta dies in office and is succeeded by Vice President Moi, who is also elected president of KANU, the ruling party.
1979	Daniel arap Moi is elected president in his own right.
1982	The National Assembly officially declares Kenya a one-party state. In August the air force leads a coup attempt that is quickly suppressed.
1987	Opposition groups are suppressed, and international criticism mounts over political arrests and human rights abuses.
1990	The death under suspicious circumstances of Dr. Robert Ouko, the minister of foreign affairs, results in increased antigovernment agitation.
1991	The Forum for the Restoration of Democracy (FORD) is formed by opposition leaders, including Oginga Odinga, but it is outlawed by the government and its leaders are arrested. The international community condemns these actions and suspends aid. KANU holds a special conference and agrees to introduce a multiparty political system.
1992	FORD splits into two factions. In December with a divided opposition, Moi is reelected and KANU wins a solid majority.
1995	Richard Leakey launches a new opposition party, Safina, but is refused recognition until late 1997.
1997	The World Bank withholds $5 billion in credits. Moi is reelected president for another term in widely criticized elections.
1998	A bomb explodes at the U.S. embassy, killing more than 230 people and wounding hundreds more; the vast majority are Kenyans. Moi appoints Leakey to head a government campaign against corruption.
2001	Moi reshuffles his cabinet and appoints opposition party leader Raila Odinga, son of Oginga Odinga, as energy minister in Kenya's first coalition government.
2002	Mwai Kibaki is elected Kenya's third president, leading the opposition National Rainbow Coalition to an overwhelming victory over Moi's handpicked successor, Uhuru Kenyatta, a son of the late Jomo Kenyatta.

1

Introduction

KENYA IS A COUNTRY OF SUCH GREAT DIVERSITY—geographically, culturally, and linguistically—that a single book can only hint at this range. As anyone who has ever been in Nairobi, the country's capital city, can testify, it is nothing special to encounter people from every continent and discover they are all citizens of Kenya. With a population of nearly 30 million people drawn from at least forty-two different ethnic groups, a number of "Asian" communities, remnants of European "settlers," and more recent expatriate communities, the country is a mosaic of cultural and racial diversity. Its environments extend from the tropical Indian Ocean coast through temperate highlands and forests to the semiarid deserts of the north. Christianity and traditional beliefs dominate its religious practices, with a growing Muslim population that includes Asians whose community members also include many Hindus. Of today's population of 29.4 million people, 43.5 percent are less than fifteen years old, and 11 percent of children die before they reach the age of five. The median age is 17.9 years, and only 4.2 percent of the population are over 65 years of age. With one of the highest fertility rates in the world (4.7 percent) and a population growth of 2.3 percent between 1995 and 2000, Kenya's population has been projected to be over 34 million in the year 2025. Today, this figure is less certain because of the high mortality of young adults from HIV/AIDS. With more than 2 million people infected, both the fertility rate and the life expectancy of forty-nine years are in decline.[1] In addition, Kenya must contend with more than 200,000 refugees seeking asylum from Ethiopia, Eritrea, Somalia, Sudan, and as far afield as Rwanda, Burundi, and the Congo. On average the country's population density is fifty people per square mile, but this number is deceptive since the range is quite wide. The

Kenya's modern capital of Nairobi began life in 1899 as a repair and storage stop on the railway from the coast to Uganda. On the Kapiti plains where the Maasai once herded their cattle, the city's suburbs and slums continue to sprawl and spread as people, especially young people, migrate in search of jobs and a better life.

density in and around Nairobi, and in the region northeast of Lake Victoria, is in excess of 260 people per square mile. The per capita income is between $250 and $500.

Kenya is a country of rich and poor, of haves and have-nots. This dichotomy is captured in two words: *wabenzi* and *wananchi*. The *wabenzi* are, as the word's origin from "benz" suggests, those who drive a Mercedes-Benz or similar cars associated with the upper classes. Those who drive these cars as chauffeurs, who wash them, who fill them with gas, or are the security guards that protect them in the garages attached to large homes behind high walls and fences are the *wananchi*. These people, along with those who farm or herd or who labor in factories and shops, constitute the majority of Kenyans. In contrast to the upper-class *wabenzi*, the *wananchi* are the lower and middle working classes and the unemployed and underemployed. Never-theless, Kenya is a modern country with thousands of kilometers of paved highways and roads that reach deep into rural areas, as do electrical power, radio and telephone service, public health facilities, an extensive educational system of primary and secondary schools, and increasingly, colleges and universities.

THE LAND AND THE PEOPLE

For comparison purposes, Kenya (582,650 square kilometers, or 224,961 square miles) is about the size of France (nearly 550,000 square kilometers, or 212,000 square miles), similar in size in the United States to Lake Michigan and the surrounding midwestern states of Wisconsin, Illinois, Indiana, and Michigan. Yet of all this land, only 14 percent, or approximately 80,000 square kilometers, is well suited for agriculture or ranching. Although the land can be divided into a number of climatic zones, two major ones are predominant—the savanna and semiarid plains—with the central highlands rising from the savanna forming a third zone, and the coastline of some 536 kilometers making up a fourth. Kenya's famous game parks, which are the destination of so many tourist safaris and the major source of photographs in brochures and coffee-table books, are generally found in the savanna plains. The coast, another well-known tourist destination, is home to peoples who for centuries have traded with, influenced, and been influenced by the peoples of the Indian Ocean rim. Kenya's well-known tea and coffee grow in the central highlands. In each of these three zones, the coast, the central highland, and the savanna, there is heavy competition for one of Kenya's scarcest commodities, farmland. The bulk of the land, however, nearly 70 percent, is not suitable to agriculture and is instead home to pastoralists, who are also known as herders. These are people whose existence is based not on farming but on keeping herds of cattle or camels, along with large numbers of sheep and goats. Despite the amount of land they occupy, most of which is semiarid, these herders make up only about 1.5 million of Kenya's nearly 30 million people. The vast majority of the population, or nearly 20 million, are farmers. In the highlands they grow beans, maize (a type of corn), millet, sorghum, and wheat; in the lower areas, which are often better watered, farmers produce bananas, cassava, sweet potatoes, yams, and sugarcane. Another 9 million people, or nearly a third of the population, live in urban areas, of which 2 million are in Nairobi.

The coast is home to the urban-dwelling Swahili, whose name is familiar to many because their language, which has long been one of Africa's major trading languages, is so widely spoken inside and outside of Kenya. Moving toward the interior, the land begins to rise. Here the Mjikenda live as farmers, planting crops along the coastal plain and the drier savanna lands that adjoin it to the west. From here the land continues to rise, eventually flattening out into a plateau. Farming dominates the areas around Mount Kenya and Lake

Only 14 percent of Kenya's land is suitable for agriculture and ranching, with the most fertile land found in the Central Highlands; the rest of the country is semiarid scrub and desert.

Victoria. The ethnicity of these groups include the Kikuyu, Meru, and Embu in the central highlands, the Kamba on the plains to their east, and the Luo and Luhya in the southwest. In the semiarid plains that conjoin the savanna and the central highlands live the pastoralists. To the south and across the international boundary into Tanzania live another of Kenya's better-known peoples, the Maasai. In the north are the Maasai-related Samburu, the camel-herding Rendille, the Turkana, the Gabbra, and the Borana, many of whom also straddle Kenya's other border with Ethiopia, Sudan, and Uganda, while the Somali herd animals astride another border in the northeast. In the west are other herders who also farm. These agro-pastoralists include the Kipsigis, Nandi, and Pokot. Whether herders or farmers, all of Kenya's peoples must today contend with rising populations, the migration of people to the urban areas, the overuse and deteriorating quality of the land, privatization of land into small-holdings, and political and ethnic conflict.

The formation of much of the land on which these peoples live is directly related to the geology of the Great Rift Valley. Extending from Turkey to southern Africa across 70 degrees of latitude, the Great Rift Valley is so prominent that it is visible from outer space. It is also scarred by some of the deepest lakes on earth, including the many lakes of East Africa, from Lake Turkana in the north to Lake Malawi in the south. Volcanoes are also part of this landscape, with Ol Doinyo Lengai in the rift southeast of Nairobi having spewed ash as recently as 1967. The snow-capped peak of Mount Kenya is also a part of this diverse landscape and would also have included Kilimanjaro in the south, only that Queen Victoria responded, it is said, to the pleading of her German relative, Kaiser Wilhelm II, to have one of these snow-capped peaks in his territory. As a result, the boundary drawn between British East Africa and German East Africa was positioned so as to place Kilimanjaro in the latter, in what is today Tanzania.

Lake Victoria in the southwest, whose bounty is also shared with Tanzania and Uganda, is rather young in geological terms. Formed some 400,000 years ago as part of the fracturing and lifting that created the Great Rift Valley, it is no more than 270 feet deep, compared with other lakes of the Rift that are thousands of feet deep (such as Lake Tanganyika, which is the deepest at 4,823 feet). A number of these lakes, as well as the source of the Nile River, were the destination of many of the eccentric travelers who in the late 1880s acquired fame on what have come to be called the great African journeys of exploration. Many of their "discoveries" bear either the name of a sovereign who was sitting on the throne at the time of an expedition or, in some cases, the traveler's own name. Lakes Victoria after England's Queen Victoria and Lake Rudolf (now renamed Lake Turkana) after the crown prince of the Austro-Hungarian Empire are examples of the former; Thomson's Falls, named in 1883 after the twenty-five-year-old Scotsman, Joseph Thomson, who first traversed Maasai country, is an example of the latter. The accounts that these early travelers wrote of their journeys, along with political conditions of the times, later unleashed a diplomatic frenzy that led the European powers to claim these interior lands for their commercial potential. Similarly, Thomson's descriptions of the fertile and temperate plains excited the imagination of the Europeans who would soon immigrate to East Africa to settle on these areas to ranch or grow coffee.

THE ECONOMY

Kenya's economy is largely based on agriculture, which employs nearly 80 percent of the labor force; of the rest, 7 percent are employed in industry and 13 percent in the service area. Almost 65 percent of all export earnings are from agriculture, with tea, coffee, and horticultural products—including cut flowers, fruit, especially pineapples, and nuts such as cashews—the major sources. Coffee and tea both flourish in the highlands of Kenya, where they were introduced during the colonial period. In that period coffee was grown exclusively on the farms of white settlers, with Kenyans barred by law from growing it. In reality, of course, it was Kenyans growing it since they were the ones working on these farms. For a long time coffee, which requires great care and constant attention to be grown successfully and can be picked only twice a year, was the country's major export crop. And although it is still grown on a half-million farms, it has been surpassed by tea as the major export, which is the crop of choice on both small and large farms. Once established, the leaves of the tea plant can be picked year-round every fourteen days. Today, only China and India grow more.

Despite world recognition of Kenya's excellent coffee and the high price it commands on the world market, Kenya's production is not a great money-maker for those farmers who currently grow it. With a history extending back to the 1890s, and coffee in the United States alone an $18 billion industry, some are beginning to question how much longer Kenyan farmers will be able to afford to grow it. Most Kenyan farmers grow and sell as part of a coffee grower's cooperative. In exchange for a portion of the price the freshly picked coffee will realize at market, the cooperative supplies the grower with fertilizer and insecticides, processes the crop, and ships the dried coffee berries to the Kenya Coffee Board to be sold at auction. Whereas once this coffee sold for $10 per pound, the past few years have seen it realize only $1.50 per pound. A major reason for this was the collapse of an international agreement between coffee-consuming and coffee-producing nations, which had tended to guarantee a higher, more stable price, combined with entry into the market of cheaper, lower-quality coffee from countries in Asia, especially Vietnam. Mismanagement of the cooperatives and the Kenya Coffee Board is also a factor. After taxes and fees have been deducted, farmers today often receive a profit of as little as a penny a pound, if they receive anything at all. When roasted Kenyan AA arabica coffee beans cost upwards of $10 per pound in a local U.S. or European coffee shop, and a latte sells for $3, one gets a sense of the various markups that occur between the Kenyan farmer and the U.S. consumer and who is the beneficiary. As a result, the coffee industry in Kenya is collapsing. With little incentive to continue growing this labor-intensive crop, each year more coffee farmers are planting red beans and potatoes amid their coffee trees or are completely abandoning its production and cutting down their trees.[2]

Today, most Kenyans acknowledge that corruption is one of the major problems facing their country. When speaking about bribes, graft, and corruption, Kenyans often do so in euphemistic terms, making reference to a local politician as one who "eats" or "drinks tea." Also widely used is the expression "TKK." Generally, the Swahili for TKK would have been explained as *towa kitu kidogo,* or "take something small." More recently, however, TKK has come to mean *towa kila kitu,* which translates as "take everything." As a result, many of the parastatals, those companies owned wholly or in part by the government, are in serious financial difficulty. A few years ago, even with a guaranteed monopoly for milk and all milk products, Kenya Cooperative Creameries went bankrupt, and Kenya Power and Lighting Company has been on the edge of following the same path.

Most recently, cut flowers have emerged as an increasingly important income earner, surpassing coffee and tourism as Kenya's second most important source of foreign exchange. Kenya has become the European Union's principal source of flower imports. Most, nearly two-thirds, of Kenya's supply is shipped to the Netherlands by chartered aircraft and auctioned in their well-known flower markets to be re-exported around the world. Increasingly, flowers are being shipped directly to the United Kingdom and other countries, where they arrive cut and prepackaged in bouquets ready to be dropped into supermarket vases and sold. As with those who grow and sell coffee and tea, the 50,000 workers in the horticultural industry, including those who grow fruit and vegetables and whose wages support roughly another 500,000 people, earn low wages. Sometimes the pay is as little as 2,000 shillings, or U.S.$25 per month. Recently, a council of flower growers instituted a code of practice whereby members pay about $3 a day or $50 a month with transportation and health care allowances, placing these workers well above Kenya's gross domestic product (GDP) per person.

Beef and dairy cattle are also an important part of the economy, as is the fish industry. Eaten fresh near its source but also dried and sold throughout the country, some fish are also turned into animal feed for dairy cows. The other crops Kenyan farmers produce, including beans, maize (corn), wheat, millet, cassava root, rice, and yams, have until recently sustained the country's self-sufficiency in food production. Increasingly, however, the demands of an urbanized population for products such as bread have had to be balanced with the higher value that the country can obtain from exporting its wheat as compared, for example, with corn. There is less export demand for corn, which thus earns less on the world market. For Kenyans this has meant shifts in food consumption patterns.

The other principal income earner is tourism, which has proven very lucrative for Kenya. Tourism employs tens of thousands of people directly in service occupations and indirectly in the production of crafts and other goods purchased and consumed by the tourists. The major attraction is going on safari to view wild animals in the country's many national parks. Game parks, however, are not without controversy. In the parks on the plains, the grasses are reserved exclusively for the herds of gazelles, antelope, zebras, and other animals. Yet in the dry season, the herders who occupy the plains surrounding the parks will often not have enough grass for their cattle and will cut the park fences to find grazing for their animals. In those areas near forests, there is also conflict between the people and animals, as people cultivate right to the edge of the forest and frequently burn and encroach into the forest itself. Forests such as those that surround Mount Kenya and are home to herds of elephants are essentially islands surrounded by densely settled farmland. The traditional fencing the farmers built was not enough to stop hungry elephants, who can severely damage and sometimes totally destroy a nearly-ready-to-harvest field in just a few minutes. Today, the Kenya Wildlife Services, working with local farmers, is erecting solar-powered electric fences that work to keep elephants out, leaving open the paths along which elephants regularly travel from one area to another.

One of the oldest components of Kenya's economy is hunting. Although hunting in Kenya has been illegal since 1977, it nevertheless represents another aspect of today's economy—the underground one. Poachers, who no longer use bows and arrows or old hunting rifles, but AK-47 and G3 assault rifles, hunt elephants for their ivory tusks and rhinoceroses for their horns. People clear-cut sections of the forests not only to create new plots of land for farming but also to burn the trees to make and sell charcoal, the cooking fuel used by so many of Kenya's rural farmers. People also brew traditional beer to sell. Once, when land was plentiful, all of these aspects of life were a reasonable part of the local adaptation to a particular environment. Animals were hunted because nearly every part of them could be used either for food, clothing, and shoes or for adornment. Similarly, trees in forests were felled and land cleared, but not to a point that their destruction caused erosion and mud slides or that they could not in time regenerate. Beer was brewed for community celebrations and rituals, and on occasion people got drunk, but not as an end in itself or to forget the pressures of daily life. Today, however, land is at a premium and its ownership highly contentious. People are desperate to eke out a living for themselves and their families, in a situation complicated by a birthrate that is among the highest in the world. And there is no government safety net to fall back on. As a result, the question of how to survive causes people to make decisions in which issues of environmental management, the destruction of natural resources and ecological niches, and the place of alcohol in a healthy diet rarely play a part.

TRADITIONAL FARMING AND HERDING PRACTICES

A typical farm, known as a *shamba,* is approximately 2.5 hectares (between 6 and 7 acres). On such a *shamba* the farmer and his family will keep perhaps three or four cows, will have a few sheep or goats, and will grow some maize, beans, greens such as kale or collard, cabbage, and potatoes. In some regions the staples will instead be sweet potatoes, yams, bananas, and tomatoes; in more tropical coastal areas it will include coconuts, oranges, and lemons. Intercropping is one of the most widely practiced methods of farming in Kenya and, for that matter, all across Africa. Instead of planting a field with single crop, these farmers plant their fields with several different crops. The advantage is that a variety of crops provide soil cover to reduce erosion while the taller crops reduce the sunlight that would otherwise encourage weeds. By growing different crops together, there also is less risk that an insect or disease will wipe out all the plants. In addition, at least some crops will normally survive a drought since different plants each require different amounts of water. Some of the land most prized by farmers is along the banks of rivers, from which ditches are dug to provide irrigation water. Even river beds that are often dry can prove productive; when they do contain water, often coming from rains much farther up the valley or in the mountains, the water that overflows the banks eventually recedes, creating a well-watered agricultural plot. When coupled with keeping some livestock that can include cows, goats, and sheep, all of which are milked, a productive pattern of subsistence can be more or less comfortably maintained.

Since independence, it has become more common for individuals to own the land on which they live and farm. In many cases the government, in land-distribution schemes," gave farmland to squatters who during the colonial period had lived and worked on the farms of white settlers. Traditionally, however, single individuals seldom owned the land on which they grew their crops. Instead, land was usually held jointly by an extended family, with different households, generally identified by a man as its head, farming plots identified as theirs and their family's. This method of holding land ensured that when the man died, the plot stayed in the extended family and would not pass out of their control. Pastoralists also held land jointly. By occupying large tracts of land that was shared by an entire ethnic group, herders could better provide pasture and water for their animals and better defend them. Having joint ownership was critical to a herder's ability to move his animals in response to their needs and the ever-changing conditions of want and plenty that characterized the land on which they lived.

For safety, herds were typically split up into smaller units or even mixed in with those of a relative or good friend (brands on the livestock allowed people to know which animals belonged to whom). In this way the different grazing needs of animals could be met and the land use could be maximized. Large animals such as cattle or camels, for example, could be taken farther away to areas where rain might have recently fallen and new grass grown. Similarly, young calves could be kept with their mothers near to the main settlement to provide the nutritious milk on which most pastoralists survived. The separation of their livestock into smaller units had the added advantage of not exposing the entire herd to the drought conditions that often plagued these semiarid areas or to a disease or to a raiding party that might capture and take the animals away.

Related to the concept of joint land ownership was a social structure that collectively provided for all the basic needs of a community's membership. Families, both nuclear and extended, clans, age groups, and other social groups within traditional society were guided by time-tested values and beliefs that ensured that the physical and psychological needs of everyone were met. These systems of overlapping responsibilities meant not only that all community members were responsible for producing goods and services that they and the community needed to survive, but also that community members would assist each other in times of difficulty and continue to have access to whatever resources the community had. Goods, whether food crops, livestock, or other locally made household objects, were exchanged or given and received as gifts.[3]

Prior to the imposition of colonial rule kinship ties, ethnic identity and the networks of exchange through which goods passed helped to determine how communities defined themselves. Often, various ethnic groups had more things in common than they had differences that separated them. For example, the well-known cattle-herding Maasai are closely related to the Samburu, with whom they share the same language. Similarly, the Samburu and the Rendille—although they speak languages from different language families (Nilotic and Eastern Cushitic, respectively) and the former herd cattle and the latter herd camels—have historically been closely linked through ties of marriage and economic exchange. Other herding societies have similar links to each other. So too do herders and agriculturists. Again using the Maasai as an example, the Maasai have always had extensive ties with the agricultural Kikuyu people who live in the highlands surrounding Mount Kenya. They traded, intermarried, recognized each other's ritual practices, and even shared a similar name for "God" (*Enkai* in Maasai and *Ngai* in Kikuyu). Yes, on occasion they fought over cattle and land. Fighting, however, was never the dominant mode of interaction, as the colonial authorities believed.[4] Sometimes, although not always, the boundaries that determined where people lived fell along geographical features, such as rivers, valley, and mountains. The permeability of social boundaries between ethnic groups led them to place less emphasis on geographic boundaries. More often than not, the nature of the land and whether it was better for the grazing of cattle or camels or growing certain crops dictated where they lived.

When the British arrived, however, they brought with them the notion that everyone belonged to a "tribe"—a culturally homogenous group following a common social system and speaking the same language. They further understood the dominant mode of interaction between tribes to be that of warfare, and therefore the only realistic colonial policy they could establish toward the local "natives" was one of keeping them separated. The boundaries they imposed were generally arbitrary and based on natural features of the land, not on ethnicity or patterns of exchange.[5] The British and Germans used a river, anthills, and even a series of large baobab trees to define the international boundary between Kenya and Tanzania. Over time, of course, rivers change course, anthills disappear, and baobab trees, even if they survive, can often no longer be identified as the precise ones used as markers in the treaty.[6] This boundary, like the ones between Kenya and Ethiopia and Kenya and Sudan in the north and between Kenya and Uganda in the east, divided ethnic groups and the land they relied on for farming or grazing. In terms of Kenya's history, such a division is a quite recent phenomenon.

HISTORY

Peopling Kenya: Archaeology, Prehistory, and Languages

Africa is the cradle of humankind; the region stretching from Ethiopia in the north to Tanzania in the south has been central to all the recent finds that confirm this. The archaeological remains spread across the East African savanna suggest that these earliest ancestors could be found here as many as 12 million years ago. Our more immediate ancestors dwelt here nearly 4 million years ago. With the most recent discovery (1999) of a near complete skull, partial jaw, and teeth, and the announcement (2001) that it was a new genus of the fossil hominid *(Kenyanthropus platyops)*, contemporary with that of *Australopithecus afarensis* ("Lucy" or Denknesh, "the beautiful one" as the Ethiopians call her), the history of human evolution became considerably more complex.[7]

Helping to unravel this history are the numerous archaeological sites in Kenya where hominids are found, and others where stone tools abound, as do butchery sites where animal bones show clearly where meat was cut from the carcass. On the edge of the Serengeti Plain at Laetoli, archaeologists have even found 3.5-million-year-old footprints preserved in what was once mud. Yet these are not ordinary footprints: the three sets suggest three different individuals who may well have been a man, a woman, and a teenage child—a family. The prints that are assumed by their size to have been left by a woman are deep enough to suggest she was carrying something. The fossil record is so rich and the evidence so extensive that scientists now believe that 1.8 million years ago, four different hominid species lived at the same time in this area. It was also around this time that these early hominids began to spread to other parts of the world; the remains of a related species dating from this time have been found in China and Indonesia (Java).[8]

Supporting evidence also comes from historical linguists, who examine words and structures that languages share to determine the relationships between them. From this they can draw conclusions about when languages separated and thus can form hypotheses about their origins. From this work they have concluded that all the world's thousands of languages can be grouped into about twenty language families. Four of the oldest of these (considered oldest because their structures suggest the fewest relationships to other languages) are found in Africa. Further, people in East Africa who have historically followed very different adaptations to the land—gathering-hunting-fishing, farming, and herding—dominate as speakers of languages from three of these four language families: the Khoisan, Niger-Congo, Afroasiatic, and Nilo-Saharan, respectively.

The Niger-Congo family includes speakers of Bantu languages, by far the largest single language family in Africa. Bantu speakers, moving across the middle of the continent from the rainforest in the west, appeared in East Africa during the early years of the first millennium C.E. With their arrival came the introduction of smelting and the use of iron tools to clear land for cultivation. In East Africa these Bantu-speaking groups absorbed speakers from the Khoisan language family and others from the Afroasiatic family, who spoke Eastern Cushitic languages and who were among the earliest peoples present in Kenya. Before the advent of the Iron Age in Eastern Africa, these early people existed by gathering, hunting, and fishing. Today, the

Elmolo at Lake Turkana, the Boni of the coast, and the Okiek (also sometimes called Ndorobo) of the highland forests are remnants of these Eastern Cushites. Other groups who followed similar subsistence patterns are recalled in the origin traditions of Bantu speakers such as the Kikuyu and Kamba as being among the peoples they assimilated into their expanding communities. Today, other Eastern Cushitic speakers, such as the Somali and Rendille, herd camels and cattle across the semiarid plains of Kenya's north and east.

Ancestors of the third major language family, Nilo-Saharan, arrived in Kenya from the north and northwest three or four thousand years ago. Initially, these migrants were cattle herders, as represented today by the Maasai, Samburu, and Turkana, but environmental changes and disease led others, including the Luo and Kalenjin peoples, to take up agriculture in combination with the keeping of livestock. Still others, like the gatherer-hunters, were absorbed into expanding Bantu-speaking communities. Today, the largest population group in Kenya, the Kikuyu, represent along with the Luhya and the Kamba the greatest number of speakers of Bantu languages. They make up 20 percent, 13 percent, and 11 percent of the country's population, respectively. The Nilotic-speaking Luo, numerically the second-largest elements in the population, make up, together with the Kalenjin peoples, 14 percent and 10 percent of the population. The rest of Kenya's people are found in communities that are much smaller in size.

Parallel to these linguistic foundations is a Kikuyu genesis story that relates the origin of the Kikuyu, the Maasai, and the Okiek (Ndorobo). According to the story, an old man near the end of his life gave each of his three sons a gift that he thought would provide for them in the future. To the first son he gave an arrow. With the arrow this son soon learned to hunt and became a Okiek. To the second son the old man gave a hoe. This founder of the Kikuyu learned to farm the land and grow crops. The third son, who received as his gift a stick, used it to herd cattle and founded the Maasai. Although these distinctions suggest cultural differences, they also suggest ecological ones, each distinguished by types of economic activity that allow communities to take advantage of naturally available resources.

Although the spread of people across East Africa is considerably more complicated than this, by the beginning of the nineteenth century not only was the heritage of the arrow, the hoe, and the stick clear, but the names generally used to identify each of today's ethnic communities were becoming recognizable. Across East Africa Okiek groups inhabited the forests. Cattle- and camel-herding pastoralists occupied the savannas and semiarid plains. And everywhere else, from the coast to the central highlands and beyond to the western region near Lakes Baringo and Victoria, was home to agriculturists. Only at the coast were there towns, and these were inhabited by the Swahili.

Early History

Stories about the discovery and exploration of Africa severely limit the ability of those in North America and Europe, often referred to as simply the West, to appreciate fully the long relationship that Africans have had with the rest of the world. Two examples from Kenya should help to dispel the notion of Africa as the "Dark Continent" without contacts until it was "opened up" by the West. In 1414 a large fleet of Chinese ships, both trading galleons (62) and smaller escort vessels (more than 100) sailed west from China. With thousands of people on board, they sailed under the command of Zheng He (sometimes spelled Cheng Ho), the most-celebrated admiral of the Ming dynasty, and crossed the Indian Ocean to the Persian Gulf and the coast of Africa. Unlike Columbus, who headed east into unknown waters in command of only three ships and ninety-some crew, the Chinese were traversing waterways they knew well to places with which they had long traded. Indeed, the Chinese were both the main producers and the main consumers of goods that were traded from the Mediterranean and the Middle East to Africa and Asia.

At a stop along the Indian coast at Bengal, Zheng He saw a giraffe brought to India as a gift from the Swahili city-state of Malindi, which was one of many prosperous trading centers on the East African coast. So taken was he with this strange-looking animal that Zheng He persuaded the Malindi ambassadors at the court of the king of Bengal to help him secure another to give to the Chinese emperor, Yong'le. The arrival of the giraffe in China so excited the imagination of the emperor and his court that Malindi and other city-states along the coast were invited to send ambassadors to the Ming court. They did so, bringing with them other exciting gifts including ostriches, zebras, elephant ivory, and rhinoceros horn and receiving gifts of spices and silk in return. Zheng He made other trips to the African coast, including one on which he returned some of these ambassadors to their home cities. The extent and length of Chinese involvement at the coast is clear from an early fourteenth-century Chinese map that shows the East African coast in remarkable detail, almost 200 years before the Portuguese "discovered" Africa.[9]

Even accounts of the well-known feats of the Portuguese, the first Europeans to sail along the African coast and then in 1498 across the Indian Ocean to India and Southeast Asia, usually ignore the critical role played by an African in their success. The credit for reaching India is attributed to Vasco da Gama, an experienced but ruthless Portuguese admiral, who was following in the wake of other Portuguese sailors such as Bartholomew Diaz, who first reached the Cape of Good Hope ten years earlier. When da Gama rounded the tip of southern Africa, he first landed at what is today Mozambique. Here he met the local sultan, who, while hospitable, also encouraged da Gama to continue northward along the coast, likely recognizing the disruptive influence da Gama's presence could have on this region. When da Gama finally arrived at Mombasa, on what is today the Kenyan coast, he recorded his positive impressions of this wealthy stone-built city with its excellent harbor and prosperous trade across the Indian Ocean. Farther up the coast at Malindi, another wealthy trading city, he resupplied his ships for the journey to India. Critically important to his journey but seldom mentioned was Ahmed ibn Majid, a pilot he took on board and who in fact was responsible for guiding da Gama and his ships successfully across the Indian Ocean to India. It was, after all, a journey the peoples of the African coast, the Arabian Peninsula, and India had long been making.

The emergence of the Swahili, both as a distinctive culture and a language, dates from the first millennium.[10] The archaeological remains found along the coast from Mogadishu in Somalia in the north to Kilwa in Mozambique to the south and on the islands that dot that coast are evidence of the thriving towns and urban centers that they built to engage in trade. The sharing of a common language, Kiswahili, and a common religion, Islam, which spread from the middle of the seventh century over the same ancient trade routes, helped provide the mutual trust that was so important in trading relationships. Muslims from around the Indian Ocean rim not only traded with the Swahili but also immigrated and became incorporated into what is today Swahili culture. The monsoon winds that dominate this region made the round-trip passage from the coast and back less difficult. From April to October the winds blow from the East African coast to the northeast and carried Swahili sailors to the Arabian Peninsula, the Persian Gulf, and India. Approximately six months later, from November to March, which allowed ample time both for the journey across and for replenishing the ship with trade goods, the winds reverse direction and blow to the southwest for the return voyage.

Generally, the family of a sultan or *diwan* and a council of elders drawn from the wealthy trading families independently ruled these urban, mercantile, and largely maritime Swahili towns. From readily available coral from the sea, they built houses, elite residences, mosques, and tombs, and from the available wood, which was often scarce in other parts of the Indian Ocean rim, they built the strong sailing ships, or dhows, that enabled them to trade. The Portuguese learned to exploit the rivalries between the independently ruled towns. Along

For 2,000 years *dhows* of various sizes have imported and exported trade goods around the Indian Ocean rim. Today, large cargo ships are replacing the *dhows*.

with raiding and pillaging, the Portuguese dominated much of the Indian Ocean trade from the sixteenth century until they were driven out in the eighteenth century by an alliance of Swahili families and Omani Arabs from the Persian Gulf. Locally, the sultan of Oman, also for purposes of enriching himself from trade, controlled a number of locations on the coast. He acquired control over the trade of some Swahili city-states through conquest, sometimes imprisoning and deporting to the Persian Gulf local Swahili leaders. However, because most of his income was derived from revenue from customs taxes, he generally continued to rule though local sultans and appointed governors. After 1840 the Omani leader, Sultan Seyyid Said, moved his capital to the island of Zanzibar. From here he ruled Oman and the East African coast and built a commercial center for the Indian Ocean trade. Everyone from the French, with whom he first traded slaves, to the British, Germans, and Americans signed treaties with him. Soon, however, the British became his principal ally as they proceeded to colonize India and control events on the Indian Ocean rim.

By the 1800s the cotton cloth from India, metalwork from the Middle East, and porcelain from China that the Swahili sought were obtained through trade in ivory, wood, and captured and enslaved Africans from the interior. Slaves were both sold and made to work on coastal plantations growing and harvesting cloves and grains such as millet and processing coconuts into palm oil. Later this thriving trade came to include guns, gunpowder, beads, and brass and copper wire. Although much of the trade focused on imports and exports at the coast, it was from the interior that the most valuable goods—ivory and slaves—originated. And the two went hand in hand as caravans returned to the coast with enslaved Africans carrying ivory tusks. Trading relationships were required with the peoples of the interior to obtain both since it was easier to purchase slaves and ivory than to capture and hunt them, especially given the large quantities of each that were being demanded by the international market. The Kamba people, who lived between the coast and the central highlands, were attracted to this trade and soon became recognized for their ability to organize and lead large caravans.

Among their destinations in the interior were three major agricultural communities: the Kikuyu in the central highlands, the Luhya (or Abaluyia) around Mount Elgon, and the Luo along the shores of Lake Victoria. Throughout the region during the nineteenth century, ethnic groups such as these dominated, and their numbers were expanding through natural population growth and by absorbing neighboring peoples, which was related directly to the need to control larger expanses of land, whether for farming or for herding animals. It is difficult to generalize about the region because each community's situation and circumstances were unique. For example, the Kikuyu continued to expand and consolidate their control over additional agricultural land on the ridges of Mount Kenya, where their dispersed communities lived and grew beans, millet, and sweet potatoes. Sometimes such expansion occurred peacefully; on other occasions they fought with their neighbors. Yet both types of interactions were part of the broader set of relationships they had with their neighbors. The Luo lived in territorial units each under the leadership of a chief, or *ruoth*, who had often acquired this status as a man of authority in community matters and war. As was the case with many such ethnic communities in East Africa, the Luo came to their dominant position through the broad range of economic, social, and military relationships with neighboring peoples. At different times these established relationships could lead to individuals or families, and even entire groups of people, being peacefully absorbed as a result of disease or famine.[11] On still other occasions people were absorbed and incorporated into communities through wars of conquest that arose from the need to consolidate control over land and control cattle, through which they stored wealth and acquired brides. This was especially the case in the nineteenth century among the Luo and the Luhya.

Agricultural communities were not the only people in the interior. In fact, the Maasai, who with their herds of cattle prevented the Kamba- and Swahili-led caravans from simply traveling at will wherever they wanted, occupied the largest stretches of this grassland savanna. The Maasai remained the "Lords of East Africa" until the end of the nineteenth century, when the "triple disasters" struck. First, bovine pleuro-pneumonia and then rinderpest decimated their cattle herds; then smallpox hit the human population. These new diseases, which were introduced to East Africa over the trade routes that continued to push deeper into the interior, left the Maasai and other pastoralist communities in disarray and fighting with each other to survive. In this considerably weakened state, these once-great warrior-herders could not mount a serious resistance to the British and Germans who arrived bent on conquest.

British Rule

Initially, Britain's interest in East Africa focused on Uganda and Zanzibar, not Kenya. Its interest in Uganda centered on the strategic need to control the Nile River, which was vital to its interests in Egypt and the Suez Canal. To the late nineteenth-century way of thinking, the only way to ensure control of Egypt was to control the Nile, whose presumed source was in Uganda. To secure its strategic position in Egypt, Britain had earlier taken control of the island of Cyprus in the Mediterranean and Egypt's southern neighbor, the Sudan. Britain's other focus, Zanzibar, and by extension the East African coast, was where the Royal Navy patrolled to put an end to Arab slaving. Suez interests also played a role because ship traffic to and from the Canal passed through the Indian Ocean before entering the Red Sea. Kenya linked these two interests since the most direct route from the Indian Ocean to Uganda passed through it.

Britain's first formal colonial involvement in Kenya came in 1885 with the granting of a royal charter to the Imperial British East Africa Company (IBEAC). This move was designed to signal to the other European powers Britain's claim to this region as part of its "sphere of influence," which was how the Europeans staked their claims to the various parts of the continent in what has come to be known as the Scramble for Africa. It was also less expensive for Britain to have the private funds of the IBEAC carry out what was essentially the country's foreign policy. When in 1895 it became clear the IBEAC was going to go bankrupt and had not done much to control this area effectively, Britain took over what then became known as the East Africa Protectorate.

To ensure its claims on Uganda and to ease communication with this interior region, as well as making certain any lingering elements of the slave trade were ended, Britain built the Uganda Railway, from the coastal city of Mombasa to Lake Victoria. Completed in 1901, it included, about halfway along, a railhead of workshops and offices that started life as little more than a tented camp only three years earlier. From these foundations the camp grew over the next three decades to become the city of Nairobi, which is today the country's modern capital. Having built the railway and taken over Kenya as a protectorate, Britain soon had to face the real issue of how to pay for both. The "hut tax" that was imposed on each African home was helpful, but it was not nearly enough. Sir Charles Elliot, who arrived as governor in 1901, pushed for Europeans to settle and colonize the rich central highlands. Elliot responded to the arguments that the British had no legal or moral right to take land from the Africans in a fashion characteristic of the time:

There seems to be something exaggerated in all this talk about "their own country" and "their immemorable rights." No doubt on platforms and in reports we declare we have no intention of depriving the natives of their lands, but this has never prevented us from taking whatever land we want for Government purposes, or from settling Europeans on land not actually occupied by natives. . . . I think it as well that . . . we should face the undoubted issue, namely: that white mates black in a very few moves. . . . The sooner [the native] disappears and is unknown, except in books of anthropology, the better.[12]

No consideration of these early colonial years in Kenya is complete without a discussion of the origins and contributions of the Asian community in Kenya. Although this community has largely remained culturally exclusive, it has nevertheless had a significant impact on the country. The earliest members of this community in Kenya are usually depicted as having arrived as indentured laborers from India, another part of the British Empire in which the transformation of a territory into a British colony had long been underway. Indeed, the need for cheap labor grew following first Britain's outlawing of the slave trade in 1807, and then its abolition in 1833, although this move certainly did not end the capture and use of slaves in East Africa. It did, however, result in an increased demand for workers to grow cotton, tobacco, sugar, and other cash crops that would generate income for Arab traders and Indian financiers at the coast and ultimately help pay for the colonial administration. Workers from India who signed three-year voluntary contracts to work sixteen hours a day, seven days a week, met this demand. The contract system declined after 1917 but was not legally abolished until 1926. Nevertheless, it was not the first time such laborers were imported from India. This dates to the Portuguese, who in the sixteenth century brought what may have been as many as 40,000 workers from western India to construct Fort Jesus on the coast at Mombasa.

Another major demand for labor, which in turn increased the Asian population, occurred in the mid-1890s when the colonial government began to expand into the interior. Itinerant traders followed this expansion, as did other skilled workers whose services were needed first to construct the administrative posts and then to make the life of the white officers stationed there as much like "home" as was possible. Clerks and bookkeepers followed the masons and carpenters, but the real impetus for the growth of this population was the construction of the Uganda Railway that began at the coast in 1895. First came those who leveled and smoothed the surface and raised the embankments. Those who built the bridges, bored the tunnels, and laid the track followed them. Then came the train drivers, firemen, stationmasters, and telegraphers who made the trains run. Well into the twentieth century, sons followed fathers and grandfathers onto the trains. The work was hard and dangerous, and of the nearly 32,000 workers who came from India, almost 2,500 died during the construction, an average of almost four workers dead for every mile of track laid. Yet in the six years between 1896 and 1901, 582 miles (931 kilometers) of track were laid from the coast to the shores of Lake Victoria in Uganda.[13]

Traversing rivers and culverts, then down one side of the Rift Valley and up the other, the railway opened the central highlands to colonial domination like no other enterprise. White settlers, whose presence was seen as the best means for making the railway pay, were attracted to the cheap land and labor through advertising. One famous poster noted, "The Highlands of British East Africa as a Winter Home for Aristocrats has become a fashion. Sportsmen in search of big game make it a hobby. Students of natural history revel in the Field of Nature's own making."[14]

Settlers were indeed attracted to the well-watered lands, especially to the north of Nairobi in the central highlands that surrounded Mount Kenya. Here, settlers from Britain, elsewhere in Europe, and South Africa established farms, never asking who might actually use the land. Some tracts were acquired by conquest through "pacification campaigns" in which troops using rifles and machine guns "hammered" the local peoples, driving them from their lands. Killed and driven off in large numbers, Africans—the Meru, Embu, Nandi, and others—abandoned their farms. With no one living and farming it, the colonial administration declared such land to be Crown land and sold it for a pittance to the white settlers. From a base of only thirteen settlers in 1901, Europeans soon controlled 220,000 acres of land in 1904 and nearly 5 million acres by 1915. The significance of this is even clearer when one remembers that so little of Kenya's actual land is suitable for farming or intensive ranching. But who actually farmed this land?

In Swahili, these white settlers were called *mzungu*. In common usage, *mzungu* has come to mean a "white person," although it may more accurately mean "a wanderer" or someone who does not stay in one place. Attached to this is the connotation of a person "with mysterious ways." Because *mzungu* also includes African Americans, everyday usage seems to have less to do with "white" or "European" and more a way to label an outsider in the general sense of being foreign. The definition of such words is in fact often arbitrary and known to change over time. For example, the Maasai call white people *il-ashumpa*, which means an individual with light skin, including an Arab or others from the coast. To make the distinction, the Maasai would sometimes add the suffix *ibor;* so the word for light-skinned people who are white becomes *il-shumpa oo-ibor.* Whatever the term, the impact of these initial foreigners from Britain was significant.

By the 1920s nearly half the men of Kenya's two largest ethnic groups, the Kikuyu and Luo, worked as laborers on these white-owned farms. How did the settlers get these Africans to work for them? Through taxation. To get Africans to work on farms, often on the very land the Africans had once farmed themselves, the colonial authorities devised and instituted a scheme of taxation. Each man paid a poll or head tax, or a hut tax, on every house a member of his family occupied. In those families where a man had more than one wife, each wife had her own house and so did the man, and so he paid a tax on each one. Required to be paid in cash, these taxes forced men who came from societies that did not use money to enter the workforce and earn cash wages from the Europeans now occupying their land.

Herding peoples were also required to pay these taxes, yet because they often moved their homes, they could more easily avoid the tax collectors. One early response to this tax dodge was to send soldiers to capture the young boys from herding groups and send them off to school. The hope was that with some education, these boys could be turned into effective tax collectors among their own people. Sending young boys off to school had the added benefit of removing them from their communities before they became warriors and raided their neighbors' herds for cattle, another aspect of traditional society that the colonial government was determined to end. Especially after World War I, the responsibility for tax collection fell increasingly to district commissioners. These British administrators arrived in East Africa devoted to the paternalistic ideal that colonial rule was a blessing for which all Africans should be grateful. Without the peace and development schemes the colonial authorities brought with them, they believed, Africans were destined to live in fear and uncertainty with poverty and disease.

Among the benefits introduced to Kenya by the British colonizers were hospitals and veterinary services, but little remembered is that these were paid for both directly and indirectly by African labor. Because taxes simply did not generate enough income to pay for the administration that the British insisted the Africans required, two additional aspects of colonial policy were introduced. For work projects such as roads and railways, forced labor was imposed. Refusal to work brought swift punishment. Such labor was but one form of the gener-

alized oppression faced by Africans across the continent. In many ways even
more oppressive was the introduction of cash crops. Cash crops are those such
as tea, coffee, cocoa, groundnuts (peanuts), sisal, cotton, and rubber that were
grown on large European-owned farms and that are not typically eaten, consumed, or even used by the local population. The purpose of growing these cash
crops, which were usually exported to and processed in Britain and Europe, was
to generate income for white farmers and industries in Europe—one of the
principle means by which Europe extracted wealth from the continent.

Growing these crops was particularly devastating to African farmers. On
the one hand Africans were forced to provide the labor to grow them, and if
they grew them on their own farms, they had to sell them to European firms
at artificially low prices. On the other hand, because they were forced to grow
cash crops, they did so at the expense of growing the food they and their families needed to eat, such as sorghum, millet, beans, and later, maize and corn.
Food crops in once-prosperous regions were in short supply, and famine
became more common. People simply did not have time to tend to their own
fields. In addition, the land on which they were still allowed to grow their
own food was usually the poorest. Eventually, the colonial system with its
seizure of land, insistence on forced or cheap labor, forced production of cash
crops, and continued treatment of Africans as inferior beings led to new
protests. In hindsight the demands being made by the Africans were actually
small. In large measure this was because those making the demands were
Africans educated in the schools of the colonized, where they began to think
like the British and merely wanted more rights within the colonial system of
which they were part.

The earliest source of Western education came from missions. Because the
colonial government found this to be an inexpensive means of providing education to the African population, they left it to the churches to provide. The
real educational interest of the missions was not to prepare workers to serve in
the colonial administration but to train Sunday school teachers and catechists
who could spread the word of God. Those Kenyans, however, who had access
to this education quickly realized that this was the means by which they could
gain access to jobs in the colonial administration and the commercial enterprises, and so they took advantage of what was offered.

Education was not widely available. Only those communities in which the
government built its administrative centers and the missions followed had
access to it. The route taken by the Mombasa-Uganda Railroad and the roads
that were built off to the interior were pivotal to determining the location of
these centers. And because the railway cut across the temperate plains below
the central highlands surrounding Mount Kenya, it was the peoples who lived
in these areas, especially the Maasai and Kikuyu, who ended up most directly
impacted by the early colonial enterprise. For the Maasai who herded their

animals on the plains, it meant being pushed south of the tracks, where they were largely peripheral to the government. Left to their own devices, they continued herding their livestock and following their cultural traditions. The Kikuyu, however, were hardly peripheral to events occurring in the central highlands. Displaced by white settlers who took over their land, the Kikuyu were critical to labor needs of these settler farms. And because the settlers were there, the government and missions that followed brought the Kikuyu education and job opportunities that later made them central to colonial development policy.

Similarly, Africans found their traditional patterns of government being "reformed" to fit colonial expectations. Principal to this was the assumption that each tribe had a "chief" and that all the colonial officials needed to do to bring about a transformation of these traditional societies was to identify that individual. With some ethnic groups this was indeed true, but in many societies the people practiced an egalitarian system of rule in which elders made decisions through consensus. Nevertheless, because the colonial authorities often insisted there had to be a chief, they found individuals willing to accept such a designation. Local chiefs were soon wielding power and authority in the name of the colonial authorities, and in time their place in villages came to be usual.

The March to Independence

Not everyone, especially individuals who had acquired an education and worked in Nairobi or the towns that were growing up around administrative centers, was so willing to accept being ruled by local chiefs. Their dissatisfaction included complaints that the chiefs gave work only to their own family members, relatives, and others who supported them as chief. Their grievances with government focused on land-tenure issues, hut and poll taxes, and the introduction of a registration system for all Africans. The *kipande* system, which required every African to carry an identity document, was designed to control the movement and labor of the African population much as passes were later used in South Africa.

Among the first Kenyans who acquired a mission education and then moved to Nairobi to seek employment was Harry Thuku. He worked on the European settler newspaper, becoming familiar with settler politics, and then became a telephone operator and clerk. In 1921, when attempts were made to cut the wages of Africans, he and other like-minded individuals decided it was time to organize themselves, with Thuku advocating civil disobedience to make their points. Soon Thuku was the leader of the militant Young Kikuyu Association, which subsequently broadened its membership and became the multi-ethnic, urban-based East African Association, whose followers included both Christians and Muslims. When in 1922 the colonial authorities arrested Thuku and deported him to the coast, rioting broke out in Nairobi. One of the leaders of this demonstration was Mary Nyanjiru, who challenged not just the British but also Kenyan men. She ridiculed the latter for the ineffectualness of their protest, telling them that if they were not going to demand Thuku's release, they should take off their trousers and let the women wear them. During this protest, she and many others were shot and killed by the authorities. This was not enough to divert local political activity, which continued to take root in many regions. Yet the real challenge was that there was no central authority among the Kikuyu or most of the other Kenyan ethnic groups through which they could present their position.

As a result, a number of ethnically based organizations took root in the mid-1920s. In the west there was the Kavirondo Taxpayer's Welfare Association, largely Luo and Luhya, and in the central highlands the Kikuyu Central Association (KCA). Among the early members of the KCA was Johnstone Kamau, another young man with a mission education working in Nairobi at this time. He later took the name Jomo Kenyatta. Some say that he became involved in local political activity inspired in part by Thuku. The KCA was a political association whose membership extended from Mount Kenya to Nairobi, and its slogan, "Pray and Work," demonstrated the important part the missions played in the early thinking of such groups. In 1925, to address the government's growing concern with these associations, and to satisfy the younger, educated Africans, the government introduced Local Native Councils (LNCs). Chaired by the district commissioner, their purpose was to advise the governor on local matters, as well as raise and distribute local revenue. Local elders and chiefs, whose own power was threatened by these nascent political associations, sought closer alliance with the colonial government and were some of the most avid supporters of the LNCs. Of course this policy suited the government well as it effectively enforced a "divide-and-rule" policy on the African population.

However, before government policy could move in this direction, there was another issue that had to be resolved. This was the desire of the European settler population to rule Kenya as "a white man's country," a claim they made on the basis that it would then enable them to be totally committed to building the country and its economy. As the settler population expanded, so too had the Asian community, and so too had the struggle between these two communities. Whether as railway worker, carpenter, smith, shopkeeper, general merchant, or newspaper founder, members of the Asian community held tenaciously to their customs and cultural traditions from India, including the establishment of their own schools, clinics, temples, and mosques. Funded by the Asian community, these and other social service organizations assisted community members in need. However, these developments were contrary to the vision that the colonial administrators and the white settlers held for the colony. Their vision was for a land that would reflect British patterns and cultural traditions, but more important, they wanted to control Kenya politically independent of the Foreign Office in London. In 1922 it seemed that this view of Kenya would actually become the official one.

The real issue, however, was the role of the Asian population. Because the Asians had come to dominate the commercial sector, the settlers wanted them excluded from having a voice in the making of government policy. This question was finally resolved with the issuing in 1923 of the Devonshire White Paper. In it, the Colonial Office reminded both immigrant populations that "Primarily, Kenya is an African territory" and that therefore the interests of the Africans were paramount. From the perspective of London, the small number of settlers, estimated in the early 1920s to be only around 9,000, could never realistically hope to rule the very large African population present in the country, and of course the Asian population was itself originally from a colony, British India. Even though independence would not come to Kenya for another forty years, this document was of major importance since the same year saw London give self-government to a small number of white settlers in Southern Rhodesia (today Zimbabwe).

By the 1930s the introduction of a cash economy by colonial rulers was a fact of life throughout Africa. Largely driven by the need to pay taxes, people displaced from their own farms went to work on settler farms or in the towns and cities that were growing up in the interior. Some people, however, managed to follow traditional patterns of subsistence in the "native reserves" that had come to demarcate those areas in which Africans could live as distinct from the white highlands, cities, and towns. Two events in 1929 had a major impact on the future. The European Protestant missionaries began a major campaign against female circumcision, considered by many ethnic groups to be an essential part of initiation into adulthood (see chapter 6, "Gender Roles, Marriage, and Family"), and Jomo Kenyatta made his first trip to England. The circumcision crisis not only gave vent to growing nationalist voices that charged the missionaries with making people ashamed of their African traditions, but it drove many African Christians away from European churches and into independent churches. Here, under African pastors, Christianity was more radical and political. Where religion had once been used by the government to control the African population and bring them to civilization, the church increasingly became the focus of protest and dissent.

The nationalists were also unhappy with the LNCs and wanted the government to allow Africans to be elected directly to the Kenya Legislative Council, which had a real policy-making function. In an attempt to change the situation, the KCA sent Kenyatta to England to make its case directly, but his repeated requests to the government were turned down. He went back to Britain in 1931 and as a student of anthropology wrote *Facing Mount Kenya*, a thesis on traditional Kikuyu cultural practices and in many ways a nationalist response to attempts to make Africans wholly European.[15] When Kenyatta returned from England in 1946, the leadership of the Kenya African Union (KAU) soon stepped aside so he could be elected its president. The KAU had emerged in 1944 as the principal African voice for independence following the government's banning of the KCA as a wartime measure.

Just as World War I had seen Kenyans who served in the Carrier Corps return from the fighting in Europe with a new understanding that Europeans were neither invincible nor as united as they had assumed, so too veterans of World War II came home, but this time trained in the use of arms as well. The postwar economy was in shatters, with unemployment among Africans high and the population pressure for land to farm unmet. When appeals for a greater say in policy formulation were rebuffed, Africans realized they were not going to achieve many rights by merely asking for them. As their impatience grew, so too did dissent, which finally burst forth in 1952 as the Mau Mau rebellion. A well-organized, largely Kikuyu fighting force, the Mau Mau guerilla army lived in the forests around Mount Kenya and targeted white farmers and Africans considered to be collaborators with the British. The government declared a state of emergency, arrested Kenyatta as the leader, and imprisoned him for nine years in the far north.

The greatest numbers of deaths that occurred during the rebellion, which lasted throughout most of the mid-1950s, were in fact suffered by the Mau Mau fighters, who lost more than 11,000, compared with 32 Europeans and 1,800 noncombatant Africans killed. The exact causal relationship between the Mau Mau rebellion and the eventual British granting of independence is still keenly debated. Nonetheless, the rebellion clearly generated fear and rumors of savagery across the country and eventually the British authorities began to make a series of concessions, including in 1957 the election of Africans to the Legislative Council and in 1959 the repeal of laws that prevented Africans from living in the White Highlands. When Ghana was granted independence in 1957, it was clear that the tide toward independence had irrevocably turned and that Kenya would soon regain the independence it had lost at the end of the nineteenth century. The state of emergency officially ended in 1960, at the same time as the delegates to a conference in London promised self-rule for Africans.[16]

Uhuru and the Kenyatta and Moi Years

Independence, or *uhuru*, came at midnight on December 12, 1963, as the Union Jack was lowered and the new red, green, and black national flag—with a shield and crossed spears in the middle—was raised. As leader of the

Jomo Kenyatta, Kenya's founding father, led the struggle for independence and was the country's first president. His over-life-size statue commands the entrance way to the twenty-nine-story Kenyatta International Conference Center.

majority party, the Kenya African National Union (KANU), Kenyatta, who was now 73 years old, became prime minister. The euphoria of independence soon gave way to recognition that the unrealistic expectations of the people could not be met. Soon it became clear that a growing African elite was reaping most of the benefits of independence while the rural peasants and urban workers were still marginalized. The "Million Acre Scheme," by which the government purchased land from the white settlers, subdivided it into small plots, and sold it to peasants to farm, was in response to this growing level of dissatisfaction. But even this could not satisfy all those who desired their own land. The new leaders faced the same problems that had plagued the British at the end of their colonial rule—unemployment and poverty. An economy based on the colonial model of cash crops and a hope of moving through the various stages of industrialization that occurred in the West was not an economic plan at all.

What became of paramount importance for these new leaders was the consolidation of their power. Kenyatta completed this in 1964, a year after *uhuru,* when members of two opposition parties joined KANU, giving the government the votes it needed to amend the constitution. Later that year Kenyatta became the president of what for all practical purposes was now a one-party state. One-party states receive bad press in the West, a view that is often justified. However, it also important to note that one-party states turn far more people out of office at election time than occurs in multiparty elections in the West, by a considerable margin. In a one-party state, multiple candidates run for the same position, but all from within a single party. In the first few years after independence, Kenyatta shrewdly shifted the control of power and authority from KANU to himself and the civil service. In this he was aided by the infighting that soon began among the other leaders of the struggle for independence.

When the focus of the nationalists had been exclusively on achieving independence, the leaders of this movement could ignore their differences. After *uhuru* the unity they had forged began to give way to factionalism. In parliament the opposition came to be identified with Oginga Odinga, a Luo from Nyanza in western Kenya. An integral part of the original movement for independence, he was the first vice president of Kenya. Soon, however, he was leading a faction that was particularly vocal about the need for the government to speed up the Africanization of jobs, the nationalization of business and industry, and a fairer distribution of the country's land and wealth. The government moved swiftly to push Odinga to the sidelines. In 1966, at a special meeting of KANU, he was forced from office, but not silenced. Odinga founded an opposition party, the Kenya People's Union (KPU), and continued to hold a seat in parliament. His disagreement with the policies of his old friend Kenyatta continued to grow. When the dissent of he and his followers caused an incident in 1969 that threatened the life of the president and resulted in the police shooting and killing eighteen people, Odinga and many of his followers were placed in preventative detention for eighteen months.

The year 1969 proved fateful for the leader of another opposition faction as well. Tom Mboya, who was the general secretary of KANU and the minister of economic planning, had been the strategist and fiery orator who led the crucial struggle of the trade unions in the run up to *uhuru*. Despite his position in the government, it was this background that soon caused him to part from certain government policies and led him to be caught up in the government's moves to curb the power and influence of the unions. Mboya, like Odinga, was also a Luo, but somewhat ironically, it was he who called the special KANU meeting that expelled Odinga from the party. Unlike Odinga, however, Mboya enjoyed a wide base of support that was not exclusively identified with any one ethnicity. His popularity was especially strong in Nairobi, and many thought him the likely successor to Kenyatta. When this popular leader was assassinated in 1969 on the street in Nairobi, many concluded it was because he had become too powerful.

In 1975 another opposition leader and self-styled man of the people was assassinated. As a member of parliament J. M. Kariuki emerged in the early 1970s as the principal critic of the government. Known widely simply as J. M., this populist faulted the government for its inability to forge a single nation from the country's many ethnic groups. His fiery rhetoric can be heard in his comments on nation building: "It takes more than a National Anthem however stirring, a National Coat of Arms however distinctive, a national Flag however appropriate, a national Flower however beautiful, to make a Nation." It can also be heard in his calls for social and economic justice when he talked about the people's rights to free medical service, education, and land: "A small but powerful group of greedy, self-seeking elite in the form of politicians, Civil Servants and businessmen, has steadily but surely monopolized the fruits of independence to the exclusion of the majority of people. We do not want a Kenya of ten millionaires and ten million beggars."[17] Although his grizzly death in the hills outside Nairobi did not silence all opposition to Kenyatta's government, it did cause widespread public fear and limited the dissent of its critics.

When President Kenyatta died in 1978, he was succeeded constitutionally by the vice president, Daniel arap Moi. As president, Moi set aside Kenyatta's calls for working together, or *harambee,* and put forth a philosophy of *nyayo* (footsteps). The footsteps that were to be followed were those of Kenyatta, which made good political sense for Moi, who came from a tiny ethnic group among the Kalenjin peoples. He had in fact been selected as vice president precisely for this reason; it would have been far too divisive and threatening to Kenyatta to have had a vice president from one of the more populous groups.

For the first few years of Moi's rule, government opposition was relatively quiet, and there were even signs that the rampant corruption that had characterized the last years of Kenyatta's rule was being held in check. Soon, however, these same forces began to resurface and cloud the government, and once again a critical opposition made its voice heard. Student strikes at the university may have been over calls for better food and living conditions, but at the heart of these demonstrations was opposition to any number of factors that had come to characterize Moi's rule—single-party rule, government corruption, economic misrule, and the list went on. The greatest threat came on August 1, 1982, when young officers of the air force led a bloody coup attempt, but this too was turned back. After that, Moi built a cult of personality for himself, and privatization "meant selling state-owned enterprises to his political cronies at very low prices, while antipoverty organizations were shut down and their leaders arrested for claiming that corruption permeated the uppermost ranks of the Kenyan state."[18]

By the election in December 2002, the economy had continued to decline and unemployment to rise. Corruption scandals were rampant, and donor nations had all but cut Kenya off from any further credit and refused to provide debt relief. The resulting situation led to a range of citizen responses, from those who simply dropped out to others who fueled domestic political violence. Among opposition politicians, though, it finally led to organizing common cause to defeat President Moi's handpicked successor, Uhuru Kenyatta, whose only real experience was being a son of the former president (Moi was required by the constitution to step down after twenty-four years in power). The opposition National Rainbow Coalition (Narc), led by the well-respected seventy-one-year-old economist Mwai Kibaki, won a resounding victory. In what Commonwealth election observers described as orderly, free, fair, peaceful, and transparent elections, 56.6 percent of voters casting ballots gave Narc 62.2 percent of the vote and 125 seats in the parliament to KANU's 31.3 percent of the vote and 64 seats. Following twenty-four years of Moi's rule, the challenge facing Kenya's third president is the extreme sense of optimism among the people: the expectation that he can immediately turn the economy around and bring an end to corruption overnight. If the challenge is unmet, social unrest will return.

"TRIBALISM" AND ETHNIC HARMONY

The villages and towns that dot the countryside, where the overwhelming majority of Kenyans live, are nearly all ethnically based. The people who live in them are from the same ethnic group, they share the same language, the preferred marriage partner is someone from the same group, and they live together peacefully. This homogeneity of population does not carry into the large cities. Here, as already noted, the population is widely diverse, yet people generally live together harmoniously. This reality is often in contrast to the more commonly assumed fighting that is presented popularly as the only form of tribal interaction.

This is not to deny that tribal clashes do occur; the local papers all too often carry headlines that refer to the victims of "tribal clashes." In the rural areas these conflicts usually focus on issues of land usage or preferential treatment perceived or given by local administration to a rival community. These clashes are often characterized by armed gangs using spears and old guns to attack villagers returning from a funeral or some other community celebration. When the arms used to drive people from their farms or grazing lands are military assault rifles, or the fighting that erupts does so over rent in the overcrowded slums and squatter settlements that surround Nairobi, then the police move in with tear gas and live ammunition.

The clashes in urban areas more typically result from the hardship and stress that urban dwellers must face resulting from low wages and high living costs to joblessness and malnutrition. Issues related to the resettlement of political and economic refugees also exacerbate such conflicts. With little hope of extricating themselves from the urban poverty, squalor, and over-crowding that all too many city dwellers face daily, some people again start to identify themselves through the prism of their ethnic identity, or what is sometimes called political tribalism. Other aspects of the rapid social change that Kenya has experienced since independence include inadequate access to health care, education, and other community services. The continuing demand for land and the pressure this puts on the environment have had disastrous effects on forests, water supply, and the sustainability of Kenyan agriculture. With individuals and communities so severely limited, and an economy that seems to increase the gap between the rich and the poor, there may seem little cause for optimism.

Kenyans, however, remain rich in indigenous knowledge and wisdom. All too often this expertise is dismissed, especially by the so-called experts who are responsible for designing "development" projects, as mere old-fashioned culture and custom. Yet these are the programs that are supposed to improve economic conditions, stabilize environmental changes, aid the delivery of social services, and more generally improve the lives of Kenyans. If this indigenous knowledge was not ignored, but instead tapped for the light it can shed on traditional underlying cultural patterns, the chances for success might be dramatically increased, and many of the negative consequences of urbanization, with its increased reliance on the individual over the community, could be reversed.

Nation building from such a diverse base is always fraught with difficulty and, not infrequently, with severe outbreaks of tension between different communities. Kenya has not been immune to this; it happened in the pre-colonial period and during colonial days, and it has on occasion burst forth since independence in 1963. The basic issue faced by so many relatively newly independent states is how to allow the expression of ethnicity and yet contain it so that differences are not exaggerated and exploited for the gain of some or a few over the many.

NOTES

1. *The Economist Pocket World Figures 2002* (London: Profile, 2001).

2. Chris Tomlinson, "Kenyan Coffee Growers Wonder Where All the Money Is Going," *Chicago Tribune,* 29 July 2001, sec. 5, p. 7.

3. Neal Sobania, " 'Feasts, Famines and Friends': Nineteenth Century Exchange and Ethnicity in the Eastern Lake Turkana Regional System," in *Herders, Warriors, and Traders,* ed. John G. Gallaty and Pierre Bonte (Boulder, Colorado: Westview Press, 1991), 118–42.

4. Godfrey Muriuki, *A History of the Kikuyu 1500–1900* (Nairobi: Oxford University Press, 1974), 98–100.

5. Sobania, " 'Feasts, Famines, and Friends.' "

6. A. C. McEwan. *International Boundaries of East Africa* (Oxford: Clarendon, 1971), 141.

7. Available at www.kenyantrhopus.com and www.museums.or.ke/paleodiscovery.htm.

8. John Reader, *Africa: A Biography of the Continent* (New York: Random House, 1997), part 2.

9. The most accessible account of early Chinese relations with Africa is found in Philip Snow, *The Star Raft: China's Encounter with Africa* (London: Weidenfeld and Nicolson, 1988).

10. *Swahili* is the term most generally used to refer to the people who speak the language that bears the same name and who live on the East African coast and is the name that will be used throughout this book. More correctly, however, the language is referred to as *Kiswahili* and the people as the *Waswahili*.

11. See, for example, Neal Sobania, "Fishermen Herders: Subsistence, Survival, and Cultural Change in Northern Kenya," *Journal of African History* 29 (1988): 41–56.

12. Quoted in W. R. Ochieng', *A History of Kenya* (London: Macmillan, 1985), 104.

13. Pheroze Nowrojee, *The Asian African Heritage: Identity and History* (Nairobi: The National Museums of Kenya, n.d.).

14. Illustrated in Thomas Spear, *Kenya's Past: An Introduction to Historical Method in Africa* (Harlow, U.K.: Longman, 1981), 142.

15. Jomo Kenyatta, *Facing Mount Kenya: The Tribal Life of the Kikuyu* (London: Secker and Warburg, 1953).

16. John Lonsdale, "Mau Maus of the Mind: Making Mau Mau and Remaking Kenya," *Journal of African History* 31 (1990): 394.

17. Quoted in Ochieng', *History of Kenya,* 154.

18. Peter Schwab, *Africa: A Continent Self-Destructs* (New York: Palgrave, 2001), 133–34, also 69–71.

2

Religion and Worldview

A WORLDVIEW is a grand explanation of what life is all about. To the members of a particular ethnic group, for example, the Luhya, Turkana, or Kamba, it provides a reasonable explanation of why they are expected to behave in a particular way—behaviors considered appropriate in their cultural system. If this way does not appear to outsiders as entirely rational, it is because any given individual in such a group (and everyone belongs to such a group) quite naturally questions the effectiveness of other worldviews. Individuals acquire their religious beliefs as part of their worldview. Anthropologists call the process by which people learn all the rules of their own culture "enculturation." People are not converted to their culture in the way they might be to a new religion.

It should come as no surprise, therefore, that the peoples of Kenya do not share a single worldview. The vast majority of Kenyans grow up either as Christian, Muslim, or traditional believers, yet they do so within the context of a particular cultural or ethnic community, which adds still more elements to their particular worldview. To provide a simplified example, a Swahili Muslim has a different worldview from a Mijikenda Muslim, even though both are from the coast. And a Presbyterian Kikuyu has a different worldview from a Methodist Meru, even though both are Christian and come from the highlands surrounding Mount Kenya. Add to this mix Roman Catholic believers in the Lake Victoria region to the west, or Christians or Muslims from the arid plains in the north, and the point should begin to be clear. To complicate the issue still further, many Christians and Muslims in Kenya, especially when a situation seems dire, may also consult a traditional healer to satisfy their concerns about the role of the ancestors and spirit world.

TRADITIONAL BELIEF SYSTEMS

For many Africans Islam and Christianity are traditional religions. However, to outsiders, practitioners of traditional belief systems are typically associated with terms such as *witch doctors, shamans, spirit mediums,* and even *voodoo priestesses* and *priests.* In "traditional" systems such functionaries are specific to particular ethnic groups, and not all types are found in Kenya. In addition, the terms *diviner* and *healer* are more useful because they incorporate most of the skills these other functionaries claim to describe. To make the other labels useful and accurate would require too many qualifiers. For example, a "witch doctor" is more correctly an "anti-witch doctor" because the true function of those who are consulted regarding matters of witchcraft is to identify witches and prevent their having any impact on community members. What they offer is advice on how to get rid of a problem and restore harmony. The term *shaman* has quite specific use in anthropology. As religious specialists, shamans are widespread in the world, are rarely women, and communicate face to face with the supernatural world by traveling to that world while in a trance. Voodoo is a quite specific religious practice and not all that common on the continent—and not at all in East Africa.

The basic difference between the practices of a Western-trained medical doctor and an African diviner-healer is that the latter seeks the explanation for what is causing illness in factors found outside of the human body. Although Western medical doctors may consider external factors, their real focus is determining what within the body is causing a particular illness. When illness or misfortune occurs, a diviner-healer is called upon to help discover the cause and to determine if a witch is involved. For example, witches often become witches involuntarily as a result of jealousy, greed, and hatred. But once a diviner identifies a witch, the afflicted can be freed of this curse by performing an appropriate ritual act. Thus divining or the acquiring of knowledge and healing are really two aspects of the same phenomenon—the diviner's knowledge provides the basis for understanding what is causing the problem, and with this knowledge the same individual, now acting as healer, provides a remedy or cure.

Especially critical to any understanding of traditional religious practice in many societies is the role played by the ancestors. Ancestors are not worshiped, but they are revered and understood as being able to play an active part in the everyday lives of the living. Because ancestors who remain close at hand can influence events, they are regularly offered gifts. And when illness or misfortune occur, the reason may sometimes be because they are angry at having been neglected. Gifts can include the sacrifice of an animal, but more typical might be the spilling of a little beer or tobacco at the beginning of an assembly of elders who are meeting together to discuss community events or issues. Similarly, a newborn child might be given the name of a grandparent, with the idea that the old spirit can now live in the body of the new baby. The inclusion of the ancestors is one of the reasons that traditional belief systems are often described as placing primary emphasis on unity and harmony. They are essentially communal in the way they see the world, which is different than the way Islam and Christianity emphasize the role of the individual in religion and society. Africans who become Muslims or Christians often find this one of the most troubling aspects of their new faith because the worldview into which they have been enculturated leads them to still think first in terms of maintaining harmonious relationships with their family, clan, and ancestors.

Among the factors that the traditional diviner-healer may discover to be the cause of an illness are an angry ancestor, failure to perform, or incorrectly perform, a ritual sacrifice, the violation of a cultural taboo, or a curse cast by a disaffected neighbor or family member. Cures can range from taking a medicinal herb or mineral to performing a sacrifice to placate the ancestor or neighbor. Another way to think of this is in terms of herbal remedies to treat physical ailments and ritual treatments to absolve social or moral transgressions. The latter are not all that different from the performance of a penance designed to correct a particular behavior so that such behavior or its outcome does not occur again.

One common misunderstanding associated with traditional religion is the notion that all such belief systems include a multiplicity of gods. However, in many such systems there is a belief in one God, just as in Christianity and Islam. Monotheism, or the belief in a single God, is common among the majority of Kenya's peoples. For many of the peoples who live around or near Mount Kenya, this snow-capped peak is understood to be the home of *Enkai* or *Ngai,* or a similar variation of this name. Among many of the peoples who live in the north, and who speak Cushitic languages, God is called *Waq* or *Waqqa.* Although the creator of the world, as in Christianity and Islam, a common difference between the Christian, Islamic God and *Ngai* or *Waq* is that this God is not omnipresent. A ceremony that includes the ritual sacrifice of an animal is therefore periodically required to summon *Enkai or Waq* to a particular location, thus ensuring that appropriate attention is being paid to the community, especially in times of crisis. Communal prayers are often sung to *Enkai* and *Waq* as the creator of heaven and all things on earth, especially "the people," which is often the literal translation of a people's ethnic name. Prayers typically ask *Enkai* or *Waq* for strength, for rain and good harvests, for the birth of healthy children, lambs, and calves, for protection from enemies, and for resting places free from spirits who are said to bring trouble to people when they sleep.

Each ethnic group has beliefs specific to its religious tradition. However, trying to define these religious beliefs or worldviews is not easy for outsiders since the ideas are often imprecise and elusive. Easier to describe are the cultural practices associated with these belief systems. Aspects of these are described here for five such groups—the Borana, Maasai, Turkana, Kipsigis, and Kikuyu.

The Borana World

The livestock-herding Gabbra and Borana, who live in the north of Kenya, each see themselves as a unique ethnic community even though they are part of a much larger Oromo cultural group found in both Kenya and Ethiopia. In the past the Oromo were often referred to as "the Galla," but this is a pejorative term used only by outsiders and is not appreciated by the Oromo themselves. In their belief system *Waq,* who is often called the Sky God by others, is not of the sky but found beyond it. As the creator God, *Waq* caused the heavens and the earth and all things found in them to come into existence. A long time ago *Waq* lived closer to the people and provided ample rain and stock for them, but because of the many divisions the people have created among themselves, *Waq* has drawn away from them. It is this that is said to be the cause of the drought, famine, disease, and war all too often suffered by the Oromo. Unity and harmony, or the "peace of the Borana" or "peace of the Gabbra" is what they strive for and seek in their communal prayers and the blessings they offer to *Waq.*

These prayers are offered at worship sites, which are traditionally associated with high places, such as mountains and hilltops, and always under sacred trees. Here, Oromo perform rituals that can include the sacrifice of small animals, such as goats and sheep, and on rarer occasions of cattle. The roasting of coffee beans and the use of incense, especially myrrh, are also associated with these rituals. Ritual specialists known as the *qaalluu* represent religious authority among the Oromo. The *qaalluu* live near permanent wells located in the mountains on the Ethiopia-Kenya border, and it is to here that Oromo, especially groups from the Borana and the Gabbra, make pilgrimages. Although the *qaalluu* do not hold significant political power, they are directly involved in blessing those in Oromo society who do perform political functions, including councils of elders and war leaders.

The world of the Oromo is strictly ordered in what to an outsider is an exceedingly complicated system of time keeping. At the heart of this system are two distinct yet closely related ideas. Using the Borana peoples as an example, everything in space and time is structured by the concept of *ayyaana*, which molds the destiny of all people and things. *Ayyaana* explains the world in which the Borana live—the relationship between the creator and the created, between the individual and the time into which the individual has been born, and all the events that occur in that lifetime. In addition, time is divided equally into five units of eight years each, a *gada*, and the sum of these five eight-year groups makes up a generation, or *luba*. In a rather simplified description of these Borana structures, political power passes successively through each *gada* group as the men who belong to it age and pass through the different stages of life from birth to death. Belief in an afterlife for the Borana and Gabbra involves their rejoining the ancestors who died before them in a land where the grass is green, the cattle are fat, and the milk always flowing. (More details on such cycles are found in chapter 7, "Social Customs and Lifestyle.") Every eight years, as a new *gada* prepared to assume political power from the *gada* that preceded it, representatives of the new *gada* made a pilgrimage to the *qaalluu*, who conducted the necessary rituals and gave the appropriate blessings. In this way the *gada* can be seen as representing the temporal authority of the Borana, and the *qaalluu* representing the spiritual. Having described this pattern, it is necessary to say that this traditional system seems to be disappearing as each year more and more Gabbra and Borana convert to Islam, as has already occurred among the Orma near the coast and among many other Oromo groups who live in Ethiopia.

The Maasai and the *Laibons*

The Maasai and those closely related to them, such as the Samburu and Arusha, have few beliefs associated with an afterlife or a role for the ancestors. They do, however, believe in a supreme being, *Engai*, to whom they appeal in times of need. *Engai* is understood to govern those elements that shape the Maasai world, including rain, thunder, lightning, and fertility. Thus the same word, *engai*, can also be used to refer to rain, thunder, and lightning. And although *Engai* is a distant force generally not too concerned about everyday events in Maasailand, prayers and ritual sacrifices are directed to *Engai* for blessings and good fortune. As has already been noted regarding herding communities such as the Maasai, the ritual slaughter of a sheep or goat, and sometimes cattle, is a common feature of such prayer, appeals, and curative rituals. Similarly, prayers and rituals are a common occurrence at those major ceremonies that mark an individual's transition from one social status to another, such as from uninitiated to warrior or unmarried to married.

More directly related to events of everyday life is the widespread belief in prophecy and divination. Among the Maasai-speaking and Kalenjin-speaking peoples of Kenya, this belief is associated directly with the powerful institution of prophets, the *laibonok* and *orkoiik*. To avoid the use of many terms that might otherwise confuse, the Maasai term *laibon* will be used here when speaking of these prophets. Given the nature of what *laibons* do, they are understood to be operating outside the authority of the elders and sometimes even outside the moral order of the community. The status as prophet or diviner that each one acquired thus depended on the recognition each managed to achieve in the particular community in which they lived and worked. Often this included how their prophecy and divination fared against those offered by their rivals in neighboring communities.

In the everyday life of a herder and his family, events can occur for which the average person has no clear explanation. These can include the large-scale loss of livestock, infertility (always associated with women), and illnesses such as blindness, epilepsy, and insanity. It is also believed that individuals can cause harm to others as a result of jealousy, resentment, and greed. Because sorcery is often thought to be the cause of such an event, Maasai and others turn to a *laibon* for protection. As one scholar has pointed out, this is particularly true the more isolated a community is from access to a town, hospital, and police protection, and especially in times of stress that threaten their existence as herders, such as drought, famine, or stock diseases that decrease their herds.[1]

Turkana Diviners

The livestock-herding Turkana, just as the Borana, believe in one great God who is understood to live in the sky above the clouds. Their God, whom they call *Aakuj,* can be both kind and malevolent. When being generous, *Aakuj* brings rain to make the grass green, keeps the Turkana free from hunger and want, and protects their homesteads and animals from disease and enemies. On the other hand, if individuals or groups of Turkana in any way break the community's moral code, *Aakuj* can punish the people. The results of this can be seen in events such as the appearance of illness, the spread of famine, and the failure of the rains. The people then respond, either as individuals or in groups, by praying for *Aakuj*'s blessing at community rituals and ceremonies. However, unlike the Maasai, who have little sense of an afterlife, the Turkana believe that in death they join *Aakuj.*

Diviners can be of greater or lesser standing, but all serve primarily priestly and mediatory roles in the Turkana community. The diviners of God, or *imuron Aakuj*, are the diviners of the highest standing and are understood to be earthly representatives of *Aakuj*. The great mystical powers of these diviners are often recalled with powers ranging from making rain and foretelling the future to the more common providing of medicine. Typically, *imuron Aakuj* came from a particular clan known for producing such diviners. Their powers, however, were always said to come from *Aakuj*, and acquiring them often came during a period of ritual isolation when they withdrew to a remote and isolated part of the country.

The power of diviners to foretell the future is understood to come to them through dreams, through the tossing of sandals, or from reading the entrails of animals such as goats. Whereas the less-important diviners, *imuron eki-toit*, were traditional healers who could tell the future by using just one of these techniques, the *imuron Aakuj* were often proficient in all three. Both types of diviners could break spells associated with witchcraft and sorcery, remove curses from people, and provide ritual cleansing, but because the *imuron Aakuj* were far fewer in number, the less-important diviners often handled these tasks. In the late nineteenth and early twentieth centuries, a few of these diviners used their power of prophecy to establish themselves as military leaders who were consulted before raids both big and small. The reputations of some spread across Turkanaland, and they developed a position of centralized leadership that led the Turkana to have a greater sense of corporate identity.[2] There is also evidence that the Turkana once had women diviners, *amuron*, but little is yet known about their source of prophecy and its efficacy.

The Turkana also hold a widespread belief in nature spirits, whose world is that of the mountains, rivers, and other natural places. However, because these spirits are not thought to be able to cause evil, they are not especially feared. Among the Kipsigis, however, every aspect of life is understood to be related to the environment.

The Spirit World of the Kipsigis

The world of the Kipsigis seems to be one of layers of belief drawn from different times in their history. There is a belief in a supreme being known as *Asis*, which is also the word for "sun," but *Asis* is not understood to *be* the sun. At other times the supreme being is called *Ngolo*, "up above," but there is also the name *Cheptalel*, which translates as "pure white girl." All of these names probably relate back to earlier eras or the different peoples who today make up the ethnic community known as the Kipsigis.

The traditional belief of the Kipsigis is that the human body is but a temporary home for a spirit that is immortal. When the body dies, this spirit simply moves on to a new body and is reborn in a baby, who is usually given two names—the name of the child and that of the individual who is understood to be reborn in that child. Kipsigis society includes a variety of specialized practitioners whose tasks hold the society together. These include *laibons* who can foretell the future, *chebsogeyot,* or female healers, who practice traditional medicine using herbs and other natural objects, and *kokwotinwekor,* who are mediators or judges who resolve issues at the village level. Kipsigis society also includes *ponindet,* who are strong magicians associated exclusively with black magic and evil. The principal religious leader of the Kipsigis is the *Boyot ab Tumba.* It is this individual's responsibility to lead annual rituals and officiate at the various ceremonies that maintain Kipsigis social order. Not surprisingly, such occasions include blessings and prayers for the birth of healthy children and the successful raising of livestock and crops.[3]

The Kikuyu and Oaths

There is often considerable overlap between aspects of religious belief and the maintenance of order, especially in communities in which ancestors and spirits are understood to play a significant part. The arrival of disease or drought or other forms of ill will that might befall an individual are often seen as expressions of their unhappiness. Similarly, such misfortune is often understood to result from people not following the rules of moral or ethical conduct, or somehow upsetting the balance between the natural and the supernatural. Just as rituals are sometimes conducted to heal or rid an individual or community of an affliction or condition that is causing suffering or distress, others are performed in an effort to prevent misfortune or disasters such as drought, famine, warfare, disease, or social disruption. Oaths or ordeals, which might be described as solemn promises to supernatural powers, were traditional means by which people demonstrated that they were not acting outside community standards. Typically used to bind persons to their decision upon pain of death or worse, oaths were also used to chase away evil spirits, to identify people using witchcraft against others, and to protect property rights. Because there was such moral and religious fear of the consequences of taking an oath and then not being truthful, they were an effective means to drive people to take responsibility for their actions.

Today, oaths are best known for their use by resistance and nationalist groups in the fight for freedom from colonial rule and are sometimes thought of as a reversion to the superstitions of an "uncivilized" past. However, in the 1950s, during the period known as Mau Mau, the Kikuyu and other Mount

Kenya peoples used them to create and enforce community solidarity. At a time when these highland peoples were fighting against their land being taken by the white colonial government, and against the imposition of rules that dramatically impacted their traditional social customs, they used oaths as a force to create and sustain both social and moral solidarity. Although they were originally administered only to top leaders of the movement, it quickly became apparent that taking this oath to the countryside and even forcing people to take the oath by persuasion or intimidation provided a further significant asset to the movement. Administering the oath to people throughout the rural communities in which these guerilla fighters operated imparted to the population a greater sense of unity and solidarity to the cause. Swearing to assist the movement and its members, to collect funds for the cause, and to never reveal anything about Mau Mau and its organization, upon threat of death ("may this oath kill me"), gave new recruits courage. The ceremony at which the oath was administered and the symbolism that surrounded it allowed those leading the event to secure vows of loyalty to the resistance they had mounted against the British. Such collective vows were made even more enduring when each oath taker understood that their oath was backed by supernatural sanctions drawn from traditional Kikuyu belief.[4]

ISLAM

The role of Islam, as already indicated in chapter 1, has had a long and influential history in Kenya. The obvious starting point for any consideration of Islam in Kenya is among the Swahili towns of the coast. The Indian Ocean coast has long been a crossroads where peoples and cultures from Africa, the Middle East, and Asia have met. In fact, Swahili civilization was born from these seafaring exchanges. Here, the coastal peoples of Africa encountered and mixed with peoples from the Arabian Peninsula, the Indian subcontinent, and beyond. Aided by monsoon winds that blow half the year from the African coast to India, and the other half of the year in the reverse direction from India to Africa, they engaged in the trade of a wide variety of goods. From the Kenya coast, ivory, wooden poles of mangrove for construction, and slaves went eastward in exchange for decorative pottery, metalware, and other household goods. As time passed existing cities became increasingly Islamicized, and new cities were founded by Muslims from Arabia and especially the region of the peninsula occupied by the Omani. Islam was a natural consequence of the expansion and immigration of Muslims from the Indian Ocean rim to the East African coast and from the intermarriage of Arab, Persian, and other Muslim settlers with the local population. However, intermarriage and proselytizing did not extend to the interior, since this was

Nearly all Muslim men wear small white embroidered caps, *kofia,* as a sign of their commitment to Islam.

the area from which slaves were captured, and Islam strictly forbids enslaving other Muslims, which of course includes converts.

Exchanges were not exclusively of the commercial variety. Although the marketplace certainly included the exchange of goods, it was also a marketplace for ideas from which people could pick and choose. Such an exchange of ideas can lead to an evolution in people's thinking and, from this, to changes in their worldviews. Sometimes these changes have come from the introduction and borrowing of foreign ideas or models. Just as often, they have led to a new synthesis that draws from both local roots and outside influences in a dynamic process of integration and transformation. What results is often a new tradition; such is the fluidity of cultural change.

Islam among the Swahili has been characterized by great artistic creativity (see chapter 4) and rather strict orthodox practices. Only the orthodox or most conservative female practitioners wear the long, flowing black gown and veil, with which Muslim women are so often identified. However, nearly all Muslim men, regardless of their branch of Islam, wear a small white embroidered cap, *kofia,* to indicate their religious commitment. This commitment to the faith is also recognized by active participation in the practices that surround the five "pillars of Islam." The central tenet of Islamic belief is in one God, Allah, and the public declaration of this: "There is but one God and Allah is His name, and Muhammad is His prophet." The Qur'an, which is the sacred text of Islam, was revealed to the Prophet Muhammad in the Arabic language. After his death in 632, the text was initially transmitted orally. Later, when it was written down, it became known as Qur'an, which is derived from the Arabic word meaning "to recite."

The second pillar of Islam is to pray five times each day, with each prayer beginning with the repeating of the public confession, "There is but one God and Allah is His name." During these prayers a Muslim repeatedly lowers his head and body in the direction of Mecca in modern-day Saudi Arabia because it was there that the Archangel Gabriel revealed the Qur'an to the Prophet Muhammad. These prayers occur after washing the hands, feet, and face, including the ears and mouth. Prayer does not need to be done in a mosque, although on Fridays this is most desirable, but can be done wherever one is, by creating a personal sacred space using a carpet or mat placed to face Mecca. The five times for daily prayer are at sunrise, midmorning, midday, midafternoon, and sunset, when a muezzin can be heard calling the faithful to prayer from a mosque's minaret of a mosque.

Another of Islam's five pillars is to fast during the daylight hours of the month of Ramadan. This form of ritual purification is done in remembrance of God's divine revelation some 1,400 years ago. The fourth pillar is giving alms to the poor, and the fifth is to make the pilgrimage (hajj) to Mecca if humanly possible. Whereas the Swahili tend to be conservative, or what is sometimes described as orthodox, in their practice of Islam by their rigorous adherence to all five of the pillars, other followers of Islam express their religious commitment less overtly. For example, following the public declaration of their faith, many may attend Friday mosque and wear a *kofia* but do not regularly fast or pray, and accept that they will never have the funds necessary to make the hajj. Similarly, Islam does not require baptism as in Christianity, or the renunciation of all traditional beliefs; some of the latter have been more

The Jamia Mosque in the heart of downtown Nairobi has long been the site of Friday prayers and the education of young people to the faith.

or less absorbed into various aspects of African Islam. However, there are also within Islam conservative brotherhoods whose declared goal is to purify Islam and bring it back to the basic tenets of its founding.[5]

Education has always been one of the fundamental attractions of Islam. This is because, although it is possible to become a Muslim without being able to read, Islam places great importance on the necessity of learning Arabic in order to read the Qur'an, which is not translated. This is quite different from Christianity, where great emphasis has been placed on translating the Bible into local languages so that people, wherever they live and whatever language they speak, can have access to the Bible. Because mosques were initially established in urban areas, and those engaged in trade lived and settled in urban communities, the influence of literacy as an aspect of Islam has historically been a largely urban phenomenon. Qur'anic schools, where students learn the 114 chapters or *sura* of the Qur'an by oral recitation and studying under a teacher, have long been a popular feature of Islam. Today, with broad elementary education found across Kenya, children often attend the Qur'anic school after public school or on the weekend. Initially, they are introduced to reading and writing Arabic through the rote learning of the Qur'an's first ten chapters. Often sitting on the ground, the children read and recite in unison from the verse(s) written on a white-washed wooden board. With this foundation they are later introduced to Islamic law, literature, social practice, and religious history, including the life of the Prophet Muhammad.

The importance of the written Qur'an can also be seen in the protective amulets many Muslims wear around their necks. Verses from the Qur'an are wrapped in these small sewn leather amulets. Typically, these verses have been inscribed on a small piece of goatskin parchment. Writing and reading from the Qur'an can also play a role in healing, when a practitioner incorporates these verses into his prescribed treatments for illness or pain. This can include instructing a sufferer to soak in water a piece of paper containing written verses from the Qur'an. With the written word of Allah now infused into the water, patients can, depending on the instruction and the nature of the illness, pain, or distress, either wash the affliction from their body or drink it as a cure.

The spread of Islam to the interior of Kenya is a relatively recent phenomenon and dates from the mid- to late part of the nineteenth century. It occurred about the same time as the expansion of Christianity to the interior and for much the same reason. As the British authorities moved off the coast to conquer and occupy the interior of the country, they required the support of Africans. When the British needed guides, bearers, armed retainers, domestic servants, and cooks, they turned to those they saw most like themselves. For this purpose, the Swahili fit the bill. They were literate and from an urban environment and had an understanding of economic exchanges, such as labor for goods or wages. They also had a strong sense of community and a system of government that included notions of justice. And although not Christian, they were religious in a sense the British could understand, which was far different from the belief systems the British found beyond the coast in the interior. Thus, as the British colonial occupation moved, so too did Islam. Later, with the development of Nairobi at the beginning of the twentieth century, the location of government shifted to that city. As it did so, the significance of Mombasa, and Islam, declined, and the role of Christian missions came to prominence. Unlike the spread of Christianity, Islam's ties to the colonial conquerors is far enough in the past that they are not generally associated with the imposition of this alien rule.

The economic success of Muslims as traders is another reason that many of their inland neighbors have adopted Islam. These believers are not generally as conservative as those found on the coast. For example, fewer of these more recent converts pray five times a day and instead allow Friday prayer at the mosque to suffice. But it is in these inland areas that Islam has seen the greatest expansion. To many outsiders Islam is often seen and generally presented by the media as a monolithic religion, with everyone acting and thinking the same. It is, however, like Christianity, a religion complete with internal divisions. Islam at the coast is dominated by the Sunni branch of the faith. Only a small minority of believers are of the Shi'ia branch, whose followers are generally from the Asian community, originating on the Indian subcontinent. Even among these main divisions there are subdivisions. Although most of the Shi'ia sects are present in Kenya, the Ismaili, who are followers of the Aga Khan, one of the richest men in the world, are among the most numerous. Also contrary to the stereotypes held by many outside of Islam, this rather more liberal sect of Islam is strongly committed to the education of women and their participation in the world of business.[6]

CHRISTIANITY

The role of organized religion in Africa is part of the ongoing debate over the precise role played by colonialism. As such, religion is regularly indicted as a coconspirator in the European master plan to bring "commerce, Christianity, and civilization" to a continent of Africans once viewed as "heathen." The place of Christianity in Kenya is merely part of this larger debate. However, equally important is that since independence, the outreach arm of the Church has played a vital role in improving the living conditions of many average Kenyans. And most recently, church leaders have been some of the most vocal critics of political corruption and strongest advocates for democratic government.

The earliest Christian arrivals were Portuguese sailors and traders in the fifteenth century. Their religious influence lasted until the Portuguese ouster from Mombasa in 1729. A Christian presence did not reappear in Kenya until the arrival in 1846 of Johann Ludwig Krapf, an ordained minister of the British-funded Church Missionary Society (CMS). For ten years Krapf and two other CMS missionaries who arrived shortly after him lived, ministered, and recorded their observations of the Mijikenda people who lived in the areas surrounding their mission station at Rabai. Krapf's letters, journals, and other writings provide a unique and early record of the culture and customs of the Mijikenda, of the Swahili language in which he took particular interest, and of the practices of the surrounding Muslim community. As evangelists, however, the Rabai mission had almost no impact. Krapf concluded that the Mijikenda had little interest in Christianity, not because of the Muslim influence that had surrounded them for at least a couple of centuries but rather because they took Christianity to be just another form of Islam, a religion from outside.[7]

The United Methodist Free Church mission, established in 1862 in this same locale, had no more success at converting the Mijikenda than the CMS. Eventually, both these mission groups turned their attention to evangelizing and providing homes for fugitive and recaptured slaves. By 1888 an ethnically and culturally different community of literate, Swahili-speaking Christians was living alongside communities of traditional Mijikenda and Muslim Swahili. This pattern was not all that different from the one experienced by most early missions. Almost always, what the mission experienced was the total indifference of the local population. Their earliest converts were typically individuals who were, for whatever reason, outcasts or the disinherited of the local community or a nearby community. Soon these early converts became dependent on the mission, whether for food or labor in exchange for their basic needs, and yet because of their social status in the local community, these individuals were largely unsuccessful at evangelizing to their own people. However, this situation would change in the twentieth century.

During the early colonial period missionary efforts were wrapped up in part of the overall justification for colonialism's "civilizing mission." For the British this phrase provided justification for the conquest and confiscation of Kenyans' land and was a useful pronouncement for public consumption. As one Kenyan scholar has described it, the civilizing mission was "a vague, convenient, but terribly reassuring attitude of mind, which could be used to explain away glaring injustices to the few people in the metropolitan who were anxious of the black man's welfare, as well as to quell the doubts voiced by future generations, who questioned the validity of the colonizer's presence in their land."[8] This lofty goal provided the fund-raisers of these large mission organizations in Britain with all they needed to make a powerful argument for what missions could accomplish with appropriate support. After all, in Africa, Christianity was directly confronting the evil of Satan. That their achievements were few initially was not really an issue.

The end of the nineteenth century and the early decades of the twentieth century saw the spread of mission stations into the interior to the highlands and beyond. However, this move was not a uniform effort. Among the Protestants in Kenya the British Anglican CMS competed with Scottish Presbyterians and American Baptists, and within Roman Catholicism British Mill Hill Fathers vied with American Holy Ghost and Maryknoll Fathers. It is not surprising that some Africans interpreted this array of denominations and orders, religious theology and ritual practices, and nationalities and languages as representative of European "tribalism." More important to the bringing of Christianity to Kenyans were two additional factors. First was the individual personalities of the missionaries themselves, as well as their particular beliefs, strategies for conversion, willingness to learn the local languages, and the degree of cultural tolerance they had for local customs and social practices. Equally important, however, was the position of the African community being proselytized. Factors that need to be taken into account to understand the impact of missions must also take into account the values and the experiences of the Africans encountering Christianity. What degree of colonial authority was present in their community, and what impact was it having on their lives? What sense of advantage did individuals see themselves acquiring through affiliation with a mission or conversion to Christianity, for example, materialistically, politically, or socially? And to what extent would individuals have to abandon or renounce traditional beliefs? As scholars have rightly pointed out, to truly understand the place of the mission enterprise in East Africa, one must consider the specific historical situation of each mission and the colonial context in which it evangelized, as well as the circumstances of the local community.[9]

For some people the missionary arrival proved both opportunistic and divisive. For example, the arrival in 1898 of the East African Scottish Industrial Mission among the Kikuyu, near what is today Nairobi, assisted the Kikuyu greatly during a devastating period of disease and famine. By caring for the sick and organizing famine relief, the missionaries earned a grateful welcome. Their efforts were rewarded when a great number of the sick and hungry converted to Christianity. A positive reputation then preceded the missionaries as they moved north toward Mount Kenya establishing new missions. Soon the Scots were joined by missionaries from the Church Missionary Society (1900), the African Inland Mission (1901), and Roman Catholic priests (1903). On one level this laid the foundation from which the Kikuyu were able to attain the role as the principal ethnic group on which the British built their colony. This position became particularly clear in the middle decades of the twentieth century, when they were among the main players in the lead up to and then the initial government following independence in 1963.

The early history of missions in Kikuyu also illuminates the splits that later occurred in this society and that were made manifest in the 1950s Mau Mau rebellion that so dramatically shaped Kenya nationalism. The African Inland Mission (AIM) emerged from late nineteenth-century American evangelical revivalism, in which individuals would come to accept divine revelation in all facets of their life following a personal encounter with Christ. The goal of this nondenominational Protestant evangelical mission was the establishment of self-sufficient communities of faith. They considered the social and religious customs of the local communities from which their converts came to be the works of Satan. Confident that backwardness and ignorant superstitions dominated the people they had come to convert, the missionaries felt that all the objects associated with such beliefs needed to be destroyed. This included the burning of sacred trees and the destruction of paraphernalia associated with divination and ancestor blessing. Only by spreading the light of the Gospel could these evils be wrested away from social practice.

As elsewhere in Kenya, at least some early Kikuyu converts to Christianity were motivated by access to land, opportunities for education and jobs, and the avoidance of colonial labor and taxes. The first catechists or "readers" were known as *athomi*. They lived in the self-sufficient mission compounds that the AIM established, dependent on the missionaries and with a growing sense of superiority over the general Kikuyu population whom they also came to believe remained in a backward world of traditional belief and thought. By the 1920s, however, these *athomi* had increased in such numbers that they moved out into the general community, where colonial rules and regulations had led to significant change in traditional society. Outside the mission compounds, the *athomi* were also subject to colonial rules and regulations regarding labor, tax, and land, and they began to take a more sympathetic view of their peers. With little support from the AIM for their new situation, these Christian converts began to criticize the mission for its lack of interest in and support of the plight of the general Kikuyu population. For the missionaries, who spent little time learning about or attempting to understand the local culture and customs, and whose only interest was in preparing for the life to come, this was entirely consistent. Their focus was on the saving of individuals' souls and not on their present condition.[10]

The response of the AIM to criticism from its converts was to impose new rules and even stricter adherence to regulations already in place. The mission paid particular attention to polygyny (the practice of a man having multiple wives) and circumcision. Both were highly charged issues that pertained to social control and issues of authority in Kikuyu society. Arguments from the Kikuyu converts that the Old Testament, which they could read in their own language, is full of polygynous patriarchs, and that the circumcision of both men and women can be understood to be prescribed, were to no avail. Indeed, these issues led many missionaries to resist translating or even teaching the Old Testament.

To further deal with the criticism, in 1928 the AIM required its converts to take a loyalty oath. Eventually, however, more than 95 percent of their converts left the AIM to establish their own churches and schools. Those who left came to be known as the *aregi*, or "those who refused" to sign the loyalty oath. The few who stayed became known as the "thumbprint" or *kirore*, after the traditional method of inking a thumb so that those who are unable to write can make their "mark," presumably on the loyalty oath. Then in 1947, nearly twenty years later, even those who had remained left over the AIM's resistance to ordaining African pastors and its continued paternalistic control of mission activities. Scholars who have examined this history argue that most Kikuyu did in fact become Christian, but that issues such as doctrinal interpretation, church governance, ordination, education, and cultural tolerance sharply divided the community. Later these splits were reflected in the divisions that occurred within Kikuyu during Mau Mau, when the *aregi* supported the Kikuyu Central Association and the *kirore* sided with the government.[11]

Another interesting example from mission history comes from western Kenya, where Christianity arrived before missionaries did. The Buganda people who live in what is today Uganda were among the earliest East African mission converts. Luo peoples, who moved freely across the political boundaries of that time, became Christian followers while in Buganda. When they moved home in to what is today Kenya, they established prayer communities modeled after traditional Luo homesteads. When the CMS missionaries arrived in Maseno in the first decade of the twentieth century, they found an established Christian community. They quickly took advantage of this, employing Luo catechists to help them spread the Gospel. However, beginning in 1912 people began having charismatic experiences, including speaking in tongues and having dreams and visions. Increasingly uncomfortable with the popularity of this Holy Spirit movement, the theologically more conservative CMS missions expelled its followers. Despite this ostracism, followers in the Holy Spirit movement grew at a significant rate and soon began to establish their own independent churches and schools. Scholars who have examined this religious phenomenon have concluded that the Holy Spirit movement drew from both Christian beliefs and traditional African religious practices to create an indigenous African Christianity under the direction of local African leaders. For local Luo and Luhya communities of followers, prophecy and healing by the Holy Spirit were effective and meaningful ways for them to fight effectively against the evil that is ever present in the world.[12]

The evangelization of whatever community or ethnic group the missionaries settled among was paramount to the missionaries. The means to accomplishing this goal was through what have been often seen as acts of good works, especially the establishment of medical clinics and the founding of schools. The spread of education created the literate workforce needed by both government and mission alike. The initial impetus for education grew from the need for catechists or local evangelists called "readers" who could travel throughout the countryside reading and introducing the Gospel. Soon, however, the missions were also introducing what came to be known as "industrial education." Initially, this was to meet the need for new mission buildings, especially churches and homes for the European missionaries. Occupational training was also required to staff clinics, run printing presses, sew the European-style clothes everyone was to wear, and raise the crops and animals that were to make the mission compound self-supporting. And of course, the government needed clerks to man the lower levels of the administration.

These skills were also required if the standards the missionaries assumed for their converts were to be met. For example, if the mission insisted on monogamous marriage, which they did, and the living of a Christian family life, then their converts needed to have houses consisting of two rooms, not one. If the converts were to read their Bibles daily, as they were supposed to, then their houses needed to have windows to give them the light to do so. If the children were to attend school regularly, then they would not be able to provide labor for their farms and the converts needed to acquire agricultural skills that would increase their harvests so they could sell some of their harvest in the market. Selling surplus production in the marketplace, or selling one's labor to earn a wage from work, was also necessary if the convert was going to tithe to the church and pay school fees and government taxes.

Medical practices formed an equally important aspect of evangelism programs if the demands of a changed lifestyle were to be supported. The greatest threat to missionaries and their introduction of new beliefs were the people they referred to as witch doctors and sorcerers. Missions saw that their only way to counter these traditional practitioners was to replace the practitioners at the local village level with Christian trained nurses and medical assistants. The service and treatment provided by missions, from helping people respond to small matters such as eye and ear infections to helping them in times of epidemics including influenza and smallpox, all worked to weaken and undermine the value of traditional beliefs and medical practices.

Improving health and reducing death rates were particularly critical among children since the missions prohibited polygynous marriages, which reduced the number of children normally expected from marriage to more than one wife. The medical missionaries soon discovered that even small improvements in health care resulted in significant and rapid increases in the population. This, coupled with an increasing number of literate young people who moved into the colonial workforce and earned an income, albeit small, had dramatic effects on local society. Lifted out of the traditional societies into which they were born, Kenyans soon found themselves entwined in the cash economy of the Europeans. New class structures rose as young people with cash incomes were no longer dependent on their extended families for goods and cattle to marry or participate in other ceremonial activities. New leaders emerged to challenge the rule of elders. In general, it seems clear that the introduction of Western ideas and ways of thinking created upheavals in basic social structures that led to significant changes in traditional patterns of community, belief, and governance.

Unlike the various levels of commitment that were allowed those who became Muslim, conversion to Christianity had strict requirements, not the least of which soon came to include literacy. Still, for many Kenyans the the-

ology of Christian doctrine came relatively easily. In large measure this may
have been because, as already noted, the traditional belief systems of most
ethnic groups included the notion of a supreme being. Nevertheless, missionaries often complained of nominal Christians and regularly denounced
polygyny, witchcraft, dancing, and drink, with members of their congrega-
tions often disciplined for transgressions in these areas. It has been suggested
that this perception of a nominal commitment was in large part because the
morality associated with Christianity was much harder to grasp and was regularly undermined by traditional value systems.

In summary, Christianity is fundamentally different from African religious
beliefs. Where Christianity focuses on the life to come, African traditional
systems focus on the here and now. Where Christianity focuses on the individual, African belief systems focus on the community. Where Christianity
focuses on salvation, African belief systems focus on health and moral order
in the present. And as Christianity spread, where the European Christians
focused on Christ's sacrifice for the redemption of all, African Christians
placed greater emphasis on Christ's healing ministry. The reasons for conversion were as varied as the individuals who made this new commitment. At
missions one could receive an education, which often led to new economic
opportunities. For those who lost land through colonial or white-settler
takeovers, or who were freed slaves, some missions could provide land for
farming. For those facing the results of social conflict or drought, famine, and
the loss of crops or livestock, missions provided a refuge, both physically and
psychologically. Initially, the numbers of converts were few. However, these
numbers soon increased, and once trained as catechists, evangelists, and
teachers, these converts left the mission compounds for villages and towns
where they preached the Gospel and taught school in local languages. This
marked an important shift in mission work; the evangelistic message was no
longer that of European missionaries to the few, but of Africans who translated the Bible and preached the Gospel far and wide from an African context. Eventually, this shift led to issues of authority and control.

To maintain control European missionaries often imposed new rules
about belief and behavior that, if not accepted or followed to the letter,
resulted in children not being baptized, marriage blessings withheld, or the
elimination of possible ordination to the ministry. Quite understandably, the
leaders who were at the core of these new and vibrant churches—the catechists, evangelists, teachers, and clinic workers—resented this interference. It
was but a small step for them to assert their independence by breaking away
from mission churches to found semiautonomous or even wholly independent churches. Just as the spread of Christianity went hand in hand with the

expansion of colonialism, so too did Christianity's role in various efforts to throw off the yoke of this foreign control.

INDEPENDENT CHURCHES AND MOVEMENTS

Missionaries generally saw themselves as independent of the colonialist order, but in addition to converting Kenyans to Christianity, it is clear they were also converting people to a broad range of Western values, including literacy and education, medicine, wage earning, and social mobility. Equally, missionaries preached about and required absolute adherence to Christian law—one wife, avoidance of "heathen" medicinal practices, and certainly no mixing of traditional beliefs. Further, although such knowledge allowed some individuals access to the lower rungs of government and church administration, the vast majority of people continued to live in rural communities. In those areas where mission churches were strong and vibrant, such people often felt cut off from traditional rituals that were important and often crucial to their family and community identity. When coupled with being confined to subordinate positions in the Western hierarchies of the mission operations, especially when Christianity speaks so clearly about equality of Christians, a number of African Christians begin to assert their independence. One way of expressing this independence was to break away from an established Western church and found an independent one.

What characterized most of these independent churches was not a major shift in theology, worship, or even structure but rather a separation from mission support and control. In many parts of Africa these independent churches incorporated "Ethiopian" into their name. In part this was because of the early biblical identity of Africans as Ethiopians and the ancient roots of Christianity in that country. In addition, however, it recognized the independence that Ethiopia fought for and retained on a continent where one region after another had fallen to conquest and colonialism. Other independent churches took various names that included "prophet," "Zion," and "Spiritual." As independent churches took on a life of their own and more were established, many also began to include aspects of traditional religious ritual and practice. For the mission churches this development represented a serious challenge, but for many Africans, especially those who moved to urban centers without the traditional support of their extended families or rural communities, an independent church provided needed and relevant support in their daily lives. With an emphasis on a prophet-led community and rituals that were not totally alien but which had elements of easily recognized traditional practices, independent churches quickly attracted significant numbers of believers and followers.

These independent churches, also sometimes called "separatist" churches, are not linked to either Protestant or Roman Catholic bodies. They are, however, typically under the leadership of a Christian-trained or strongly Christian influenced head. Because the Holy Spirit plays a particularly important role in these churches, they are sometimes called Pentecostal, but they have no direct link to Western Pentecostal churches. Prominent in their praying is the laying on of hands for physical and social healing. Their worship services are lively and enthusiastic, making liberal use of dancing and singing to African drums and musical instruments. In Kenya groups representing independent churches are easily recognized as they gather on a Saturday or Sunday and process under banners, wearing distinctive white clothing with their heads covered by a scarf or twisted piece of cloth. Just as in traditional belief systems in rural areas, independent churches emphasize the importance of unity and fellowship among believers.

One such group, which is widely known in Kenya, is the Legio Maria Church. Led by Baba Ondeto, this sect's followers believe that reincarnations of both Jesus Christ and Mary live among them in a makeshift settlement on a mountain they call Calvary or *Got Kwer* in South Nyanza in the southwest. The group's beginning is reported to have been in 1965 when Gaudensia Aoko, who was said to be the reincarnation of Mary, the mother of Jesus, saw a vision that told her to go and preach the word of God. The group, which broke away from the Roman Catholic Church and has a similar hierarchy that includes a pope, is a close knit but materially poor community. They believe that everything will be theirs in the afterlife and that through prayer, which often includes speaking in tongues, they cure the sick. Followers live a pure life and have strict rules against blasphemy, drinking beer, and committing adultery, and they wear colorful clerical robes of black, green, or white, depending on their status within the community.[13]

Today, both Islam and Christianity are a vital part of everyday life for believers and continue to grow at a significant rate. Increasingly, especially in urban areas where tribalism continues to break down, Islam and Christianity have become what some refer to as a super-ethnic fellowship. Periodically, however, as more and more traditional patterns and practices are discarded, there are calls for a return to "authenticity." Typically, these calls come from two very different sources. One source consists of those with a university education, who have often earned their degrees in the West. While in Europe and North America, these Africans have experienced Western life firsthand and seen the problems faced by people, rich and poor, in these regions. They have also often been witness to, or at the very least heard about, the role of religion in creating, exacerbating, or not seeming to help seriously to solve the issues of poverty, hunger, education, and moral living. And so they call for a return to traditional religious practice with its emphasis on harmony, unity, and respect for clan and community members. The other source has been traditional leaders. This is especially the case in some rural areas where these leaders have been displaced as the result of the spread of government and democratic movements and in general have been pushed aside by community members who now put their own interests ahead of the group's on the road to modernization.

RELIGION, MISSION, AND POLITICS IN KENYA TODAY

Islam and Christianity continue to grow today. The AIM has grown into the strong and vigorous Kenyan-led African Inland Church (AIC). It still has American and European missionaries who dominate the unofficial headquarters in the Rift Valley at Kijabi and staff mission stations in the more remote regions of the country, but its churches and outreach programs are increasingly under local leadership. Since independence, the AIC has played a significant role in establishing primary schools and medical clinics, and in developing water resources. This has been especially the case in the semiarid north, where the government under President Kenyatta tended not to invest as heavily as it did in other regions of the country. In this same period in the north, the AIC competed with the Catholic Church, which was also active in establishing primary schools and clinics at its missions. Under Kenya's second president, Daniel arap Moi, who was a product of AIM schools and the church, the north was allocated more resources for development projects. Since 1980, although the missions still provide significant support, the government has administered all the primary school and clinics.

Despite these changes, the mission stations themselves still look very much like the self-sufficient communities striven for by early missionaries. The Catholic missions consist of large churches surrounded by separate living quarters for the priests, nuns, and African workers and are almost invariably surrounded by a fence. Sometimes the church will have a local look to it, such as the large, round, Rendille-like structure with a traditional roof at Korr, but otherwise the buildings are of locally made cement blocks and roofed with corrugated tin. Inside the fenced compound will also be a small garden and some combination of clinic, school, motor vehicle garage/workshop and famine-relief distribution and storage shed. Overall, an AIC mission station has the same look to it—modern cement-block house for the missionary family, a workshop/garage, clinic, and primary school. A nearby airstrip is also common so missionary planes can supply the station's needs from Nairobi

A Roman Catholic mission church at Korr is an enlarged version of the traditional house in which the Rendille people of northern Kenya have long lived.

and regularly bring a doctor or nurse practitioner for the more serious medical cases.

Whether Italian Roman Catholic or American Protestant, these humble, generous, and hardworking missionaries must be admired for their commitment to their faith and their singular goal of bringing the local peoples to Christ. However, their familiarity with the local culture and customs of the people they serve remains limited, and their attitudes toward the people they serve are not all that different from the patronizing ones recorded at the beginning of the twentieth century. This is reflected in what one scholar who has looked at these issues in considerable depth recorded with a Roman Catholic priest in an interview in the 1970s: "The Rendille are very primitive, they are real children."[14] Interestingly, given the missions' focus on winning converts and saving souls, there is a near-total absence in mission activities of programs associated with livestock production, even though herding animals is the principal focus of the people among whom the missionaries live and work. What better way to build bonds of confidence, familiarity, and cooperation? Even the argument that peoples of the Old Testament were in fact pastoralists who herded animals left the missionaries unconvinced. And so the missions continue their work but without veterinary clinics, vocational programs in livestock production, or efforts to organize cooperatives that could

Shree Swaminarayan Mandir, a Hindu temple, built of stone imported from India and locally carved wood and completed in 1999, is indicative of the large Asian population that has lived in Kenya since before 1900.

assist these herders and their families in marketing their livestock so they might become more self-sufficient.

Just as Kenya is made up of a multiplicity of ethnic and racial groups, so too it is composed of believers from many faiths following the wide range of practices found within each one. Every lunchtime in downtown Nairobi, parks like Jeevanjee Gardens are witness to loudspeaker music and prayers led by evangelical preachers armed with electronic megaphones, each competing to attract a crowd. Signs along the road in the country and in small towns announce the location of churches, from mainline Protestants that include Presbyterian and Baptist churches to parishes of the Roman Catholic diocese. But the signs also announce independent churches, from old established ones such as the Legio Maria Church and Ruwe Holy Ghost Church to the more recent "Jubilee Harvest Church" and "Full Gospel Church." In addition, evangelicals come to Kenya from the United States and Europe and hold revivals that attract thousands of people to Nairobi's Uhuru Park. On Friday especially, Muslims assemble for prayers in large numbers and once rather quaint mosques such as the Jamia Mosque in downtown Nairobi today include newly constructed minarets, entrance gates, and education buildings. Similarly, new temples have been built and older ones refurbished by Hindus, Sikhs, and Jains. As the national economy has declined and people despair, religion provides many with hope and may for a while even help them forget they are hungry. Today, the outreach programs of churches, mosques, and temples play an important role in many aspects of society. They feed, clothe, and care for refugees and orphans, support democratic institutions with their leaders speaking out for human rights, and are critical of politicians whose actions are not grounded in the best interests of the poor and working class.

NOTES

1.   Elliot Fratkin, *Surviving Drought and Development: Ariaal of Northern Kenya* (Boulder, Colorado: Westview Press, 1991), 25, 28.

2.   John Lamphear, *The Scattering Time: Turkana Responses to Colonial Rule* (Oxford: Clarendon Press, 1992), 30–40.

3.   Abdul Karim Bangura, *Kipsigis* (New York: Rosen, 1994), 23–26.

4.   Benjamin C. Ray, *African Religions: Symbol, Ritual, and Community* (Englewood Cliffs, New Jersey: Prentice-Hall, 1976), 165–71; and Jomo Kenyatta, *Facing Mount Kenya: The Tribal Life of the Kikuyu* (Secker and Warburg, 1953), 223–25, 301. On how the British exaggerated and sensationalized the use of these oaths, see John Lonsdale, "Mau Maus of the Mind: Making Mau Mau and Remaking Kenya," *Journal of African History* 31 (1990): 399.

5.   There are a number of general books on Islam, such as Rene Bravmann, *African Islam* (Washington, D.C.: Smithsonian Institution Press, 1983).

6. Many of the subdivisions within Kenya's Asian Muslim community are detailed in Cynthia Salvadori, *Through Open Doors: A View of Asian Cultures in Kenya,* rev. ed. (Nairobi: Kenway, 1989), 181–271.

7. David Sperling, "The Frontiers of Prophecy," in *Revealing Prophets: Prophecy in Eastern African History,* eds. David M. Anderson and Douglas H. Johnson (London: James Currey; Athens: Ohio University Press, 1995), 85–86.

8. See Godfrey Muriuki, *A History of the Kikuyu, 1500–1900* (Nairobi: Oxford University Press, 1974), 177–78.

9. Thomas Spear and Isaria N. Kimambo, eds., *East African Expression of Christianity* (Oxford: James Currey; Athens: Ohio University Press, 1999).

10. David Sangren, "Kamba Christianity from Africa Inland Church to African Brotherhood Church," in *East African Expression of Christianity,* ed. Thomas Spear and Isaria N. Kimambo (Oxford: James Currey; Athens: Ohio University Press, 1999), 169–95.

11. Thomas Spear, "Toward the History of African Christianity," in *East African Expression of Christianity,* eds. Thomas Spear and Isaria N. Kimambo (Oxford: James Currey; Athens: Ohio University Press, 1999), 14–15.

12. Ibid., 15–17, and Cynthia Hoehler-Fatton, *Women of Fire and Spirit: History of Faith and Gender in Roho Religion in Western Kenya* (New York and Oxford: Oxford University Press, 1996).

13. "Inside the Secret Sect," *Drum* (May 1983); reprinted in *Kenya: The National Epic from the Pages of Drum Magazine,* ed. Jim Bailey (Nairobi: Kenway, 1993), 310–11.

14. Fratkin, *Surviving Drought and Development,* 81, and chapter 5, "The Impact of Christian Missions," 75–94.

3

Literature, Film, and Media

LITERATURE

Any introduction to the literature of Kenya, and for that matter the entire East African coast, must begin with Swahili. This is because old Swahili towns dot the coast from Somalia in the north to Mozambique in the south, representing the history of not only a people but also a language. Just as people have ancestors, so too do languages. Through the close study of related languages, historical linguists have traced a group of modern-day languages from the coast back to a common ancestral language called Sabaki. Because the vocabulary, sounds, and grammar of Swahili are similar to those found in the languages spoken by their nearby neighbors, linguists convincingly argue that a long time ago, they all once shared Sabaki as a common language. In turn, the Sabaki and Swahili languages are similar to other languages once spoken in parts of central Africa and across and into West Africa. Together all these make up what is known as the Bantu language family.

For a long time, however, it was thought that Swahili, or more correctly, the Kiswahili language, was a foreign import to the East African coast. There were a few reasons for this. First, Swahili contains a large number of Arabic words, which neighboring inland languages do not share. Also, the Swahili people are urban dwellers—traders and artisans—whose culture differs markedly from that of the surrounding farmers and herders. In addition, the Swahili are followers of Islam, but in the course of language development, this is a relatively recent development. Together, these factors suggested to many that Kiswahili and the Swahili came from outside Africa, perhaps from the Arabian Peninsula or the lands surrounding the Persian Gulf. Today, we know this is not true.

From their study of languages around the world, linguists know that languages develop very slowly. Employing various techniques to document these changes, they discovered that Swahili and the other languages to which it is related separated from Sabaki more than a thousand years ago. Their separation in such a time period is consistent with what archaeologists tell us about the founding of the first coastal towns in the ninth century. However, because these towns were on the coast, the Swahili speakers who lived in them emphasized fishing over farming and herding, and traded with merchants from the Middle East who sailed down the Red Sea and around the Arabian Peninsula to the East African coast. As trade increased, different social classes developed and so too did the urban communities in which they lived. Soon these towns included a wealthy merchant class, middle-class artisans, and lower-class fisherman and farmers. The merchants in particular began to follow the practices of Islam, the religion of their influential overseas trading partners. Some even adopted traditions of having foreign origins to make their claims to wealth and prestige more convincing. In the process people also borrowed the Arabic words they needed to talk about, describe, and explain their new lifestyle of seafaring, trade, and Islam. That the Swahili should have borrowed so many Arabic words is no different from the way people and languages borrow from others today. At the same time, the words used for many of the activities they practiced before these changes in their lifestyle, such as the vocabulary associated with fishing and ironworking, can still be found in the language.[1]

Literature in Arabic

As a result of their early overseas contacts, the oldest writing in East Africa is found among the Swahili people, with the Arabic script in use since at least the seventeenth century and the Roman alphabet since the beginning of the twentieth. For the Swahili, most of whom can read and write, the written word also has important status. In part this is because as Muslims, the Swahili understand Arabic to be the revealed language of God because it is the language in which the Qur'an, the sacred scripture of Islam, is written.[2] It is also because the Swahili have a number of written "chronicles" that are understood to document their history. The histories presented by these chronicles are in fact a series of tales that have been adjusted over time to conform to present circumstances. Each time Swahili society changed, the reformation of the society was incorporated into a new version of the story to present the Swahili to others as the Swahili want to be understood.

For example, some of the most important chronicles concern Fumo Liongo. Whether he was a historical person is unclear. According to different accounts, he was Muslim, he was a ruler during pre-Islamic times, or he was a Christian. His actual identity is in fact not as important as what the chronicles present, which is how he moved between three distinct population groups—Swahili townsmen, neighboring herders who today are called the Orma, and the nearby hunter-gatherer Boni—and formed marriage bonds between each one. These marriage bonds helped to forge unity and established the legitimacy of the relationships between the communities that represent island and mainland, and urban and rural. These chronicles thus help to fix the basis of the trading relationships that shaped Swahili society. Their tales relate the uniting of local peoples and rulers with Muslims and sometimes even with Muslims who originate in parts of the Middle East and Asia.

Taken together, these chronicles preserve for the Swahili a tale of their origins that they find acceptable and by which they want to be known to others. They are understood to be true even though a more objective historical view of each reformation of Swahili society needs to document the incorporation into their community of diverse ethnic, political, and social groups. It also needs to address events at the coast before their adoption of Islam. Yet for the Swahili, their identity is that of a coherent, proper Muslim society, and thus the story of their origin does not need to include any of this information. Instead, the Swahili accept what scholars call the "standard Islamic myth," which fixes people into the categories of man or woman, free or slave, and distinguishes between the realm of the living and that of the spirits.[3]

Literature in Swahili

Today, literature written in Swahili comes in many forms, but traditional Swahili literature is in the form of epic song poems, proverbs, and stories passed orally from generation to generation. Only recently have these been written down and translated. The Swahili are especially fond of poetry, *ushairi,* and those skilled in its writing. This admiration comes from recognizing the challenges the poetry's meaning(s) presents to the listener and the knowledge of words and imagery required to express oneself in poems.

One of the more interesting epic poems is "Conquer the World," composed by Mwana Kupona. Written in 1858–60, during the last two years of her life, the 102-stanza poem is full of moral teachings for young people, especially for Swahili girls of marriageable age. To heed the words of the poem was to live a trouble-free life and ensure entry into the world to come. The following stanzas are representative of the wisdom found in Mwana Kupona's poem. The first (stanza 62) is also presented in Swahili to illustrate the traditional *utendi* form of this poem—four lines of eight syllables in each, with the last sound of the first three lines ending in the same sound, and the fourth rhyming with the fourth lines of all the other stanzas in the poem.[4]

> Sipende wenye jamali
> na utukufu wa mali
> fuqara ukamdhili
> cheo ukamvundia.
>   (stanza 62)

> Do not love too much
> those with wealth and good things
> while you despise the beggar
> and scorn his low status.
>   (stanza 62)

> Do not express opinions
> about things you do not know
> guard against talking
> and gossiping around.
>   (stanza 19)

> First hold on to your religion,
> do not reject the laws of God;
> and follow the Traditions
> as closely as you can.
>   (stanza 12)

Other poems that are essentially stories were recited at family gatherings as a form of evening entertainment. For children and adults alike, they explain why things are the way they are in Swahili society, carry a moral, or address serious religious matters. For example, in "How the Cat Became Domesticated," children learn that cats once lived in the wild, as do lions and cheetahs today. But the cat, being ever curious, moved closer to where the hunters lived to observe better how men and women lived. By doing so, the cat discovered that when the hunters came home, they were met at the door by their wives, to whom the hunters always gave their spears, bow, and arrows. From this, the cat concluded that a wife must be very brave to disarm so easily a hunter, and so determined to make friends with the powerful wife who would protect the cat from the hunter. The next time the man left to go hunting, the cat entered the house, where the wife treated him kindly. And from that time on, the cat has been happy to stay at home, especially in the kitchen, with the wife.[5]

In a much more serious vein is the old poem *Ngamia na Paa,* or *The Camel and the Gazelle,* which tells how the Prophet Muhammed was in a mosque praying when he heard a faint voice calling to him, praising his name, and asking for help. Outside the mosque the Prophet discovered the voice calling him belonged to a camel, who told him how her master, who was an unbeliever, had abused her and now planned to kill her. After weeping for the camel, the Prophet went to the camel's owner and asked to buy the camel. The owner refused. The Prophet replied that he knew the owner had been cruel to the camel, because she had told him so, and he would take the camel. The owner did not believe him and challenged the Prophet to prove the camel could speak.

On the way to the camel the owner and the Prophet passed a cage that contained a gazelle wearing an iron collar. The gazelle too praised the Prophet and told him of her plight—she had four babies in the forest with no one to feed or care for them. As with the camel owner, the owner of the gazelle, who was also a nonbeliever, refused to sell the gazelle but agreed to let the Prophet take her place in the cage while she went to feed her young. When the gazelle returned, its owner was so amazed that he announced his belief in Allah and let the gazelle go free to take care of its young. The owner of the camel remained unimpressed. However, when they reached the camel and the camel again related how cruel the owner had been to her, the owner announced his belief in Allah and let the camel go free. From that point on, the camel and the Prophet remained good friends, and when the Prophet left this world for the next, the camel wept at his grave.[6]

For the Swahili the issue raised by this poem is not why the men let the animals go, or why they so suddenly began to believe in Allah, but rather, who is the gazelle? Who is the camel? The answer is that both represent the soul because they belonged to unbelievers who treated them badly just as people treat their souls badly. But it is the Prophet who tries to save souls, and when nonbelievers accept Allah and become believers, their souls are freed.

Proverbs and Riddles

Proverbs are an important part of oral literature across the African continent. Like many traditional poems and stories, they represent a distillation of traditional wisdom. Described by an authority of Swahili proverbs as a "piece of human experience couched in a beautiful phrase," proverbs have for generations taught the collected human wisdom of ages past.[7] Not only can proverbs color everyday speech, but they have also found their way onto clothing as decoration. Swahili proverbs, *methali*, are an important element of the *khanga* cloth that is so much a part of everyday wear for women on the coast.[8] When translated, the meanings of these adages are clear to all. For example, *Mtaka yote hukosa yote* (One who wants all usually loses all), *Ujana ni moshi: ukenda, hauji* (Youth is smoke: it goes and does not come back), *Rahdi ni bora kuliko mali* (Blessings are better than possessions), and *Mapenzi ni kikohozi, haiwezi kufichika* (Love is like a cough; you can't hide it) do not require additional clarification. In fact, they sound remarkably similar to expressions parents and grandparents say to children everywhere.

Proverbs often reflect on the unexpected change of events that occur or aspects of human nature that individuals must learn to live with. This focus can be seen in proverbs such as *Yaliyo mumo ya mumo* (What is inside is inside) and *Mshika mavi, hayaati kumnuka* (The one who touches dung, it will inevitably smell on him). Many proverbs that are associated with issues of wealth and poverty are especially common in Swahili, in large measure because one's status is understood to be reflected in the efforts one makes to achieve wealth. Whereas industriousness leads to success, *Haba na haba hujaza kibaba* (A grain plus a grain fills a bushel), laziness results in failure, *Ukulivu huvuta ufukara* (Laziness causes poverty). Other proverbs comment on men and women, love and marriage; *Mwenye ishiki kalewa* (Some one in love is drunk), *Mungwana ni kalima* (A gentleman is as good as his word), and *Waalimu wawili hufundana* (Two learned men will learn from each other) are truisms no matter which society repeats them.[9]

Proverbs are found in most languages, each encapsulating a small piece of cultural knowledge. The proverbs for which the Swahili are particularly famous are often taken from their epic poetry. In fact some poets compose their poems and songs so that every line of it is a proverb. Others take existing proverbs and build them into the verses of their poems. Still others who are knowledgeable in reciting poems and proverbs love the challenge of being asked to recite them alphabetically beginning with one that starts with an A, the next with B, and moving through the entire alphabet. Still other proverbs are found in written sources, especially manuscripts in Arabic. Today, Swahili proverbs remain an important part of everyday language usage and are comparable to Shakespeare's in the English language and those from Ecclesiastes and Proverbs in the Bible. A few examples will suffice to give a sense of the way these preserve traditional cultural wisdom:[10]

Akili ni mali	Brains are money.
Kuuliza feza	A good question is silver,
Jawabu dhahabu	a good answer is gold.
Dhibu Matuhumu walakini	The wolf is suspect even though
Amelala mwanue njaamasikini	the poor creature slept hungry.

Tales and proverbs such as these are of course not exclusive to the Swahili but are found everywhere in Kenya (and for that matter, all across Africa), instructing and reminding listeners of their culture, patterns of acceptable behavior, admired personality traits, and even the geography of the region. The following proverbs have been recorded among the Kikuyu: *Andu matiui ngamini* (Men do not know liberality) means that one does not give without hope of return; *Hita itanakira* (Resist the beginnings) suggests that the indulging of small faults is the first step to allowing for larger ones; and *Irio hiu itiumaga mburi* (Cooked food is not sold for goats) advises people that food is to be given to friends and visitors. Others have clear parallels in Western proverbs. For example, *Muukiri tene ainukaga tene* (He who gets up early returns early) sounds very much like "The early bird catches the worm." And *Kuhika ni kuuna* (Hurrying is breaking) is essentially "Haste makes waste.[11]

Just as proverbs are used to entertain and instruct, especially children, so too are riddles. Depending on the ethnic group, there are illusions and images that relate to traditional lifestyles. Among the Maasai and other groups that have historically existed by herding animals on the plains of East Africa, references to the outdoors and to meat are common. For example, the answer to the riddle, "The two of us cross the wilderness without talking to each other" is "You and your shadow." And the correct response to "Who is the first to eat when an ox is slaughtered?" is "a knife"; and "What part of the meat can be denied to no one?" is "the smell of roasting meat." Such culture specificity is also clear in the riddle "Which tree is cruel and hates all the others?" The answer is the tree that is used for making fire sticks, since the Maasai use these objects to start fires and burn wood. Similarly, the response to "They moved homes and the red one was born" is "the fire," referring to the Maasai custom of burning their old villages when they shift their settlements to follow the grass for their herds.

Oral Literature

Oral literature is not limited to proverbs and riddles but has also long provided the means by which communities have recorded and recalled their history. Oral literature, also called oral tradition, is a part of the rich heritage retained by each of Kenya's ethnic communities. To a large degree oral tradition recounts in different forms the history of a people, but such histories are not always understood or appreciated. Tom Mboya, who was a leading trade unionist and member of parliament in the 1960s, noted how colonialism devalued, even dismissed, this important aspect of people's cultural identity:

The educational system and the teaching received in the schools during colonial days were ... designed to belittle African traditions and customs and replace them with habits and attitudes developed in Western Europe. The folk stories and rhymes and jingles of African society were neglected in primary schools. Instead wholly inappropriate fairy tales and verse of an alien culture were imported at an early stage. The minds of children were confused by having to cope with Zeus and Saturn instead of Ngai or Lwanda Magere; with King Arthur instead of Gor Mahia or Odera Akang'o; with Thor and Heyda instead of Kikuyu na Mumbi; with bears and wolves instead of lions and giraffes.

Traditional tales of this kind grow up with a society and lose a great deal if transplanted. In the true context they play an important part in instilling basic moral and social concepts in the mind of a child. So later on, the pupil is taught a set of attitudes and social values which do fit with the traditional ways.[12]

The origin histories, known as "traditions of genesis," tell how people locate themselves in time and space and make clear what is still relevant to a community in the contemporary world. Essentially, they are versions of the past upon which different elements of society all agree. Many of these traditions purport to deal with the origins of an entire ethnic group. Yet when one records and examines the origin histories of individual families, clans, or sections, these more-localized traditions recount a much more complex history of where people have lived, the movement of new people into the regions, and even the exit of others. In other words, what those versions that claim to tell the historical origin of community are really all about are core values. They are especially concerned with detailing unity and showing the consequences of breaking accepted cultural norms. By presenting traditional wisdom as stories, the grandparents and elders, who usually have the exclusive rights to tell such stories, remind the community of the common rules of behavior, attitudes, beliefs, and taboos that the society must continue to follow if they are to survive in the world. This was Mboya's point about Gor Mahia, Kikuyu na Mumbi, and the other figures he cited.

The origin stories of the Luo are all about the migrations of families, lineages, and clans to western Kenya, and their impact on non-Luo-speaking peoples who already lived in the area. And while they contain threads of historical detail that can be teased from them, they are really as much about the present as the past because they are describing present-day circumstances and relationships, including the many "diverse and incongruent elements" that are found in today's Luo society. As a result they can be seen to be not just about the construction of a Luo people or nation, but also about other collective identities. Stories about lost spears and lost beads, or references to rivalries between cowives, or the use of witchcraft by one brother against another are in fact about fissures within Luo society with families dividing and brothers separating to go their own way.[13] As one scholar has influentially argued, the construction of ethnic identity is an ongoing and "unfinished process of coming to be."[14]

At the same time these migration stories also address a broad range of issues that are typically about what people encounter in their daily lives. Tolerance is one theme of many Luo stories, and another is jealousy and how to respond to it, for example, when a neighbor treats your child less well than another's. The Luo view of women is made clear in a story about a mother who faces a hyena that is threatening her children. When her helpless husband behaves like a child, she exhibits physical bravery to defend her children. In this story the woman exhibits not only maternal devotion but also courage and intelligence, and the message at the end is clear—do not disrespect a woman merely because she is a woman. In a similar vein, stories about strange offspring are appeals for tolerance toward children who are physically challenged.

Often, those traditions that recount broad histories do so by recalling the names of individuals identified as founding heroes. Some, such as Gikuyu and Mumbi of the Kikuyu, are well known. According to Kikuyu tradition, God appeared to Gikuyu and gave him all the land southwest of Mount Kenya. Here, he and his wife, Mumbi (the Adam and Eve of Kikuyu) made their home and raised nine daughters. Later, the land that God gave Gikuyu was divided among the nine daughters, each being the forebear of one of the nine Kikuyu clans. Today, the Kikuyu still farm this land that was given to them by God.[15] The message in genesis traditions, as it is in this one, is that ethnic groups did not evolve but have existed as a cultural unit from time immemorial, with rights to the land they occupy. For people without written history, these traditions help to explain where they came from. Although some cultural heroes are likely based on real people, others clearly are not. Still others present the very interesting issue of whose cultural hero they are. For example, Fumo Liongo is a great cultural hero of the Swahili, yet Luo legends recalls a person named Liongo whom they claim as their own. Is there in fact some linkage, or is it mere coincidence? This is the sort of challenge that faces those who work with this first type of tradition, traditions of genesis.

Those stories that are more likely to recount actual historical shifts and movements of people are usually particular to a certain geographic area, a clan, or a section of a larger ethnic group. Typically, such stories also identify the pattern of economic adaptation that was followed by this group in earlier days, such as farming, herding, or gathering and hunting, although these may not be common to the community today. An example of this second type of oral tradition is found in the north of Kenya among the Dasenech people. Dasenech society is made up of eight territorial sections. The arrival among the Dasenech of two of these territorial sections, the Kuro and the Randall, can be traced back to the late nineteenth century, at a time when some groups of people who were originally from the cattle-herding Samburu (Kuro in the Eastern Cushitic language of the Dasenech) and the camel-herding Rendille (Randal in the Dasenech language) moved northward. Suffering greatly from the ravages of famine that resulted from the loss of most of their livestock to diseases, these immigrants moved north along the eastern shore of Lake Turkana and settled among the neighboring Dasenech. They picked up and moved in order to survive. Their intention may have been to do so only temporarily until the bad times passed, but ultimately, they stayed and did not return to their own people. Today, oral tradition recognizes them as being more recent immigrants to the larger Dasenech society in which they live.

A third type of oral tradition, reminiscence, is the easiest to use in reconstructing history. These traditions are usually straightforward and relate the life histories of individuals who are presently elders or stories that they heard from the generations of their fathers and grandfathers. Such reminiscences focus on daily life, politics, and events that were actually witnessed by those telling them or were heard from an earlier generation that witnessed them. They recount times of famine and drought, warfare, and migration, as well as the arrival and use of trade goods and technological changes. Because these accounts are typically related as having occurred in the time of a named warrior age-set, they also provide, albeit unintended, a chronology of events that serve those retelling the stories as a kind of mnemonic device. For example, the Samburu relate that at the time of *mutai,* which is their word for the time when the disease of rinderpest killed thousands of their cattle, the *Merikon* age-set were the warriors. Historians have recorded much Samburu oral tradition and know a great deal about how their age-sets work, including the order in which they were inaugurated as warriors. As a result, we know that the *Merikon* were warriors between 1879 and 1892 and that the time of *mutai* occurred during this period.

Many of the peoples of East Africa, including the Maasai, the Borana, and the Gabbra, have such age-sets. For historians the age-set system of the Rendille is the easiest to use because the Rendille follow a calendar in which they name each year after the day of a week. Each new age-set is inaugurated in a "Friday" year and given a unique name. After that age-set has been warriors for a cycle of "two weeks" of years, or fourteen years, they inaugurate a new age-set, with a different name. In addition, certain ceremonies occur in particular years of the age-set. Thus by working backward from the present, and relating named Rendille years to the Western or Gregorian calendar, it is possible to determine when a particular age-set was initiated into warriorhood and in what years the various ceremonies they follow took place. So when a Rendille elder relates that a particular battle occurred between the Rendille and the Laikipiak section of the Maasai during the second Saturday year after the *Dismala* age-set was initiated, a historian can with reasonable confidence know that this fighting took place in 1889.[16]

Oral traditions provide access to the life experiences of all kinds of people similar to that found in published biographies and autobiographies, except that oral tradition "publishes" ordinary people, and not just the political, social, and intellectual leaders of a society. This has exciting implications for social history everywhere, but especially for documenting and writing the history of Africa, in places where individuals know their history but have no access to publishing and often do not know how to write.

Contemporary Literature in English

Comprising approximately 20 percent of the total Kenyan population, the Kikuyu are the largest ethnic group in the country. Because their homeland covered the lower slopes of Mount Kenya in what became known as the White Highlands following the settlement of European farmers there, the Kikuyu were among the first to be colonized. They were among the first to be brought into colonial structures through paid farm labor and education at mission schools, both of which accompanied the spread of white settlers. And the Kikuyu were also among the first to develop a political consciousness aimed at confronting the policies of their colonizers. They quickly came to recognize the value of education and the advantages that accrued to those who spoke English. Soon, however, there were not enough schools to meet the demand, and yet at the same time there was a growing dissatisfaction with mission schools, which taught that many important traditional cultural practices, including polygyny and circumcision, were evil and should be abandoned.

Because many Kikuyu saw advantages in speaking English over their own Gikuyu language, and even Swahili, Kikuyu-born authors began writing in English, rather than their vernacular language, the policy promoted by colonial government to keep Kenya's various peoples further separated. Among the earliest of these Kikuyu writers was Jomo Kenyatta, with his 1938 anthropological study of the Kikuyu titled *Facing Mount Kenya*.[17] The first real burst of writing in English came in the 1960s with a series of autobiographies, most recounting the experience of Mau Mau freedom fighters, and the first novels and plays of Ngugi wa Thiong'o (b. 1938). Somewhat ironically, but perfectly logically, Ngugi decided in the 1980s to write only in Gikuyu. At one level this commitment can be seen part of a campaign to help preserve traditional cultures, but equally important to him is that his writing be more broadly accessible to his own people, whether they are urban office workers or rural farmers. Such a decision may not be quite as realistic a choice for a less well established and commercially successful writer.

Acknowledged internationally as Kenya's foremost author, Ngugi, once chair of the Department of Literature at the University of Nairobi, has written novels, dramas, short stories, and essays. Ngugi's writings and outspokenness on a range of social issues, but especially the role of land ownership and the ever-widening gap between wealthy and poor Kenyans, led to his arrest in 1977. The catalyst for his arrest appears to have been his play *Ngahiika Ndeenda* (I Will Marry When I Want To), which was first performed and published in the Gikuyu language. Using local villagers as actors, the play tells the story of a poor village laborer and his wife who are duped by their wealthy Christian neighbors into mortgaging and ultimately losing their plot of land in order to afford a ceremony to cleanse their marriage in the church. The reason the neighbors covet this land and perpetrate this unholy hoax is because they want to build a factory with foreign capital that will make them even more wealthy. With its theme of land, the play was both authentic and relevant to the local population. It also included catchy songs that the audience went away singing, adding to the play's popular appeal. The government, however, found all of this so threatening that they revoked the theater's performance license, dismantled the theater, and detained Ngugi without trial. The real threat, of course, was that the audience was hearing dialogue and songs in their own language, Gikuyu.

Until this time the Kenyatta government had been quite tolerant of criticism by its intellectuals, but until this play in Gikuyu, such criticism had always been leveled in English or Swahili, which was understood by only a small percentage of the population. When there emerged the possibility that the criticism would be understood by a majority of the population, the government felt truly threatened. As Ngugi explained, "If you see that you are poor because God has willed it, you are more than likely to continue to pray to God to right your condition. But if you know that your poverty is not God-conditioned, but is socially conditioned, then you are likely to do something about those social conditions that are assuring that you will be poor."[18] Released after a year, Ngugi continued to write and have his work published in Kenya. However, when his latest and even more radical play, *Mother Sing for Me,* was banned in 1982, Ngugi, who at the time was out of the country, stayed out of Kenya to take up teaching posts in England and the United States.

The road that led Ngugi to being an expatriate began with a mission school education and baptism as James Ngugi, the name under which his earliest novels first appeared. His first novel provides a historical perspective of early Kikuyu history on the verge of Britain's colonial occupation. *The River Between* (1965) is set at the beginning of this period, when the introduction of outside customs was only starting to be felt in Kikuyuland, although no white colonialists had yet arrived in the area. Detailing the story of two villages divided by a river, which both unites and determines the villages, the novel relates the importance of ritual and tradition in everyday life. Through its story and characters, *The River Between* expounds the contentious issues with which a changing society must contend. Ngugi emphasizes two such issues—the balance between the need for community and the desires of individuals, and the challenge to youth of obtaining an education. This latter theme explores a desirous school-based education that allows students to make their own informed decisions versus the rigid indoctrination of a mission-based one, which requires them to denounce tribal traditions or be barred from school.

In *Weep Not, Child* (1964) Ngugi again looks at the Kenyan, and for that matter the African, experience, when land was appropriated for colonial farms and modernity forced the abandonment of one's traditional heritage. The contentious issues that surround land ownership date back to 1915 when the British Imperial Land Act transferred ownership of all land to the British Crown. As a result the Kikuyu were forced to work as squatters or *ahoi* on land now owned by white settlers but which was once their own. Although Ngugi's characters contend with bewildering forces that disrupt their traditional way of life and seem beyond their control, his stories always present a challenge for present-day Kenyans: "All white people stick together. But we black people are very divided. And because they stick together, they have imprisoned Jomo [Kenyatta], the only hope we had. Now they will make us slaves. They took us to their wars and they killed all that was of value to us."[19]

Whether in other early novels such as *Grain of Wheat* (1967), the backdrop of which is Mau Mau and the split within communities between the "homeguards" who were part of the British effort to put down the rebellion and the freedom fighters, or more recent novels, such as *Petals of Blood* (1977), set in a small village just after independence and confronting the growing gap between rich and poor Kenyans, Ngugi is outspoken and uncompromising in his critique of exploitation and oppression. From the precolonial period through the colonial period to independence and beyond, Ngugi confronts the impact of events on local politics and traditional values. With Kenya as his backdrop, he describes the impact of European conquest at the local level and the emergence of inequality in a colonial system where Africans could not win, to the acquisition following independence (*uhuru*) of personal and economic power by a few at the expense of the majority. Certain themes dominate Ngugi's criticism of Kenya and Kenyans. Among the most biting are those aimed at land-hungry politicians who cheat peasant farmers out of their land (e.g., *Grain of Wheat*) and a capitalism that impoverishes the already underprivileged causing further misery and suffering (e.g., *Petals of*

Blood). Christianity is certainly not immune when Ngugi asks, "Why is it that the church is always preaching humility and forgiveness and non-violence to the oppressed? ... Why is it that the church does not concentrate its preaching and efforts of conversion on the very classes and races that have brutalized others, manacled others, robbed others?"[20] And his suggestion of a solution cannot be comforting when he writes about a messianic leader who concludes that true liberation can only come through the taking up of arms (*Matagari*, 1987).

Grace Ogot (b. 1930) is another well-recognized author, although she has not had the same acclaim given to Ngugi. Primarily known as a writer of short stories, she often engages themes of village life and the place of women in these traditional communities, as in her first short-story collection *Land without Thunder* (1968) and her novel *The Promised Land* (1966). Like Ngugi, Ogot wants her writing to reach a broader Kenyan readership. So she has published some of her work in Dholuo (Luo), the language she grew up speaking. A founding member of the Writer's Association of Kenya, she has also served Kenya as an ambassador to the United Nations and UNESCO (United Nations Educational, Scientific, and Cultural Organization).

Kenya also has other women writers of note, some of whom have only recently entered the field. Among the established writers is Marjorie Oludhe Macgoye. Among the more recent is Margaret Oglola, also a pediatrician. Her insight into the way young people, especially young girls, think makes her first novel, *The River and the Source* (1995), particularly noteworthy. This award-winning novel traces the strong women of an extended family across three generations as they confront the shifting values and changes in cultural tradition that have marked the Luo people of western Kenya as they have moved from precolonial rural villages to postindependence urban towns. Stela Kahaki Njuguna's first novel, *Labyrinth* (2000), confronts head on the various roles, chores, and obligations that girls, mothers, and wives perform with devotion and sacrifice, but without recognition or compensation. Some male writers are also producing novels and dramas that have women as strong central characters. Included in this group is the playwright and actor Francis Imbuga, whose *Aminata* (1988) and other plays are often performed at the Kenya National Theatre.

Still other novels and short stories that have been published by Kenyan authors, although they have not garnered the "great literature" label enjoyed by Ngugi's works or found a wide international readership, are also of a high standard and worthy of note. In this category are the popular work of Charles Mangua (b. 1939) and Meja Mwangi (b. 1948). Their writing hits at the raw hardship and urban poverty that shape the lives of so many of the common people who live, work, and love in urban centers such as Nairobi. Mangua's initial success came with the publication of his entertaining *Son of Woman* (1971). A form of social commentary on Kenyans' struggle to deal with rapid social change, it is told by Dodge, the son of a prostitute, whose shiftlessness takes him from the slums of Nairobi to the good life as a corrupt government employee and finally, to jail. Similarly, Mwangi's *Going Down River Road* (1976), which is an actual street in downtown Nairobi, tracks the life of a young man through the wretched underside of living poor in the nation's capital.

In his tragic tale *Carcase for Hounds* (1974), Mwangi presents the overlapping lives of three men: a Mau Mau general, who was once a goverment chief, his boyhood friend who is now a local chief collaborating with the colonial police, and a British officer trying to put down the rebellion. The Mau Mau struggle is often the backdrop for Kenyan writers.

Among the next generation of authors is David Mulwa. His 1987 novel, *Master and Servant,* is set against the other major backdrop in Kenyan writing—the colonial era—and traces the life of a youth growing to manhood.

Published locally at relatively reasonable costs, these novels go through a number of multiple printings, which gives a sense of their popularity and wide readership. Also popular among the Kenyan reading public are what might best be described as pulp spy adventure stories and tales of love and betrayal. Mwangi Gicheru's *The Ivory Merchant* (1976) is representative of this genre. In many of these stories being right, even if the hero or heroine is on the losing side, is part of the key to the protagonist's success. The writings of Kenyans remain rich and varied with many new emerging writers continually being published. With increasing numbers of Kenyan authors being read as part of secondary school literature curriculum alongside recognized European and American classics, Kenyan literature has a promising future. This short introduction provides only a glimpse of some of the highlights and is far from exhaustive.

FILM

Kenya has and continues to provide spectacular locations and captivating subject matter for films, but seldom is the screenplay developed from literature written by Kenyans. Instead it draws on popular literature written by non-Kenyans. The most widely known of these is *Out of Africa* (1937), the romantic memoir of Karen Blixen, who wrote under the pen name of Isak Dinesen, in which she writes about her eighteen-year struggle (1913–31) to succeed as a coffee farmer in the white highlands of Kenya. Included in the memoir is her adulterous love affair with Denys Finch-Hatton, an aristocratic English playboy (she was Danish), and her relationship with her husband,

The home of Karen Blixen, whose romantic memoir *Out of Africa,* which tells of her struggle to succeed as a coffee farmer in the early twentieth century, was made into a film of the same name starring Meryl Streep and Robert Redford.

Bror Blixen, which through marriage made her a baroness. Her tale of struggle as a woman managing a coffee farm leaves unexplained the reason coffee was so profitable—cheap land, which the colonial government deliberately undervalued, and cheap African labor, to whom the land on which the coffee was being grown originally belonged. In 1985 *Out of Africa* was turned into an epic film starring Meryl Streep and Robert Redford and directed by Sydney Pollack. Visually beautiful and finely acted, the film also leaves unexamined the place of Blixen and other white farmers whose upper-class lifestyle was built on their being colonizers of the Kikuyu people who worked hers and their farms. This omission makes inconsequential the complaint that Redford portrayed the British Finch-Hatton as an American since, unlike Streep, his portrayal was accent free.

Although this blockbuster was quickly followed by two more films about Kenya, *Kitchen Toto* (1987) and *White Mischief* (1988), neither of these films had the same commercial success. Absent Hollywood stars, writer-director Harry Hook's low-budget film *Kitchen Toto* explores the relationship between colonizer and colonized and the ways in which colonialism destroyed lives on both sides. It does so by providing episodes in the lives of a district commissioner and the small child (*toto* in Swahili) who works in the district commissioner's house and kitchen during the 1950s Mau Mau uprising (see chapter 1 for more on the Mau Mau rebellion). The child takes the kitchen job when Mau Mau rebels murder his father, a Kikuyu Christian minister. While serving in the official's household, the child becomes a victim first of colonial racism and then by the Mau Mau who force him to take an oath to kill all whites. Although this film had the potential to be a significant critique of colonialism, it is slow moving with characters that never really develop. Even less satisfying is the colonial critique, which is left to the viewer to make, based on the repetitive sufferings of the kitchen *toto*. With its focus on Mau Mau, it recalls Robert Ruark's *Something of Value,* which in 1957 was turned into a movie of the same name. *Something of Value* is but one of Ruark's many adventure/big-game-hunting novels full of dangerous Africans and tribal ritual and ceremony.

White Mischief, directed by Michael Radford, again focuses on the white upper classes that dominated aspects of Kenyan life in the 1940s, relating the real-life murder of a wealthy, but most unpleasant British aristocrat. As a period film about such aristocrats' decadent lifestyles, it could have shed light on aspects of the colonial situation at this time. However, as presented it is simply an unmemorable murder mystery in which Kenya is little more than a backdrop.

The earliest films of Kenya were taken by Osa and Martin Johnson and focus on the country's wildlife. Their first film, *Trailing African Wild Animals* (1923), was followed by the release of many others during the 1920s and 1930s, ending with *I Married Adventure* in 1940. The early films were taken near a volcanic crater lake the filmmakers called "Lake Paradise," which was near Marsabit in northern Kenya. These tremendously successful films gave many people their first look at Africa. When in the 1950s they were shown on television, a new generation was introduced to Africa. But the image everyone saw was that of wild Africa. When later filmmakers introduced story lines, Africans were portrayed as primitive caricatures of themselves. Missing entirely are rural farmers displaced as the result of colonial policies that left them squatters on their own land, or the underclass of urbanized town folk subject to pass laws (*kipande*) not unlike those imposed in apartheid South Africa. In the 1960s and 1970s a second generation of wildlife films captured the Western audience's imagination. These included John Wayne's *Hatari* (1962), *Africa Texas Style* (1967), and the hugely successful films *Born Free* (1966) and *Living Free* (1972), about George and Joy Adamson with Elsa the lioness and her cubs.

Although the release of *Out of Africa* heralded a period of time when the Kenya film industry was strong, demonstrating its significant potential, by the mid-1990s this budding film industry faced significant problems from two different directions. The first was from Hollywood, where movies associated with Africa are generally either of the "Tarzan of the Apes" type or tales of adventure and big-game hunting. Both types support the stereotyped image of Africa as "the Dark Continent" full of "dangerous savages." This is certainly the Africa presented in *The Mountains of the Moon* (1990), another historical drama filmed in Kenya, which tells the story of Richard Burton and John Speke's search in the 1850s for the source of the Nile. However, the major challenge to the Kenya film industry comes from southern Africa. Since the resumption of majority rule, South Africa especially and Zimbabwe to a lesser extent have used their significant already-in-place filmmaking infrastructures to attract film crews. Because South Africa and Zimbabwe have far less government bureaucracy and red tape to be cut through before shooting can begin, Kenya has serious competition. The stark reality of this situation was made especially apparent when the immensely successful film *Ghost in the Darkness* (1996), starring Val Kilmer and Michael Douglas, who also produced it, ended up being filmed in South Africa. The film is based on a true story of how in 1895 two man-eating lions at Tsavo in eastern Kenya held up the construction of the Mombasa-to-Uganda railway. Much in the film is invented, including Douglas's American white hunter character, who leads a group of lion-hunting Maasai warriors who come to the rescue of the British engineer building the railway's bridges. Of course, the Maasai would need a white hunter to lead them in a lion hunt even less than the British engineer needed someone else to shoot the lions, which in the event he accomplished quite successfully. The featured group of Maasai and Samburu warriors, all of whom were flown to South Africa for the film, led one scholar to describe this film as playing on "Western stereotypes of primordial masculinity and glorious blood-drinking savagery."[21]

Following the success of this film, Africa, including Kenya, again became a desired film subject as witnessed by two more commercial successes, *The Air Up There* (1994) and *Ace Ventura: When Nature Calls* (1995), neither of which did much to add to the audience's understanding of modern-day Africa. *The Air Up There* is billed as a comedy about an American university basketball scout who heads to Africa in search of another Akhim Alijawon, who in fact hails from Nigeria. *Ace Ventura: When Nature Calls* is little more than a vehicle for Jim Carrey to act up while playing off one stereotype of Africa after another, from sensual African maidens and strange food to savage blood-thirsty warriors and stupid tribal leaders, all in need of a white man to make life better.

While Africa as a whole may still lag behind the West in a number of areas of film production, Kenya has talented actors, writers, and production personnel, unbelievably beautiful and diverse landscapes, and plants and animals that can provide fascinating scenic backdrops for the film industry. The evidence for this can be found in films that have been shot in Kenya and the growing local production of films and dramas being made. Among the latter is Sao Gamba's direction of the film *Kolormask* (1985), which confronts the issue of Kenyan students returning home from abroad with both university degrees and white wives.[22] This exploration of the significant cultural differences between Kenya and England speaks directly to a Kenya that is still sorting out its present from its past. Also noteworthy is the work of the Gallamoro Network. Founded by the actor Joseph Olita (who acted in films including *The Rise and Fall of Idi Amin* [1979] and *Mississippi Masala* [1992]), this nongovernmental organization uses film documentaries and theater dramas to tackle African social issues related to HIV/AIDS, poverty, women, and the environment. Through a mobile cinema project, these documentaries, as well as popular films, are shown without charge to hundreds of thousands of people in the rural areas, paid for through advertising attached to them. Nevertheless, the conclusion reached by one authority on African cinema remains troubling: "It is as if the camera has matured to the point where it can see Africans, but it cannot accept them as they are."[23]

MEDIA

Newspapers and Magazines

Newspapers have a long history in Kenya. Prior to the present day, the most vibrant period was probably the years from the end of World War II up to Mau Mau. In this period there was a populist press, a moderate nationalist press, and a regional press publishing mostly in Swahili, Gikuyu, and Kamba. Many were weekly or biweekly publications, and others were monthly, but all were at some level expressing the political hopes and aspirations of the African population. The first two focused largely on national issues, with the moderate nationalist press, edited by an educated elite, campaigning for constitutional change. The populist press, largely in the hands of less well educated men active in grassroots politics, was more interested in independence. The regional press was less concerned with issues at the national level and tended to focus on local concerns. Some papers achieved what can be considered a large circulation, and because they were passed from reader to reader, many more people read than actually bought the paper. In the end they all suffered from a lack of funds and experience, and many folded. Under the State of Emergency declared in 1952 in response to the Mau Mau uprising, the colonial government closed down most of these publications, labeling them a danger to public order. When in the 1960s newspapers in local languages tried to make a comeback, they discovered the competition from the English and Swahili national dailies, each being published by financial powerhouses, to be too strong.[24]

Dominating the press today are three English-language dailies—the *East African Standard,* the *Daily Nation,* and the *Kenya Times*—and a Swahili-language daily, *Taifo Leo.* Recently, a fourth English-language daily, *The People,* has become a serious player in the market, appearing under the banner "Fair, Frank, Fearless." The oldest of these dailies, the *East African Standard,* has been publishing since 1902 and in the 1950s published two Swahili papers, *The Baraza* and the *Tazama.* Today, the Lonrho Group, a British multinational, owns the *East African Standard.* As well as covering local, regional, and international news, it prints financial news and Nairobi stock exchange closings. The *Daily Nation*—with the largest circulation of more than 150,000—and its sister publication, *Taifo Leo,* are owned by Prince Karim Aga Khan IV. Founded in 1960, each maintains and prides itself on a high level of reporting. Their coverage, which includes national, regional, and international news, also features a large number of photographs, good sports coverage, serious columns by local commentators, and letters to the editor. For many years the *East African Standard* and the *Daily Nation* were the only papers in Nairobi. However, when in 1983 both papers became increasing critical of the government and its policies, for which its journalists and editors suffered harassment, arrest, and detention, the ruling Kenyan African National Union (KANU) political party founded its own daily, the *Kenya Times.* Kenyan news and the party line dominate the *Times.* There are also Sunday papers to go with the dailies: *The Sunday Standard,* the *Sunday Nation,* and *Taifa Jumapli.* Mombasa has a weekly publication called the *Coast Weekly* that caters to local news, including shipping information.

Kenya has also seen the publication of a number of highly regarded magazines. The most enduring is a popular monthly called *Drum.* Originally founded in South Africa, it was introduced in Kenya in 1952 at the beginning of the Mau Mau emergency, from which time it has regularly provided a forum for contemporary political issues. It does so with good and timely writing and excellent photographs. As well as publishing in South Africa and Kenya, *Drum* has a long history of reporting from offices across English-speaking Africa.

The most recent addition to the Nairobi scene is the magazine *Quest: Kenya's Lifestyle Magazine.* Like *Drum,* it includes advice columns and feature stories of local interests. Recent articles have reported on housing projects for orphans, the global issue of HIV/AIDS, and the rising recording artist Mercy Myra. Similar to North American and British lifestyle magazines, it covers fashion and the arts and includes movie reviews, recipes from chefs using local ingredients, weekend getaways to scenic locations and game parks, product tests (e.g., liquid soaps and savories such as vegetarian *samosas*), horoscopes, and sports.

Another glossy, four-color, high-quality magazine is the music quarterly *Phat!* Billed as "Africa's First Music and Entertainment Magazine" and popular from East Africa to southern Africa and also distributed in Europe, *Phat!* is *the* inside source on all things related to the African and world music scene. Kenyan produced and edited, *Phat!* profiles African recording artists and bands, presents feature articles on music festivals and styles (e.g., "Pure Angolan Style" and "Drummers of Burundi"), reviews of recently released CDs, and in regular columns the latest "buzz" on everything from the hip-hop and rap scenes to Gospel, fashion, and Web links.

Television and Radio

Only twenty-some years ago radio and television in Kenya was essentially a monopoly of the Voice of Kenya. Today under its new name, the Kenya Broadcasting Corporation (KBC), it faces considerable competition, and not only from satellite dishes and video rental stores. The Kenya Television Network (KTN), the first private station granted a license to broadcast, came on the air in late 1989. It broadcasts beginning with the news at noon to midnight; when not airing local shows it is linked to CNN centers in Atlanta and London. STV (Stellagraphics, Ltd.) has South African and British connections, with a range of programming that includes South African soap operas, the BBC World News, and Sky International. M-NET has broadcast links that show Super Sport and Movie Magic programming, as well as the Cartoon Network. When not airing various American and British television evangelists, Family TV brings the Christian World News into Kenyan homes.

Prior to this liberalization the government kept a tight reign on broadcasting, beginning with the first radio station set up in 1928 by British East African Broadcasting. The Kenya Broadcasting Service, established by the colonial government in 1954, eventually pulled together the previously segregated services set up for European, African, and Asian broadcasts. Then in 1961, with independence on the horizon and fearful of all broadcasting falling into the hands of the African population, the British organized the KBC, which introduced television to Kenya in 1962. But in 1964, the newly independent government nationalized the KBC and reorganized it by an Act of Parliament as the Voice of Kenya, which it remained until 1991 when it was reinvented as a new state cooperation and again named the KBC. Although Kenya currently has nine private television broadcasters and nineteen radio stations, they tend to be focused on the Nairobi area, with a couple of stations in Mombasa. The stations sending their signals across the country remain those operated by the KBC, with forty-three VHF/UHF television stations and twenty-two AM and seventeen FM radio stations.

Today, KBC radio competes with an ever-expanding range of privately owned and operated FM stations, many of which sound like Kenyan versions of English-language pop music or talk radio found in many other parts of the world. No longer is it necessary to have short-wave radio and to search from band to band and megahertz to megahertz, depending on the time of day, to try and locate English- or Swahili-language broadcasts. It is now all on the FM radio dial. Local news competes with the World News on BBC's local FM station.

Two stations seem to dominate the contemporary music scene, although more and more are moving into this market and establishing their own identities. Capital FM, the first private radio station to be licensed (1996), plays a full array of Western contemporary music with DJs who sound as if they are broadcasting on London's Capital Radio. Hip-hop, the local music scene, and Congolese bands provide the staple of 101.9 FM. Other stations include Family Radio, which has a Christian focus, and an AM dial that is the center of numerous ethnically based stations.

A relatively new focus for radio has been the development of soap operas to educate the general public to health issues. For example, the twice-weekly radio soap opera *Ushikwapo Shikamana* (If Assisted, Assist Yourself) has been used for the past few years to address a variety of social issues from domestic violence and substance abuse to urban migration and the low status of women, but especially HIV/AIDS prevention. Using drama and intrigue to highlight the choices people can make in their lives, *Ushikwapo Shikamana* presents the lives of everyday people in three different settings—a rural area, an urban one, and at a city's edge. *Ushikwapo Shikamana* also currently appears three times a week in a comic-strip version in the Swahili-language daily *Taifa Leo,* where the radio soap's messages are reinforced.

It seems clear that the liberalization of Kenya's airwaves will continue, although not without debate and discussion. At times ownership, control, and licensing of television and radio stations surface as contentious issues, and always more so in the months leading up to national elections. The major issues, however, that will come to dominate the debate in the coming years, undercurrents of which are already present and particularly in the music business, are those of local programming and content. Today, with the emergence on the world scene of Kenyan musicians who can record and mix their own CDs with Kenya professionals in local recording studios, the lack of play time for Kenyan-produced music on local radio is already an issue. Demands for stiffer regulation of program content are also sure to increase in the coming years.

NOTES

1. Derek Nurse and Thomas Spear, *The Swahili: Reconstructing the History and Language of an African Society, 800–1500* (Philadelphia: University of Pennsylvania, 1985).

2. The author of the Qur'an is Allah (God), and thus he is associated with the language that originates in Heaven. Islam in Kenya is discussed further in chapter 2, "Religion and Worldview."

3. John Middleton, *The World of the Swahili: An African Mercantile Civilization* (New Haven, Connecticut: Yale University Press, 1992), especially 27–40.

4. Kitula King'ei, *Mwana Kupona, Poetess from Lamu* (Nairobi: Sesa Sema, 2000), 52–66.

5. Malcolm C. Jensen, "Paka Comes Inside," *Faces* 14, no. 4 (1997): 32–33.

6. Kitula King'ei, *Mwana Kupona,* 82–90.

7. Jan Knappert, *Swahili Proverbs* (Burlington: University of Vermont, 1997).

8. More on *khanga* cloth can be found in chapter 5, "Cuisine and Traditional Dress."

9. Many more examples can be found in Knappert, *Swahili Proverbs,* and other works on Swahili language and literature.

10. Knappert, *Swahili Proverbs.*

11. G. Barra, *1000 Kikuyu Proverbs,* 2nd ed. (Nairobi: Kenya Literature Bureau, 1960).

12. Tom Mboya, in a speech, "Is African Culture Blocking Progress?" quoted in B. Onyango-Ogutu and A. A. Roscoe, *Keep My Words: Luo Oral Literature* (Nairobi: East African Publishing House, 1974), 8.

13. William David Cohen and E. S. Atieno Odhiambo, *Siaya: The Historical Anthropology of an African Landscape* (London: James Currey; Athens: Ohio University Press, 1989), 17, 30–31, 35–36, 125.

14. John Lonsdale, "When Did the Gusii (Or Any Other Group) Become a 'Tribe,'" *Kenya Historical Review* 5, no. 1 (1977), 123–33.

15. Godfrey Muriuki, *A History of the Kikuyu, 1500–1900* (Nairobi: Oxford University Press, 1974), 47.

16. Neal Sobania, "Defeat and Dispersal: The Laikipiak and Their Neighbours at the End of the Nineteenth Century," in *Being Maasai: Ethnicity and Identity in East Africa,* ed. Thomas Spear and Richard Waller (London: James Currey; Athens, Ohio University Press, 1993), 105–19.

17. Jomo Kenyatta, *Facing Mount Kenya: The Tribal Life of the Kikuyu* (London: Secker and Warburg, 1953).

18. Quoted in Albert Gerard, *African Language Literatures* (Harlow: Longman, 1981), 313.

19. Ngugi wa Thiong'o, *Weep Not Child* (Portsmouth, New Hampshire: Heinemann, 1964), 75.

20. Ngugi wa Thiong'o, *Writers in Politics* (Portsmouth, New Hampshire: Heinemann, 1981), 22.

21. Sidney Kasfir, "Slam-Dunking and the Last Noble Savage," *Visual Anthropology* 15, no. 3–4 (2002).

22.   Manthia Diawara, *African Cinema: Politics and Culture* (Bloomington: Indiana University Press, 1992), 116–17.

23.   Kenneth M. Cameron, *Africa on Film: Beyond Black and White* (New York: Continuum, 1994), 29.

24.   Fay Gadsden, "The African Press in Kenya, 1945–1952," *Journal of African Studies* 21, no. 4 (1980): 515–35.

4

Art, Architecture, and Housing

ART AND CRAFT

The world of any group of people is filled with the objects of everyday life—furniture for sitting, pots and utensils for cooking, containers for storing, and fabrics and jewelry for wearing. Usually, we appreciate these objects for their beauty, but almost never do we think of their makers as artists. Instead, if we have any appreciation at all for such items—perhaps the hand-turned pottery vase or the woven rug—we call them "crafts." This comes from a Western concept of art that is tied tightly to notions of creativity and uniqueness. As an exclusive category, it suggests that only certain objects are valued as art and that objects that are not paintings or sculptures fall outside the category. As such, items that are functional or utilitarian are labeled "craft" or "handicraft." In anthropological terms these same objects are called "artifacts" and made not by artists but "artisans." Indeed, until very recently a review of most African art books or exhibition catalogs of African art included few, if any, objects from eastern (and southern) Africa. Yet the suggestion that these vast regions are without art is merely the imposition of this preconceived Western notion of what art is. More important, this idea is not reflected in African thinking. Because everyday objects have an aesthetic dimension—that is, they are appreciated as being beautiful and in good taste—the Western distinction between art and artifact or art and craft is not very helpful. Instead, we need to broaden our gaze, especially when considering the diversity of other peoples' cultural traditions. Whether African or, in this case, Kenyan, we must seek to understand the beauty and value these people see in the objects. After all, these objects are not made only to be used; they are also made to be handled, looked at, and displayed.

To confront this issue more directly, consider the wealth of beautiful objects used in everyday life. Is Maasai beadwork art? Are the woven-grass milk containers made by Borana women art? Are the burial posts of the Mijikenda art? Are the doors of Swahili homes on Lamu Island merely an architectural feature? Just because a society has no tradition of sculpture or painting does not mean it is without art. Did one need to wait until Kenyans began to produce and exhibit contemporary painting in European- and North American–style galleries to declare that Kenya has art? When one steps beyond the realm of three-dimensional art and considers music and dance, is traditional dance art? What of drumming? (Chapter 8, "Music and Dance," looks at these genres in more detail.) And if written literature is art, how do we view oral tradition and storytelling?

Most objects that are used in traditional homes in Kenya are made locally. Some objects can be made by almost anyone; for example, most women make pots or weave baskets, and men carve wooden containers and headrests, at least in those societies that use them. In other cases particular objects require special expertise and specialists are needed, such as blacksmiths who shape and forge metal for plows and spears. Get to know a community well, and its members will tell you who among them is a good object maker. Whether or not they are aware of there being a creative process at work, people know what pleases them and what does not, what is culturally correct and what is not. Go to a marketplace and watch an individual purchasing a pot, a basket, or a piece of cloth. If any one will do, why do they take time considering which one to buy? As well as looking for quality, an aesthetic judgment—what is pleasing in the eye of the beholder—is also being made. Are the proportions correct? Are the colors correct, and have they been applied appropriately?

Three-Dimensional Art

Personal objects represent a particular kind of African art, created mostly for practical reasons as opposed to religious, ritual, or ceremonial purposes. In large measure the materials available in the local environment dictate what can be made. While providing utility, such objects also represent the artistry of their maker. Although it is not possible to be exhaustive with respect to the range of objects included in this category of personal items, the following are some important examples associated with particular regions of Kenya.

Headrests, for example, have a long history in Africa. Found in Egypt among the possessions of pharaohs, they were used across the continent. Today, they are less common but are still used in the semiarid plains of northern Kenya where people continue to herd livestock for a living. Headrests

Elders who cover their hair with decorative mudpacks sleep on wooden headrests so as not to destroy this personal adornment.

appear in a broad range of styles, often with more than one style in use in the same community. Personal and portable, they can be used when visiting, when traveling great distances, or while herding livestock. Used to support the head and cradle the neck when sleeping, they are particularly useful to those men whose hair is worn in an elaborate "mudpack." Elders of many different communities in northern Kenya adorn themselves by shaving their hair back from the forehead to create a very precise hairline. Hair from this line is then pulled back, and hair from the back of the head is pulled forward. All of it is then covered with mud to hold in place ostrich feathers and other ornaments that indicate the man's status. Because considerable time is spent creating these mudpacks, which normally last from a few weeks to more than a couple of months, it is important to not destroy them by sleeping on them; thus headrests are used.

Among the Dasenech and Turkana in the very north of Kenya, the most common form of headrest is a very smooth simple neck bar resting on a single pedestal leg. Further south among the Rendille and Samburu, two legs at each end of a longer neck bar are more common. Some headrests are incised with decorative designs, but generally they are valued for their smooth surface and the lustrous soft patina acquired from daily use. Headrests often double as stools, especially when herders are away from home in stock camps. A three-legged variety of headrest-stool is carved from a carefully selected tree with intersecting branches that become the legs.[1] These stools are often used to provide additional support for recently circumcised youths. Headrests are a response to a functional need and made for a specific purpose to an exacting standard. Most often this standard is that of the herdsman who carves the headrest himself. Increasingly, as young men abandon the practice of styling their hair with mud, the number of headrests produced can be expected to continue to decline.

Across the country, pastoralists use milk containers, constructed much like a thermos, with a bottom for storing milk and a top for drinking.

Other wooden household objects include hollowed-out containers for milk. Some of these are constructed much like a thermos, with a bottom for holding and storing the milk and a top for pouring milk into or drinking from. Containers that hold animal fat for cooking and cosmetic use are also carved from wood. If such objects are decorated at all, it is typically with incised hatched lines and a leather strap that may or may not have beads sewn on it.

For many outsiders, brightly colored beads symbolize Africa. However, beaded necklaces, earrings, and bracelets, along with other various forms of personal adornment and hairstyle, often define an individual's status within and between communities. Colors and patterns of beaded decoration can declare not only an ethnic affiliation but clan and age-group connections as well. This aspect of identity has been most extensively studied among the Maasai, where beads are a part of the material culture that defines who they are. For example, by placing strings of beads around a baby's wrists, ankles, and waist soon after it is born, a mother can observe her infant's growth as the beads tighten or slacken. A small child will also wear a necklace consisting of the small end of a gourd that often contains a piece of obsidian surrounded on each side by an old dark blue or black bead and a cowrie shell. These objects respectively signify the earth, the sky, and the sea.

For the Maasai the wearing of personal adornment immediately identifies an individual's social status—girl, eligible for marriage, or married for females, and boy, warrior, or elder for males. The status is communicated by the shape, pattern, and color of beadwork and earrings; when two people approach each other, even if they have never seen each other before, they know how to "read" the status of the other and thus use appropriate forms of address and greeting. While to an outsider the Maasai outfitted in all their beaded finery may appear to be all "dressed up" and ready for a special occasion, most such adornment is worn daily throughout the time the individual is in a particular stage of life. The high degree of sophistication and symbolic communication that has come to be attached to Maasai beadwork dates only from the end of the nineteenth century, when large quantities of colorful uniform-sized glass beads with predrilled center holes became available from what is today the Czech Republic. Prior to this, Maasai adornment consisted of metal ornaments forged by blacksmiths, and only a very few European-manufactured glass beads, but these too would have communicated an individual's particular social status.

Across Kenya beadwork is invariably the domain of women, and this is certainly so among the Maasai. Even the beads worn by men, which generally indicate warriors, are made by their mothers, sisters, or girlfriends. Maasai girls and women produce their beadwork for themselves, their families, and

From an early age young girls among the Maasai, Samburu, and other peoples begin to acquire beaded collars that make clear to all who see them that they are not yet married. The girl in this photograph is Samburu.

their friends—and only more recently for cash sale to curio shops and road-side marketplaces.

The key to understanding the Maasai aesthetic in beads is to recognize that those things which are the same cannot match. Thus each earring in a pair must be different just as for the Maasai heaven and earth are a pair, female and male a pair, and so too Maasai and non-Maasai. It is this aesthetic that produces the beautiful array of colors and patterns so closely associated with Maasai beadwork that if read properly indicate each person's social status. Young unmarried girls are easily identified by their distinctive brightly colored, wide, flat, dishlike beaded collar necklaces, which they offset with single strands of forehead beads and ornaments, and small dangling earrings worn from piercings at the top and in the lobe of the ear. From an early age girls begin to acquire these bead collars in various circumferences. Later, when worn layered and shown off in dances, the necklaces float up and down in an entrancing way.

Married women can also wear these beaded collars but more typically wear a contrasting collar made from multiple strands of a dark grass (not giraffe hair) with a series of single, oblong red beads down the center. These voluminous collars balloon between neck and shoulders and, along with their earrings, clearly indicate their married status. Their earrings, more correctly labeled earring flaps, consist of multiple strands of beads sewn in ornate patterns on leather backing. About the size of a bookmark, they are looped through a hole in each earlobe that has been slowly stretched and enlarged from a young age to accommodate such an earring. Within Maasai society these earrings communicate married status much the same way a wedding band expresses married status within Western cultures. When they are worn with a women's cloth and cloak, there is no mistaking a married woman for an unmarried girl.

Similarly, strands of beads around the neck, chest, wrist, and waist are worn as one of the indicators to signal the social status of a warrior. Over time the designs and patterns of this beadwork have changed to coincide with current trends and styles. For example, in the 1970s the Samburu, a Maa-speaking community in Kenya who live at the northern end of Maasai country, began to wear beaded bracelets, which they called a *watch*, that widened at the center into a series of circular design. A more easily understood form of personal adornment that communicates status is found in male earrings.

In a standard image of Maasai male youths, two or more are wrapped in their red cloths, called *shukas*, and have not-so-very-small white round earplugs in their ears. These earplugs, which are worn in their stretched earlobes, are made from the cross section of an elephant's tusk. To the Maasai, and to their neighbors, these earplugs immediately signal that these youths are warriors. So too does the style of hair. Warriors spend considerable time assisting each other in plaiting their hair, including adding strands of grass to make it longer, fuller, and more impressive. Red ochre is also carefully applied to the face in decorative lines. This careful primping is all the more important when one understands that the end of this period is the crucial time for them to identify a potential wife. At a major ceremony near the end of the period of warriorhood, their mothers shave their heads and give away all of their

This Samburu woman's earrings, along with the way she wraps her
cloth, communicate to all that she is married.

ornaments. The change in hairstyle and the wearing of small metal earrings
that dangle from their stretched earlobes define their new, more serious status
as elders who are able to marry.[2]

Personal adornment is both a primary medium for aesthetic expression and
a significant indicator of everything from ethnic identity, clan, and gender to
social status and personal preference. The colors, designs, and styles all add to
the complexity of these indicators that are broadly shared within each community. In Kenya, for example, many people have adopted Maasai-style beadwork,

The ivory earplugs immediately identify these young men as warriors.
Because they want to ensure they are noticed by young women, yet
appear intimidating to outsiders, these youths spend considerable time
helping each other with their hair and applying decorative lines of red
ochre to their faces.

but style alone is not enough to serve as an indicator. The patterns employed are
not arbitrary, and the use of certain colors is quite specific. Only when all the
various parameters are used together correctly are these markers meaningful.[3]

Nonetheless, these indicators have never been static or unchanging. In
fact, the import of trade goods such as beads, wire, cloth, and dyes led to
major innovations at the end of the nineteenth century and beginning of the

twentieth century in what has been called an explosion of creativity. Remember that the beaded traditions of the Maasai have only been around for a little more than a hundred years. Although red remains the dominant color desired by the Maasai, other colors have also been popular at different times, often dependent on the availability of the beads imported. And just as the Maasai once made a change from metalware to beads, new changes are on the horizon. With more Maasai going to school, and continuing on to high school and some to university, there has been a significant decline in the number of youths still willing, for example, to stretch holes in their ear-lobes and to have multiple piercings in the tops of their ears for the purpose of holding traditional ornaments. But at the same time, one must be careful of predicting any major changes among the Maasai; writers have also been predicting the "disappearance" of the Maasai and their herding way of life for nearly a hundred years, and this has yet to happen.

The Maasai are not the only people in Kenya to wear beaded personal adornment. In the west Pokot girls wear flat, wide, circular collars of incised water reeds strung on doum palm. Sometimes edged with colored beads, these collars extend over their shoulders and upper body and indicate their availability for marriage. Turkana girls send the same message when they wear multilayered beaded necklaces with three leather pendants of sewn beads at the back. Kamba have wide beaded belts they wear as part of their dress and that are associated with circumcision. And the list goes on.

In addition, personal adornment does not only take the forms of beads. For example, among the Swahili, powdered henna is mixed with water and the juice of unripe lemons to paint elaborate floral or geometric designs on the hands, arms, and feet of a bride. As many as six applications of painting and drying are sometimes necessary to ensure that the design does not fade too soon. For others, personal adornment is made of metal. Coiled wire and bracelets and anklets fabricated from brass and copper are another major form of adornment. And from time to time new materials are adopted, such as Gabbra and Borana bracelets and necklaces made of hammered aluminum from discarded cooking pots. In the same way, old forms also disappear, such as the pierced chin ornaments of ivory and copper wire once worn by Dasenech and Turkana elders.

Wood-sculpted masks and figurines such as those recognized from western and central Africa are generally absent in East Africa. One such tradition is well known in Kenya, however, and is found in the hills above the coast among the Mijikenda peoples who erect memorial planks, *vigango* (singular, *kigango*) to honor their dead. Typically, these long, narrow panels were carved from a hard wood that resists termites. With a circular disk head, short neck, and tall rectangular body, these planks were smoothed and chip-carved with triangular patterns, sometimes including facial features, and then painted red, white, and black. These are not gravestones; the graves of the dead are usually unmarked. Instead, a *kigango* was placed near the homestead of the deceased to provide a focus for eulogizing and paying respect to the spirits of important community leaders.

Such commemorative posts have a long history at the coast, where the Swahili have a tradition of constructing monumental pillar tombs. Although today people seldom recall the names of those buried there, it is widely understood that these tombs honor the men and women who helped to establish Swahili towns and brought Islam to the coast. Sometimes round, sometimes rectangular, the pillars are constructed of limestone and coral rubble and are often carved with low-relief geometric patterns or inset with niches to hold porcelain bowls. In this they resemble the ornamentation found on doorways, *mihrabs* (the niche indicating the direction of Mecca to which Muslims turn when praying), and other features of mosques and Swahili houses beginning in the thirteenth century. Like the mosques, these pillar tombs were also places of prayer and meditation.

The same geometric patterns found on the pillar tombs are also prominent in many facets of coastal art and architecture. Forged from cultural and religious roots that date back more than a thousand years, Swahili artistic traditions have been shaped in the urban environment of their coastal towns. The influences on coastal art and architecture are derived from the interior of East Africa, the coast itself, and the civilization of the much larger Indian Ocean rim from the Arabian Peninsula and Persian Gulf to India and beyond. This includes Islam, which encourages the use of intricate design over the representation of animate beings in art. Although deeply influenced by the maritime peoples with whom it has traded over the centuries, Swahili culture is not a mere copy or reflection of Arab and Islamic civilization. Like the Swahili language itself, it is a cultural tradition with its own identity and style.

Finely produced wooden Qur'an stands, boxes, bowls, and chairs exemplify Swahili craftsmanship and the establishment of Swahili and Muslim identity. The Swahili stand for holding the Qur'an, *marufad*, is similar to those found throughout the Islamic world. Constructed of two flat boards hinged in the center to form a vertical X, it can be opened to hold a Qur'an in the top triangle or closed and laid flat. In a fashion similar to the chip-carving found on Mijikenda *vigango* and the pillar tombs, the outer surfaces are incised in a style typical of Swahili decoration—geometric patterns of triangles, squares, and circles.

Perhaps more reflective of the wealth generated by the Swahili urban-maritime life and the significant achievements of Swahili culture is the "chair of power," *kiti cha enzi*. Made of ebony wood with an elaborate caned seat and back, and decorated with inlaid patterns of ivory and bone, these chairs were once used at formal gatherings of leaders and elders, and to present a bride and groom at their wedding. With its tall back, broad arms, and footrest, the "chair of power" appears to have been a kind of coastal throne. Passed from generation to generation, they were until recently still being faithfully reproduced on Lamu Island. Along with other symbols of office, such as side-blown horns (see chapter 8, "Music and Dance") and drums, such regalia gives at least some indication of the independence and prosperity from trade that the Swahili people once enjoyed before their eventual colonization.[4]

Wooden boxes with brass decoration and hardware, similar to ones found all along the eastern African coast across to India, provide another example of Swahili involvement in the trade of the Indian Ocean and the production of goods to meet the cosmopolitan tastes of these urban towns. Fitted with trays and various-size interior compartments, these small boxes, *kasha la mfuto,* sometimes called a scribe's box, held money, jewelry, and writing implements, all signs of the successful Swahili merchants, women of means, and the literate society whose admired possessions they were. Often acquired elsewhere and brought to the coast, they were commonly finished and reworked to suit local taste, including the addition of incised trays, brass hardware, and metal inlay. Larger chests, often referred to as Zanzibar chests, were used to store a family's prized clothing, linens, and fine jewelry. Small cylindrical lidded boxes, *zikakasi,* used to hold spices or cosmetics, were turned on hand lathes and stained with a locally produced vegetable dye resembling a lacquer finish. Whether these various rectangular and cylindrical boxes, as well as the formal chairs once used by elders, are of indigenous creation or an adaptation from the Persian Gulf or India, is of little matter. The beautifully incised decorations that finish these pieces give them the fine lines and high degree of refinement associated only with the Swahili coast.[5]

Today, plastic jugs, metal boxes, enamel bowls and mugs, and printed cloth are widely available in markets and shops across Kenya. As a result many of the beautiful objects once made from clay, wood, grass, gourds, and leather are fast disappearing. With increasing urbanization, greater numbers of children attending school, and better-paying jobs that are attracting more and more youth and young adults to the larger towns and cities, the days of many traditional cultural objects may indeed be numbered. Still, this should not limit our admiring and celebrating the ingenuity, creativity, and artistry of these once widespread traditions.

Contemporary Art

There is no clear definition among art historians as to what constitutes contemporary African art. The arguments generally focus on the role of tradition, authenticity, and the place of individual creativity in the works the artists produce. And of course, these issues are regularly played out in what museums and galleries exhibit. Museum collections of traditional African art seldom include works or objects from Kenya. Nevertheless, the urban and rural landscape is full of artistic expression and home to producers of art—wood and soapstone carvers, basket and banana-fibers weavers, furniture makers, sign painters, jewelers, and blacksmiths. All of these producers, whose work is acquired especially in the urban area by Kenyans and tourists alike, are part of the informal economy and generally work out of doors, as opposed to those workers in the formal sector who work in factories and offices. In Kenya they are collectively known as *jua kali,* those who work in the "hot sun" of a marketplace or crowded alleyway. Such work is rarely considered part of the world of art and rarely connected to the name of the individual creator. Rather, it is either completely dismissed or relegated to the broad categorization of folk art. Yet the artistic expression of a sign painter can be highly skilled and eagerly sought after, and not just for store or roadside advertising and slogans; some of their finest work is found on buses, trucks, and taxis. Similarly, the blacksmith as recycler makes decorative mugs and small kerosene lamps from cans and suitcases from scrap-sheet metal. The works of some curio carvers have found their way into a gallery setting, but even then, the nature of the gallery determines whether it is to be admitted to the realm of art. Such has been the case with the animal chairs carved by Mutunga, a Kamba woodcarver. According to one expert, Mutunga's work "lingers in the ambiguous space, which exists in Kenya between 'good tourist art' and 'serious art' sold in galleries."[6]

Contemporary art in Kenya also lingers between a Kenyan aesthetic and a Western one. Nairobi's leading gallery, Gallery Watatu, was founded in 1984 and run by American Ruth Schaffner until her death in 1996. The vast majority of what her gallery displayed (and continues to display) was the work of self-taught artists, not the academically trained. This distinction is one that is commonly made in the contemporary African art world, in the belief that only the work of self-trained artists living in a traditional community is authentic. For the holders of this view, the creativity of African art needs to be protected from the influences of European abstraction and certain other styles. What the market (that is, European residents and tourists) wants are scenes of rural and urban life and expressions of fantasy that clearly suggest the raw "primitiveness" that is absent in the work of African artists trained in academic circles. This was the essential philosophy of Gallery Watatu, held in the belief that this is what the gallery's clientele desired, and perhaps it is true.

Many Kenyan artists could be singled out for the significant recognition they have obtained, but four of Gallery Watatu's self-trained artists can serve

Expressions of a fantasy world inhabited by playful animals are the frequent subject of the crayon-on-paper works of contemporary artist Kivuthi Mbuno.

as representative: Kivuthi Mbuno (b. 1947), Joel Oswaggo (b. 1954), Sane (Mbugua) Wadu (b. 1954), and Meek Gichugu (b. 1968). Working in crayon on paper, Mbuno uses a playful drawing style to depict animals, such as elephants, giraffes, hyenas, and monkeys, living together in a fantasy world. He also draws rural people going about their everyday rural lives. But their features suggest a more grotesque kind of world than everyday reality. Oswaggo, who also works in colored pencil and crayon on paper, uses his knowledge of Luo oral tradition, legends, and traditional patterns of life in the countryside surrounding Lake Victoria as the focus of his work. For example, "The African Child" shows children weeding, bathing, and sleeping, and "The Preparation of Warriors" shows two warriors with shields, one blowing a greater kudu (antelope) horn. One of his recent works is quite different and offers political commentary. In it a boy reading a book titled "Education through Starvation = Overloading with Distress" is sitting atop a stack of books with titles that include "Music," "Home Science," "Mathematics," and "Agriculture," while another boy wearing a T-shirt and torn shorts carries a basket loaded with grass.[7]

Wild animals, rural landscapes, and people performing everyday tasks also appear in the early works of Sane Wadu. During this time in the mid-1980s, the people of his own town took his strange dress and carryings on to mean that he must be insane. Following the success of his first show at Gallery Watatu (1987), he responded by taking the name "Sane," by which name he continues to be known. Today, he works in oil on canvas, painting ordinary people going about their daily lives, such as riding in a bus or on a bicycle or listening to an evangelist in a park, but in a more abstract yet clearly urban environment. More recently, his paintings have also begun to take on a political nature, including people protesting for multiparty elections. Meek Gichugu, who was encouraged to paint by Sane Wadu, is best known for his oil-on-canvas paintings of interlocking figures and parts of figures (limbs, heads, necks, and torsos of humans, giraffes, antelopes, and lizards).[8]

The Paa ya Paa ("the antelope rises") Art Center stood in sharp contrast to the Western-influenced Gallery Watatu. Paa ya Paa was founded in 1965 by Elimo Njau, a Tanzanian trained in art at Makerere Art School in Kampala, Uganda, which later became part of Makerere University. There, Njau largely adopted the views of his teacher Sweeney (Cecil) Todd, a South African art educator. Their belief was that an African modernism would emerge from the interaction of twentieth-century European traditions and traditional African art. Further, they were convinced that self-taught traditional artists produced only art that confirmed exotic Western fantasies and stereotypes of what is African. He calls the paintings of lions and elephants for the tourist market "animal pornography." Thus Njau established Paa ya Paa for artists with academic training. The struggle to survive has not been easy, with many painters leaving for the more market-savvy Gallery Watatu. Lamentably, Paa ya Paa has yet to come back from a fire in 1997.[9]

Together, these galleries, along with the Gallery for Contemporary East African Art (housed in the National Museum) and other exhibition spaces that actively support the arts such as the British Council, the French Cultural Centre, and the Goethe Institute, promote the art of Kenya. They continue to attract patrons and an audience and help to establish the reputations of both well-known artists and young local artists aspiring to a career. Success by even a few has led others, especially those from the towns in which now-recognized artists grew up, to try their hand at drawing and painting. In Banana Hill, a rural town near Nairobi, it has led to an association of artists who draw their inspiration from everyday rural street life. And on the outskirts of Nairobi, the Ngecha Artist's Association began when six artists, including Wadu, each worked together on shared canvas to create six different paintings. From its humble beginning in 1995, this group today numbers more than forty artists.[10]

Two other Kenyan artists who have achieved significant recognition in the world of art are Richard Onyango (b. 1960) and Abdallah Salim (b. 1958).

Onyango, who lives on the coast, paints finely detailed works of the modern world in acrylics on canvas. The world he paints is of his own making and includes underwater airports and highway scenes with buses and trucks careening around corners and over bridges. Salim is unique to Kenya's artists in that he is making his mark as a sculptor. His installations of freestanding, carved-wood pieces, painted with acrylic, have included a soccer team and an alphabet of Maasai dancers.

Finally, in a category all her own, given the international recognition she is receiving, is the contemporary ceramic artist Magdalene Odundo (b. 1950). Born and raised in Kenya, she studied in Britain, where she now lives, Nigeria, and the United States. Although much of this education was based on Western ceramic models, her finished pieces are hybrids with clear African roots, described as "dazzling" and full of energy "embodied in the interaction between shape, color, texture and detail."[11]

The clay vessels Odundo produces are more than mere pots. Their strength and beauty give them a singularly elegant form. Often described as voluptuous, the forms her works take include traditional necks and mouths re-created in new lengths and widths. They are not thrown on a wheel, but rather hand-coiled, as are most traditional Kenyan pots. Along with coiling she uses a piece of gourd or coconut shell scraper to achieve the desired curved shapes and profiles she favors. She then burnishes the surface, sometimes using polished stones and pebbles. It is this labor-intensive process that results in the high-luster surfaces she achieves. Depending on the firing technique she then employs, there emerge what she calls "non-utilitarian containers of form and color," typically in various shades of black and orange rust. One piece can take days or weeks to complete. Odundo has not really invented something new; rather, with her creativity, she has updated something from the past.

Works in art galleries, however, are not what the usual visitors to Kenya see first. Instead, the art they encounter is either that of the boutique or souvenir craft market. African Heritage in Nairobi is such an up-market boutique that today has opened branches in other parts of Kenya, Tanzania, Zanzibar, and South Africa. Here, cultural artifacts—from baskets and bowls to carvings of soapstone and wood to restrung beaded jewelry to better match Western taste—are sold according to an ethnic label, not the identity of the object's maker. So too are the wares found in craft-market stalls and on the street.

Carvings of animals are of particular interest because they are largely produced by cooperatives organized specifically to make and market the work of their members. Perhaps more important, they create a circumstance that allows individuals to carve full time and to learn from each other new techniques and skills. The Kamba have three such cooperatives where members stay and work together, organized in much the same way as a family workshop. The largest are near to Nairobi and Mombasa, the two tourist centers, with the latter having over a thousand resident carvers. Although skilled in carving bows, arrows, and clubs for hunting, the Kamba had no tradition of figurative carving. Instead they were most widely known as the porters who carried ivory to the coast. The entire Kamba industry of carving animals, human figures, bowls, and salad sets is attributed to one man, Matisya Munge from the Kamba village of Wamunyu. When he was drafted into the carrier corps in World War I, he did a tour in what was then called Tanganyika. Here, he saw the work of Zaramo carvers, is said to have liked what he saw, and introduced it at home upon his return.[12]

The artists, galleries, and cultural centers of Nairobi, Mombasa, and other towns regularly mount shows and exhibitions to which the public is invited. Nevertheless, the resident expatriate community acquires the vast majority of contemporary painting and sculpture being purchased today. In this sense the artists are fortunate that Kenya has so many embassies, international organizations, and nongovernmental organizations based there. Ultimately, however, the limited patronage by these outsiders and a small educated Kenyan elite is holding back the further development of contemporary art in Kenya.

ARCHITECTURE AND HOUSING

Urban Housing

African architecture is a sophisticated adaptation to available local materials and the various climates found across the country. In many parts of Kenya the houses are of wood, which is then plastered with mud to keep the interior cool in the heat of the day and warm at night, when temperatures can drop dramatically. In the arid regions of the north, where trees are scarce, homes are made of dried mud, cow dung, and grasses. At the coast, where stone and coral rubble, along with the necessary skilled labor, was readily available, buildings were constructed complete with lime plaster on the interior walls. And in the modern, postindependence cities of Nairobi, Mombasa, Kisumu, and others, bold statements have been made using cement, steel, and glass. Homes often serve as an indicator of wealth and status. Just as the multistory homes of the Swahili coast were previously indicators of status, so urban skyscrapers signal the continuing development of modern Kenya.

Centers of urban life have existed in Kenya for more than a thousand years. Indeed, Swahili culture was already well established when Ibn Battuta, a Muslim traveler and chronicler, visited and recorded life on the East African coast in the fourteenth century. From present-day Somalia in the north to Mozambique in the south, a long chain of Swahili towns and cities provided the focus for their maritime trade around the rim of the Indian Ocean. Sometimes these communities were no more than walls that enclosed a small settlement, but others were of significant size, consisting of carefully planned residences whose overhanging balconies provided shade in the narrow streets below that led to shops, mosques, and monuments. As they still do in the better-preserved coastal towns today, these narrow lanes led to main streets that converged on public plazas. When abandoned (for reasons that are still not entirely clear), the surrounding tropical paradise quickly grew back to engulf and leave only today's ruins as a reminder of this former grandeur.

Beginning in the eighteenth century, the leaders who governed the cities of the Swahili coast lived in stately multistory houses called *jumba*. Constructed of coral rubble and crushed limestone, these flat-roofed houses were constructed around a frame of mangrove poles. In contrast to the thatched buildings of the town and surrounding areas, a *jumba* proclaimed the prestige, wealth, and influence of the family that lived in it. The house was in fact the domain of the woman of the family and the focus of all social and domestic activity. In a long-established pattern, the first floor was typically occupied by servants, with the better-ventilated second and third floors occupied by the parents and a married daughter's family, respectively. In Lamu, one of the better-known and best-preserved traditional Swahili towns on the Kenya coast, the way in which these houses were expanded upward from one generation to another is easily seen, although not from the street, where plain, high walls hug the town's narrow streets.

Large, brass-studdeds and often ornately carved doors mark the entrance on the lanes and streets that separates the public space of the outside world from the private indoor world of the family. Found from the northern Kenyan coast to Zanzibar, these doors were traditionally made of teak and set in a square frame. The carving of these ornamented doors reached its zenith in the nineteenth century, when outside influences, especially from India, led to some of the most intricate designs. Although the double doors themselves were not always carved, the frames and center post that surround them were. Passages from the Qur'an protected the house, chains demonstrated security, and the geometric and floral designs were filled with symbolic associations. Palms and incense suggested wealth and abundance, rosettes and lotus reproductive power.

Just inside the entrance door was a bench-lined porch or portico for greeting guests. Beyond this an open central courtyard, *kiwanda*, provided light, air, and privacy for the long and narrow rooms, *misana*. Also from this interior courtyard, a staircase ascended to the upper floor and the rooms in which the family typically lived. The interior walls of these upstairs rooms were inset with numerous niches, *zidaka,* of various sizes. The intricate plasterwork on the niches and the ornate chip-carved geometric patterns that surround them set off the valuable possessions, including copies of the Qur'an and pieces of blue-and-white porcelain from China, that were displayed and stored here. From monumental tombs and graceful mosques to beautifully carved house doors and the detailed refinement of their homes, the Swahili coast still illustrates the splendor for which it has been admired in the historical record for hundreds of years.

Unlike Lamu, where there has been a concerted effort to maintain and preserve the buildings of its formative years, Mombasa reflects an architectural mix of modern and traditional as well as the Islamic, Christian, and Hindu faiths of its multicultural population. Like so many urban centers around the world, it is a city that has been added to many times over. In the Old Town are the remnants of the city, which regularly traded with the Arabian Peninsula and beyond. Tucked between these Middle Eastern–style houses and buildings are countless mosques with their minarets from which the muezzin, using loudspeaker systems, summons the faithful to prayer. The Old Town also has its share of old colonial buildings, including law courts, banks, and a few hotels and cafes that have served the resident population and visitor alike for nearly one hundred years. In today's city center modern high-rise monoliths, initially developed in the 1980s, have begun to dominate. And along the coast and lagoons immediately north and south of the city are the modern hotels, restaurants, and shops that serve the tourists who arrive directly from Europe to this tropical paradise for their winter vacations.

Today's Nairobi is also a city of skyscrapers, contemporary office blocks, and hotels, only on a much larger scale than anything found at the coast or in the country's interior. The nearly 350-foot-high Kenyatta Conference Center, with its hexagonal tower and revolving restaurant at the top, has an interior of red-tiled promenades with cheerful graceful fountains and a plenary hall that can seat 4,000 delegates. The surrounding streets of downtown are a mix of colonial, neocolonial, and modern buildings of stone, concrete, and glass that house shops, restaurants, galleries, and cinemas. Depending on the season, the streets and parks are filled with the purple blossoms of jacaranda trees and the bright crimson, orange, and blue flowers of bougainvillea vines and other tropical flowers.

In the largest urban areas the homes in which people dwell cover a wide variety of styles and types, ranging from freestanding bungalows of colonial vintage in classic neighborhoods to the patchwork of shelters constructed of corrugated metal and other recycled materials found in Nairobi's slums. Yet each one is someone's home. Nairobi is representative of any number of Kenyan and other African urban centers in that from its very beginning it has struggled to provide housing for the people who are continuously moving into it. Founded in 1899 as a railhead for the Uganda Railway, its first citizens were a multicultural mix of African herdsmen (Nairobi means "place of cold water" in the Maa language) and farmers, European railway workers, traders, missionary and military types, and Asians from across the subcontinent. Soon this six-year, 5 million pound sterling engineering marvel, which also cost hundreds of lives and was labeled by its London critics "the Lunatic Express," was drawing immigrants from around the world. Evidence of this founding population is still seen in the stone-built Anglican All Saints Cathedral, the Jamie Mosque in the heart of downtown, and intricately carved Hindu and Jain temples. Such centers of faith continue to be built, with one of the most recent, the Shree Swaminarayan Mandir Temple, constructed of yellow marble from India and beautiful wood from Kenya and completed in 1999.

Nairobi's first houses and shops were built by and for Europeans. As the city grew and Europeans prospered, they built roomy one- and sometimes two-story homes in what are today the suburbs of Nairobi, but which fifty years ago were small communities well on the outskirts of the city. The most famous of these is Karen, which takes its name from its most famous resident, Karen Blixen, who wrote about her early pioneering experiences in *Out of Africa*. Surrounded by fences and ever-higher protective walls, these rural compounds and estates include single-room quarters in the back for domestic staff and drivers. Prominent in both city and suburbs are the ever-present metal grilles over windows and doors, burglar alarms, and security guards to help prevent increasingly prevalent crime.

The Kenyan government has always had a strong commitment to providing public services to its population. Generally speaking, the working middle class, who live in neighborhoods that surround city centers, has seen improvements in nutrition, health, education, water, and housing. Maintaining these advances and keeping the infrastructure for them in good repair continue to be problematic. The real struggle is to meet the needs of those who are not yet in, and may never reach, the middle class. Kenyans themselves tend to think of the population according to income categories such as very rich, middle-high, middle, middle to low, and the poor who today include political and economic refugees from Ethiopia, Rwanda, Somalia, and Sudan. Beginning in the 1970s efforts by the government to house those on the bottom rungs of the economic ladder focused on the construction of housing estates. Here, the one- or two-story cinder-block homes, built on concrete slabs and all with similar floor plans, looked very much alike. Today, all that has changed. Where once the government was the owner of these estates, such as Bahati, Jericho, Jerusalem, and Umoja, most of the dwellings are now privately owned, most often by landlords rather than the residents who live in them. These estate homes no longer all look alike either. Walls have been pushed out, extensions added on, and upper stories added, with each floor being rented to a different family. Few if any building codes are followed in this new construction, so it is not unusual for businesses and bars to share a wall with a private residence.

To the north and west of the city reside the upper-middle class to the very rich. Suburbs once associated with higher incomes, including Westlands, Golf Course, and Ngong, are now middle-income areas. The wealthier have moved still farther outside the city to Lavington and Langata, and on to the estates of South Sea and Bura Bura. Here, people own their own homes and work diligently to maintain local building codes in the interest of preventing the kinds of changes that have overwhelmed the formerly government owned estates. At locations such as Runda and Muthaiga, where the wealthiest members of Kenyan society live, the communities are made of fortresslike residences. Here, the norm is large wooded compounds with big yards and gardens, enclosed by tall walls with heavy metal gates. If the creativity of architectural design is at work anywhere in Kenya, it is in these locations. But as far as most Kenyans see it, there really is no Kenyan architectural style.

Traveling thirty minutes to the west of the city, you will be going through rural countryside along a ridge of the Ngong Hills, from which you can gaze down on to the floor of the Rift Valley. Cross Tom Mboya Street in central Nairobi, named in memory of the slain political leader, in a northeasterly direction, and you leave the modern downtown capital city and enter the overcrowded shanty-town neighborhoods and communities that spread to the Nairobi River and beyond. Here, in Mathare Valley, probably the most densely populated location in Nairobi, and in communities named Kibera, Laini Saba, and Korogocho, live tens of thousands of urban poor eking out a living in both the formal and the informal economy. No matter how fast the city develops and builds affordable housing along paved roads with sewers, electricity, and telephone, the population grows faster, and the need for adequate shelter is ever greater. Along unplanned, helter-skelter dirt tracks and pathways, houses and shelters are built, sometimes from proper building materials of brick and cement, other times from whatever can be gathered together. Sometimes to save money, or merely to have a roof over their heads, people crowd into single rooms. Without basics such as clean water, sewage, and electricity, the health of the residents in these areas suffers, which then limits their ability to work productively or to stay awake in school.

Not all recent efforts to build affordable housing have focused on the urban poor and people of lower income. "Own a home in a day or two" slogans advertise the introduction of modular designs from the United States and Europe for the middle class. Still, the demand for affordable urban housing and services continues to present enormous challenges to city and national government alike.

Rural Housing

In the agriculturally rich highlands and western regions of Kenya are found the farms or *shamba* on which the majority of Kenyans live. Traditionally, many of the peoples who once lived here were hunter-gatherers or livestock keepers. These include the Kipsigis, Luo, and Nandi in the west and the Kikuyu, Meru, and Kamba in the central highlands. Today, nearly all have evolved into agricultural communities. Historically, these communities grew millet, bananas, sugarcane, and yams. However, in the colonial period they were pushed into raising cash crops such as tea, coffee, and sisal and introduced to the beans, maize, and potatoes that today are the principal crops of the highlands, as well as the rice, pineapple, and peanuts that predominate in the west. Maize is grown nearly everywhere in Kenya, while along the shores of Lake Victoria fish and rice are principal staples.

In these intensively farmed regions, land is at a premium. Where once these communities held land in common, especially when they herded cattle, land today is increasingly divided into small plots on which families work to be self-sufficient. Housing, however, has remained surprisingly consistent. Whereas in Europe and North America homes are designed for a family to live under one roof, the African pattern is more one of a series of buildings, each with a different function—sleeping, cooking, and eating—surrounding an open courtyard. It is in the open courtyard space where much of daily life takes place. Other small buildings are usually for storing grain or keeping chickens. Those built on stilts have added protection from pests and predators. In those communities where a man may have more than one wife, each wife and her children have their own home in the compound or what is sometimes called a homestead. In some locations a small homestead might consist of three structures—a parent's house, grandparent's house, and a structure for cooking. It is usually only in the cities where poor and working-class families crowd into small one-room houses.

The materials with which such houses are constructed can be stone, wood, grass, or mud, depending on what is most readily available in the local environment. They are also built with less permanence and a sense that they can easily be altered. If the number of family members change through death, marriage, or the arrival of more family members, then new building materials are gathered and new buildings constructed, or parts of existing houses

The typical compound of a rural family often consists of a parent's house, sometimes a grandparent's house, and structures for cooking and housing animals.

are enlarged, but social and physical needs were always met. Houses can be circular, rectangular, or square. This is usually a matter of local custom and adaptation to local conditions. A floor of beaten earth is not unusual, although concrete is becoming increasingly common. Rural houses such as these are simply furnished with locally made furniture. A few stools, woven mats for sitting on, and a bed with wooden bars or a cord frame to hold a mattress is typical. A cooking fire may be found inside a house but is more commonly found in a separate cooking house. Hung from the walls near to the cooking fire will be common kitchen utensils—bowls, baskets, and storage containers carved from wood or made from a gourd. Standing on a wooden shelf will be cups, glasses, and plates; on the ground nearby will be found a mortar and pestle for pounding grain and clay pots of various sizes for storing water. More often than not, such homes are without running water; if they have electricity, it is likely to be a single bulb hanging from the center of the main room.

Nowadays, many people are building larger houses of stone and cement. Both outside and inside walls are plastered and whitewashed, and doors and windows are of better manufacture, offering more security. Roofs are no longer of thatched grass but made of corrugated iron sheets that are either left plain or colored green or red. Either way, they collect and hold in much more heat than did a thatched roof, but offer greater protection from the rain and other natural elements.

A Herder's Home

Like a Swahili *jumba* from the coast, the houses of Kenya's herders are the domain of the woman of the family and, in some cases, such as among the Somaili, are owned by the women. All these houses are light, easily portable structures whose size varies according to the family's need. Basically circular, such houses are generally between nine and ten feet in diameter and six feet high, allowing an average person to stand upright in the central living area. The framework is constructed of long sticks bent and tied in the desired shape. Once the framework is in place, the house is covered with woven or hand-knotted roof mats. Over time these wear out, but are easily replaced because all these materials are naturally available in the local environment. For example, the Rendille use framing sticks made from the trees that line riverbeds and roof mats woven from wild sisal collected on the mountains that surround the lowlands where they live. To complete the Rendille home, two half skins cover the doorway, which is positioned on the western side of the house, and a few cow skins hang as a wind block against the inside back wall (the eastern side).

For the Rendille, as for every other herding group, the interior living space of each house provides more than shelter. It affirms the family and community that is the core of their identity. Divided into quadrants demarcated by purpose and gender, the Rendille house demonstrates the multiple connections between family members and generations. The two western areas circumscribe a more public place, with the cooking and firewood storage areas in the northwest and a visitor's space in the southwest. The two eastern quadrants mark the private space, with the wife's portion in the northeast and the husband's in the southeast. Two mats cover the ground in this back part, which are then overlaid with cow skins for sitting and sleeping. Children sleep between their parents on these same skins.

When this more-or-less circular house is considered in terms of a north-south axis, the northern half can be seen to be the woman's, with her private space and kitchen, and the southern half the man's, with his private space and the visitor's section. The center of family life is the cooking area, with its six hearth stones (two rows of three) on which pots for cooking are placed. Seated in her private area, the woman of the house can cook, reach the water and milk storage containers that hang along the inside wall, and get to any of her personal belongs such as clothing and personal adornment. Although in Rendille society the man is the head of the household, the house itself is for all practical purposes the territory of his wife, and only a married woman can have such a dwelling.[13]

Most commonly, a settlement of herders consists of as many as 200 to 300 people in twenty, thirty, or more houses. Although not the usual way of seeing such a settlement, the best vantage point is from the air. From this perspective it is obvious that the houses form a large circular enclosure. Where the animal kraals are placed depends on which ethnic group lives in the settlement and each is quite distinct. For example, the kraals that hold the Rendille camels, sheep, and goats are constructed in the interior space between the houses. The small stone enclosure found at the center of these kraals is called the *naabo*. It is the principal meeting place for elders from where they manage the settlement's affairs. The fire that is kept burning day and night in this enclosure provides the focus for the community's ritual activity. The kraals of most cattle-herding societies are just the opposite, with the livestock kraals providing a protective perimeter around the houses on the inside.

Just as the doorway of each Rendille house faces west, so the entire settlement is oriented to the west. Homes are placed according to seniority beginning immediately to the north of the settlement's western entrance. When other members of these clan-based settlements want to join an already-established settlement, they do so by attaching their houses in small semicircles on the periphery of the main circle. Because the placement of houses is based on seniority, there is rarely any question about where this smaller semicircle of new homes is to be built. A settlement does not always house all members of the community. At certain times of the year the unmarried warriors, accompanied by unmarried women and their younger sisters, move with many of the camels, goats, and sheep to smaller stock camps, *fora*, in better-watered pasture lands, returning to the settlement only for ritual festivals or when the grazing is depleted.

In the past the Rendille and the other herding communities had to defend their animals and territory from livestock raiders and moves by neighboring communities who sought to occupy their lands. When the pastureland on which the animals browsed or grazed dried up, or the water supply could no longer support the settlement or was found at too great a distance to travel to, these highly mobile communities dismantled their houses and loaded them on large pack camels or donkeys. Generally, two camels or two donkeys can carry the structure and entire contents of one house, with the main frame poles of the house serving as the main frames for the pack animals' loads. In two hours the women and their daughters can take down their houses, load them, and be ready to shift locations. By beginning early in the morning, an entire settlement can move thirty to forty kilometers and be settled in a new

In a matter of a few hours, a herder's home can easily be taken apart, loaded on either two camels or two donkeys, transported to a new location, and reerected before the sun sets.

location by sunset. Whereas in the past these herders might move four to eight times a year, today they seldom move, and their settlements are almost-permanent fixtures on the land.[14] Nevertheless, today's houses, whether covered by woven mats or plastic polyethylene sheeting, and filled with a mixture of both traditional wood and woven storage containers and modern enamel and aluminum ware, provide a ready reminder to all who enter of cultural history in a time of rapid change.

NOTES

1. For the range and variation in headrests, see William J. Dewey, *Sleeping Beauties* (Los Angeles: Fowler Museum of Cultural History, University of California at Los Angeles, 1993), 16–51.

2. See Donna K. Pido, "Art among the Maasai of Kenya," *Art and Life in Africa* (Iowa City: University of Iowa, 1998). CD-ROM.

3. See Donna Klump and Corinne Kratz, "Aesthetics, Expertise, and Ethnicity: Okiek and Maasai Perspectives on Personal Adornment," in *Being Maasai: Ethnicity and Identity in East Africa,* ed. Tomas Spear and Richard Waller (London: James Currey; Athens: Ohio University Press, 1993), 195–221.

4. James De Vere Allen, "The Kiti Cha Enzi and Other Swahili Chairs," *African Arts* 22, no. 3 (1989): 54–63, 88.

5. On Swahili forms and styles, see Rene A. Bravmann, *African Islam* (Washington, D.C.: Smithsonian Institution Press, 1983), 102–13.

6. See Sidney Littlefield Kasfir, *Contemporary African Art* (London: Thames and Hudson, 1999), 42.

7. These titles by Joel Oswaggo were for sale in Gallery Watatu in December 2001.

8. More information on each artist can be found in Andre Magnin and Jacques Soulillou, *Contemporary Art of Africa* (New York: Abrams, 1996); Bernd Kleine-Gunk, *Kunst aus Kenya: Sieben Ostafriaknische Maler* (Essen: Graphium Press, 1994); Wanjiku Nyachae, "Kenya: Concrete Narratives," in *Seven Stories about Modern Art in Africa* (Paris: Flammarion, 1995), 179–89 (exhibition catalog).

9. Peter Graff, "Art for Money's Sake?" *Time,* February 10, 1997, 6.

10. Interview with Wanyu Brush, one of the founding Ngecha artists, 18 December 2001, at Gallery Watatu, Nairobi.

11. See Marla C. Berns, *Ceramic Gestures, New Vessels by Magdalen Odundo* (Santa Barbara: University of California, 1995).

12. See Kasfir, *Contemporary African Art,* 107–9.

13. See Anders C. Grum, "Rendille Habitation," in *African Nomadic Architecture: Space, Place, and Gender,* ed. Labelle Prussin (Washington, D.C.: Smithsonian Institution Press, 1995), 150–69.

14. Neal Sobania, "Pastoralist Migration and Colonial Policy: A Case Study from Northern Kenya," in *The Ecology of Survival: Case Studies from Northeast African History,* ed. Douglas Johnson and David Anderson (London: Lester Crook; Boulder, Colorado: Westview Press, 1988), 219–39.

5

Cuisine and Traditional Dress

CUISINE

It often seems that the roadsides of large cities and towns are everywhere dotted with food kiosks, announced by music blaring from radios and cassettes. Convenient, selling good and inexpensive food, these kiosks are the fast-food restaurants of working-class Kenyans. Here, on a wood or charcoal fire sits a huge aluminum cauldron, called a *sufuria,* full of maize and beans. This traditional highland Kenya dish requires long, slow cooking to make the vegetables tender. Supplemented with beef, chicken, goat, or mutton, it makes a tasty stew. It is often served up in an enamel bowl with a mug of smoky Kenyan tea on the side. Another favorite food for those who can afford it is roasted meat, or *nyama choma.* It can be fixed in a variety of ways and is often made more tender by marinating it in curry and other spices before roasting. Also sold on the street is grill-roasted corn on the cob and deep-fried yams, both of which are served with a squeeze of lemon juice and sprinkling of a hot pepper mixture (*pilipile*). The indoor counterpart to these street kiosks are *hoteli,* basic restaurants that serve good milky tea, local dishes, and a local unleavened flat bread (*chapati*) made from flour and whose origin is in India. A good filling lunch, typically the main meal of the day, can be obtained here for a reasonable price.

Even those farmers who grow their own produce cannot grow or process everything they use in the kitchen. They, like so many Kenyans, turn to the outdoor markets that abound to buy the vegetables and fruits they need and want. These are laid out for display in small piles so that interested buyers can look and examine them, or they are available from large sacks to be ladled out

Colorful outdoor market stalls have long been where Kenyans buy the vegetables and fruit that make up a significant portion of their diet.

with a tin can in whatever quantity the customer wants. Sometimes the display will be on a straw mat spread on the ground; other times it will be in stalls on wood tables. For still other shoppers, the shopping is done in small shops and increasingly, in local supermarkets. On display are vegetables that include potatoes, yams, beans, maize (a form of corn, but not the sweet corn eaten in the West), plantains, bananas, and tropical fruit almost beyond imagination from mangoes and papayas to pineapples and guavas.

Many of the foodstuffs that go into Kenyan cooking are easily recognizable to Westerners, but the combinations are not necessarily those that most Westerners put together, nor are the names familiar. *Irio* (*kienyeji* in Swahili), for example, is a highland dish typically made with potatoes and corn, all mashed together and served hot. In some areas, the same name is applied to a mixture made with a green vegetable such as peas and potatoes or with beans. If roasted or grilled meat is served with it, it is called *nyama na irio*. *Sukuma wiki* is a stew of greens such as kale or collards, with onion and tomato. As the literal translation of *sukuma wiki*, "push the week," suggests, it is mostly eaten when cash is low and next week's paycheck is still a few days off. Inexpensive, healthy, and easy to cook, it can also be eaten with meat or eggs when times are better.

Regional variations in cuisine are widespread. Students at boarding schools are served a dish called *githeri,* made of boiled potatoes, maize, and red beans. But, especially in the western part of the country, they would rather have fish, which is believed by many to make one intelligent. Fish is a staple of some peoples' diets, particularly in the west where tilapia are caught in Lake Victoria and Nile perch in Lake Turkana. Tilapia are eaten fresh as well as salted and dried and transported to other parts of the country. Fish (*samaki* in Swahili) is also a staple on the Indian Ocean coast. Here, it is cooked by baking or grilling, *samaki wa kupaka,* or prepared in a sauce or gravy, taking advantage of the many cultural contacts that have influenced this region. When fish is served in a curry sauce, it becomes *mchuzi wa samaki.* Chicken prepared using coconut milk is *kuku na nazi.* Everywhere a key to the local cuisine is to have a full stomach, using foodstuffs that are affordable. As a result the meals eaten by a majority of Kenyans are heavy on carbohydrates.

Across the country people consume potatoes, rice, and breads, but the most widely prepared and eaten meal throughout the country is based on a foundation of maize meal. Maize meal, called *posho,* is mixed with water and cooked to make porridge. When made into a thin porridge, called *ujii,* it can easily be spooned from a bowl or drunk from a mug or gourd and consumed as breakfast. Bread often accompanies *ujii.* When served as the main meal, the *posho* is added to boiling water and then stirred continuously. When it is finally ready, this heavy, thick mixture, now called *ugali,* is cut into chunks and served. *Ugali,* which can also be made with millet or sorghum, can be eaten on its own or with cooked vegetables such as *sukuma wiki* or with a bit of meat on the side. Left over, it can be rolled into balls and deep fried.

In the east toward the Ugandan border, people are fond of plantain (*matoke*), another starchy food. This vegetable from the banana family is a common dish in western Kenya and is eaten wherever people from this region have settled. Unlike its sweet-tasting cousin, plantain must be cooked in order to eat it. When steamed and served with tea (black tea when money is short), it is breakfast. Boiled until tender and then fried, it can be lunch or dinner. Bread, a common staple everywhere, is another carbohydrate filler. Others include *kitumbua* (fried bread) and the already-mentioned *chapatis*. *Mandazi* and *samosas* are also widely eaten. *Mandazi* are a sort of doughnut that is sweet and typically eaten for breakfast. *Samosas,* also known locally as *sambusas,* are small triangles of thin pastry. These come in two varieties: filled with spiced ground meat, or vegetarian, filled with chopped potatoes and peas. *Chapatis, mandazi,* and *samosas* are among the many elements and influences found in Kenyan cooking that belong to other regions of the Indian Ocean rim. Swahili dishes especially reflect the long history of contact between the coastal areas of East Africa, the Arabian Peninsula, and South Asia. One result of this is the popularity of curry dishes. Basic curry powder, which can be purchased in most markets, is a blend of spices including coriander, cumin, turmeric, and cinnamon. All originating in Asia, these spices undoubtedly found their way to the coast through the early Indian Ocean trade. Later, however, curries gained popularity in the interior of the country, where such dishes were introduced either by colonial officials assigned to East Africa after duty in India or through the many people who came to work in Kenya from the Indian subcontinent.[1]

British influence is evident everywhere, but the roast beef and Yorkshire pudding and custard-drenched desserts, or "afters," have been greatly tempered by the inclusion of locally grown fruits and vegetables, as well as the use of ingredients and cooking styles from other parts of the former Empire. Today, while chutneys and curries are still commonplace, Indian influences are not the only ones reflected in Kenya's many fine restaurants. As a country that is today home to many more expatriates than it ever was in the colonial period, its international flavor is extensive. This is especially true in Nairobi and Mombasa. From Asia the choices include Chinese, Japanese, Korean, and Middle Eastern. From Europe there are cafés and bistros where one can choose from Austrian, French, Italian, and nouvelle cuisine. And from Africa there is one restaurant that serves dishes from across the African continent, and there is a also choice of Ethiopian restaurants. Coffee shops abound, as do ubiquitous fast-food options of hamburgers, roasted chicken, and pizza.

Along with spices ranging from peppers and chilies to tamarind and cloves is a wide variety of vegetables and nuts, including sweet potatoes, manioc, cashews, and almonds. Tropical fruits are also plentiful, from oranges, lemons, and limes to mangoes, papayas, and pineapples. Pineapples, especially, are grown by major agrobusinesses on plantations that have largely supplanted their former production in Hawaii. At the coast dates, coconuts, and cashew nuts are all grown. The largest plantation crops, however, are tea and coffee, which provide Kenya with two of its major exports.

Beverages and Traditional Drinks

Kenya's arabica coffee, grown especially at the higher altitudes around Mount Kenya, is one of the world's most highly prized premium coffees. Among the most flavorful, Kenyan coffee has been a mainstay of the economy and has provided employment for thousands of small-scale farmers. These farmers handpick the coffee beans and transport them to cooperatives where the beans are roasted, packaged, and sold. In the past Kenya's coffee and tea have brought high prices on the world market. Unfortunately, these prices depend on factors outside of Kenya's control. Commodities such as coffee and tea are known as cash crops, which are produced for the global market and often at the expense of food crops. Staple crops normally consumed as nutritionally valuable food and sold locally return far less monetarily than do cash crops exported for consumption in the industrialized world. Economically, the issue is further complicated because the industrialized world is the one that sets the prices for these cash crops. Importing countries can fix the prices they are willing to pay because there are so many alternative suppliers they can turn to if one or two countries try to establish a higher export price. Cash-crop exporting countries such as Kenya are made more vulnerable by this process because of their need for hard currency. Without U.S. dollars, British pounds, or Euros, which is the form of currency they are paid for their exports, they cannot continue to import the manufactured goods their citizens expect or maintain the flow of oil necessary to run their own machinery. This is because the exporting West will not accept soft currencies such as Kenyan shillings (or Ghanaian *cedi,* Ethiopian *birr,* Nigerian *naira,* or Zambian *kwacha*). As a result Kenya and the many other "developing" countries of the world that are dependent on the export of one or two cash crops must also contend with economic forces largely beyond their control. When frosts or disease hurt coffee crops in other parts of the world, such as in Brazil or Colombia, the price of Kenya coffee rises and the country's economy flourishes. However, when there is a glut of coffee available on the world market, the price often drops precipitously, the economy declines, and many Kenyans have little cash available to purchase locally manufactured consumer goods.[2]

Tea and coffee are not only typically served with milk and sugar, but they are often brewed in it. Adding tea leaves, milk, and lots of sugar to cold water and boiling these together makes old-fashioned Kenyan tea, although today in many households, the sugar is added separately into each cup. Entrepreneurs have recently begun bottling this same drink and marketing it around the world as *chai,* which is merely the Swahili word for "tea." Black tea, *chai kavu* or *strungi,* a word perhaps derived from "strong tea," is tea without milk and known as the tea served when money is short. Another variation used in preparing tea, but when money is not so short, is *chai masala.* To prepare this, tea is first brewed and then steeped with milk and spices, which typically might be ginger—*tangawizi*—or cardamom. In addition to sugar, honey can also be used as a sweetener, as it is in many African produced soft drinks. Popular soft drinks in Kenya include Coca-Cola, Fanta, and Sprite, and high-energy sports drinks are becoming increasingly popular.

Any alcoholic beverage, whether produced commercially or brewed at home, is referred to as *pombe.* Beer is readily available both in bottles and as home brew. Bottled beers such as Tusker and White Cap have even found an export market in this era of people seeking out quality microbrews. Guinness in draft form is also available in many parts of Kenya, but only the dark color is similar to the genuine Irish potable. New to Kenya is Castle Breweries of South Africa, whose many labels are now in direct competition with Kenya Breweries, which are responding by creating new brand names such as Citizen. More common in Kenya among the general population, however, is home brew, made from maize, millet, or sorghum. Any grain or vegetable that will ferment can be turned into an alcoholic beverage, such that local drink is brewed and readily available in nearly every community, especially those in rural areas. Home brew typically begins with soaking grain in water. After the grain has absorbed this water, it is left on leaves to dry. Later it is sometimes roasted. In a large clay pot, water is brought to a slow boil and the dried grain mixture and various leaves are added. Removed from the fire, this mixture is left in the covered pot to ferment. Periodically, the contents are stirred and tasted, until pronounced ready for consumption and sale.

Because grain can also now be purchased in small shops, the brewing and consumption of alcohol is no longer confined to the local agricultural cycle, when beer was only brewed at harvest time. As a result beer is available to be drunk at any time, money permitting. The quality, taste, and strength of the local brew, served in "cups" that are often recycled tin cans, is often a major topic of discussion. The consumption of home brew is very often a male activity that brings together elders and other initiated men who eat and drink as neighbors. In this setting they discuss and agree to various transactions that impact the village community.

At the coast, coconut milk, popularly known as *madafu,* is drunk, as is a popular and locally home-brewed palm wine, *tembo.* Palm wine is made by farmers who tap their coconut palms for the sap that would otherwise go to form the coconut on the tree. As the sap oozes from the trees, it is collected into containers. On its own and without heating, the sap quickly begins to ferment and becomes wine. Because newly fermented palm wine will turn sour after only a few days, it needs to be drunk soon, but always on festive and ceremonial occasions. Made in the countryside, freshly tapped palm wine is transported to cities in large gourd containers and sold by both women and men.

In most communities no ceremony or social gathering is complete without beer. It can be traded for goods or services, but more important, it is used as payment to neighbors who assist with farm labor or help construct a new house. On such occasions it is typical for the participants to gather around a large clay pot and drink communally. Among the Kipsigis, for example, governed by particular rules of drinking etiquette, people drink from a communal beer pot using long straws made from a local plant. It is at times like these that community matters will be discussed, stories told, and songs sung.

Palm wine, just as with home-brewed beer, was often a major focus of colonial officials who were concerned with the effect of drunkenness and its interference with workers' productivity. From early in the twentieth century, they developed procedures for licensing those who sold it and increasingly raised the cost of such a license in an attempt to drive up the price of palm wine so that it became unaffordable to workers. As with attempts elsewhere in the world to impose rules and regulations on alcohol consumption, these methods were largely ineffective. If there was an influence on lessening the production, sale and consumption of palm wine at the coast, it came from the Muslim prohibition against intoxicating drink, but this too was in large measure ineffective.

Milk, *maziwa,* is a staple of many diets and comes in a variety of forms. Sour milk, *maziwa mala,* has a taste enjoyed by some, especially in western Kenya where it is served cold on *ugali,* with cooked greens on the side. *Maziwa lala,* the "milk that has slept" is not quite as sour but is appreciated and desired by many. In other parts of Kenya curdled milk, *maziwa mbichi,* which resembles something similar to cottage cheese, is a treat, as is sweetened buttermilk and the cream, *mtindi,* that comes off the very top of fresh milk. Milk is used to make both butter and cheese, which although generally not part of the traditional diet, are increasingly popular. Butter is also used to make ghee, a kind of clarified butter for frying, but Kimbo, a commercial cooking fat or lard, is the most widely used for this purpose. In still other parts of Kenya, especially the semiarid regions where the herding of animals is the local pattern of subsistence, milk is the primary source of nourishment.

Herders, Livestock, and Milk

Pastoralism is the practice of raising large livestock such as cattle and camels and small livestock such sheep and goats as the principal means of supplying a population of people with the food and nourishment they require. In Kenya the most widely known group of pastoralists is probably the Maasai, but there are many more, especially in the country's northern region. These include the Ariaal, Borana, Dasenech, Gabbra, Rendille, Samburu, Somali, and Turkana. The practice of living off one's animals is not unique to Kenya or even East Africa. Ethnic groups such as the Tuareg and Fulani in West Africa follow similar patterns, while yaks are kept for the same purpose in Tibet, camels in the Middle East and Asia, reindeer near the Arctic Circle, and llama and alpaca in South America.

Herders and their families essentially live off the products of their animals, although not exclusively, as some sources suggest. They eat grain when it available, trade for it, and today even buy it in local shops. The principal sources of nutrition, however, are milk and its by-products, such as butter, sour milk that can look and taste similar to yogurt, and cheese. Although it would appear to an outside observer that meat is plentiful, it is rarely eaten, and when it is, it is the male animals that are slaughtered. The logic of this is that male animals neither give milk nor give birth to the young animals that increase the herd size and will be the next generation of milk producers. When slaughtering occurs it is typically during the dry season, when the weakest might otherwise die anyway and when grass for grazing is most scarce. Eliminating a few of the older male animals is advantageous for the entire herd and allows the female animals, the milk producers, greater access to the limited grazing and water that do exist. The other reason that the eating of meat is rare is quite obvious; if the herders ate their animals rather than drinking the renewable milk, there would soon be too few animals left for them to remain herders.

Meat Feasts

Having appropriately emphasized the importance of milk in the diet of herders and their families, it is equally important to note the other by-products consumed in this diet, as well as discuss the role of meat. In most

The main sources of nutrition in a herder's diet are milk and milk by-products such as sour milk and butter. Beginning at an early age, daughters and even young sons assist their mothers in milking the family's animals.

parts of Kenya meat, especially roasted meat, *nyama choma,* is widely desired. Indeed, one of Nairobi's most popular restaurants, whose name perhaps says it all, is the Carnivore. Here, meat of every sort, from beef and lamb to ostrich and zebra, is grilled on Maasai spears and carved straight on to the diner's plate until the diner cannot eat any more and "surrenders." The more usual source of *nyama choma* for average Kenyans is at an outdoor stand. Among herders meat feasts occur when a group of elders or warriors, *morani,* decide to have one. Commonly, these are connected to ritual celebrations associated with aging and include initiation into warriorhood and recognition of a man's status as an elder. These feasts are guaranteed to draw a crowd eager for good food and conversation, for these are village affairs.

Critically important to any meat feast is who eats what part of the slaughtered animal. Among pastoralists this is strictly regulated by custom. In Western society it is usual for the best cut of meat or the largest piece to be given to a guest or a senior male, but with herders this is not an option. Although it is true that those roasting the ox just outside the village may nibble on some choice cuts, this is little different from what the person carving a holiday roast or turkey might do in the kitchen before taking it into the dining room. However, the meat that is actually prepared for the feast is distributed ceremonially and according to a prescribed pattern. In the case of the Maasai, for example, the ox is seen as consisting of two identical sides. Therefore, there are two pieces of each specific cut—two briskets, two shoulders, two flanks, and so on. Thus in the distribution pattern they follow, the brisket of one side will go to the elders, the other to other elders or their wives; the outer thigh meat of one side to boys, the other to the elders; the inner thigh meat of one side to girls and the other to the elders' wives. Other parts of the animal, such as the tongue, which might not be considered a particularly choice piece by some outsiders, is in fact reserved for the ritual leaders or highly respected elders. On the other hand, elders want nothing to do with the innards, including such parts as the liver, spleen and stomach parts, and leave these for their wives to cook.

Slaughtering an entire ox produces a great deal of meat, and although much of it is consumed on the first day, the meat will in fact last for most of a week. The feast itself is the first day, but meat that has been roasted continues to be distributed over the course of the next few days. When only bits and pieces of meat remain, they are made into a stew for sharing with the entire village. At the very end, a finishing stew is made using whatever is left along with the jowls, feet, and local roots. Earlier in the week, the village dogs would have eaten the brain. The fat of the slaughtered animal is also shared and consumed according to a recognized rating system of delicacy and taste. However, equally important is the oil extracted from certain fats by squeezing it. This oil is used ritually as a protective blessing and applied by smearing or dribbling it over the front side of the body. As one scholar notes, this transfers symbolically the protection of God to those who have feasted on the ox. In the end nothing is wasted.[3]

TRADITIONAL DRESS

Dress, like food, is regionally specialized. However, across Kenya it is fair to say that both women and men are fond of wearing cloth wraps that extend from the neck to the knees or waist to the ankles. Whether plain or patterned, light such as cotton cloth or heavy as with a woven blanket, these rectangular pieces wrap easily around the body and stay on when folded over at the top and tucked in or tied at the shoulder. Such wraps are most common in rural areas or for indoor wear at home in the towns. Common as well are shorts for both boys and men and, increasingly, skirts and dresses for women. Outdoors, men wear trousers and shirts, and women wear dresses or skirts and blouses, just as one would see in many other parts of the world. A man's outfit is often completed with a coat and tie, even in small towns, and a woman wears a pullover or cardigan sweater. Black shoes or even tennis shoes are worn everyday. A high school student in Kenya dresses much as a high schooler does anywhere—jeans and T-shirt for casual; uniform of trousers, shorts or skirt, a shirt with a tie or blouse,

A holdover from British colonial days, schoolchildren across Kenya are required to wear uniforms to attend school.

and a jacket or sweater for school. As evidenced by the school uniform, the power of colonial practice lingers in many aspects of modern-day Kenya.

The greatest variation in clothing exists where what is often called "traditional" clothing is still worn; sometimes it is even possible to distinguish what ethnic community an individual belongs to by the distinctive clothing they wear. This is increasingly difficult as traditions change and Western-style clothes are more readily available, although it is likely to be more true for certain groups, such as the Maasai, Swahili, and Turkana. However, individuals from these same groups may just as readily be found speaking Swahili or English and wearing Western clothes: a coat and tie at work in Nairobi or Mombasa, and jeans, a sports shirt and sweatshirt on the weekend when visiting the family farm or herd.

Wraps and Colorful Clothing

Some of Kenya's most distinctive and colorful traditional dress originated at the coast, where people had the greatest contact with traders from the Indian Ocean rim. Among the Swahili and other coastal people, men wear a *kikoi,* known in other parts of the country as a *shuka.* Made of cotton, this long piece of plain or patterned material is worn by wrapping it tightly around the waist, folding the top section over a couple of times, and tucking it in toward the body to hold it up. A belt can also be worn around the waist but is not common. Traditionally, these colorful *kikois* were handwoven as a small cottage industry and completed with hand-tied fringe. Today, they are also machine made with some end seams sewn together so that they resemble a sarong. As everyday wear, a *kikoi* can be worn for work or relaxing and can double as a sleeping cloth at night. A shirt can easily be added to the *kikoi,* as can a vest or waistcoat, called a *kizibao* by the Swahili. Today, however the *kizibao* is not commonly seen. Nor is the long beautifully dark colored *joho,* which, with its richly gold embroidered shoulder decorations, was once worn much as a full-length coat would be worn over other clothing. Still being worn, however, is the one-piece *kanzu.* Made from cotton cloth, a *kanzu* is much like a white cotton dress shirt, only it extends from the neck and shoulders almost to the ground. Lightweight and white in color, it is loose fitting and airy and therefore most practical for a people who live in the hot, humid climate of the coast.

Invariably, such traditional clothing is worn with a small intricately embroidered white cotton skullcap, or *kofia,* identifying the wearer's adherence to Islam. Because a *kofia* is such a common religious marker throughout the Muslim world, it too reminds people of the long history this part of Kenya has had with the Islamic world of the Middle East and Persian Gulf. Many are so finely made that they are in themselves a kind of work of art.

A mother and child each draped in a *khanga,* a piece of brightly colored cotton cloth. Wrapped and tied in a multitude of ways, they are worn across Kenya as skirts, tops, and head coverings, as well as to create a sling to carry a baby.

When traditionally attired a Swahili gentleman makes an impressive appearance. A traditionally dressed Swahili woman, however, can still upstage a Swahili man, even if she is completely covered by a *bui-bui,* a cloak worn by devout Muslim women, together with a veil. The *bui-bui* is made of black cloth and is worn when going outside so that only the eyes and hands are uncovered. The purpose of such head to foot covering is to conceal women from the eyes of men who are not part of the family and are therefore out-siders. Historically, Swahili women wore trousers and loose-fitting dresses of richly colored fabric and shawls of imported silk and other fine material. Today inside the home, however, Swahili women can still be found wearing a brightly colored rectangle of cotton cloth called a *khanga,* similar to the *kikoi* worn by men.

The *khanga* is thought to have originated on the island of Zanzibar off the East African coast in the nineteenth century. The word itself is Swahili for a guinea fowl, a bird about the size of a large chicken and whose colorful feath-ers display a variety of subtle patterns and markings. The story of its begin-nings is that some wealthy women began sewing together six colorful cotton handkerchiefs to make much larger pieces of cloth. The colorful patterns that resulted, which could be sewn to meet individual tastes, are said to have reminded people of guinea fowls, and so the cloth came to be known by the same name. Today, a manufactured *khanga* is about five feet by three-and-a-half feet. They come in an array of colors and with a multitude of elaborate patterns and are not particularly expensive. Husbands give them to their wives, mothers to their children, daughter to their mothers, and women to their friends. Indeed, the popularity of the cloth is such that when new designs and color combinations appear, they are quickly bought up. Older ones then find their way to second-hand markets. Somewhat rough and stiff when new, a *khanga* becomes soft and smooth with washing. To set the early dyes used in these cotton cloths required a good washing in the salt water of the Indian Ocean. Much like T-shirts, *khangas* are a means of personal as well as of political, religious, and social expression, with no end to the colors and themes found on them.

The cloth is unique is a number of ways. First are the many different and expressive styles in which it can be wrapped or tied. Second, it consists of two identical pieces. Still another is the message it carries in the form of different Swahili proverbs printed on the cloth. Women and girls can wear a pair of *khangas* as a matching skirt and shawl, or as skirt and head covering. They can be tied to allow a mother to carry her baby either on her back or in front. And they can be worn at night for sleeping. Indeed, it is said that the second cloth can be placed on a husband's pillow using the Swahili expressions or messages printed on the *khanga* to indicate the wife's mood. Often these proverbs do not translate well or contain hidden meanings, but "Don't bother me" is straightforward enough. "The love of a child is in its mother's womb," how-ever, is more ambiguous and can be translated as, "A child gives no pleasure unless its mother is loved by her husband." Generally, the message of proverbs is clear, such as "When two elephants fight, it is the grass that gets hurt," "Blessings are better than possessions," or "One who grabs for all usually loses all." (A more in-depth discussion on Swahili proverbs and their meanings is in chapter 3, "Literature, Film, and Media.")

Kitenge cloth, which is now made locally by machine, is another popular cloth used in the making of men's shirts and women's dresses. In the past *kitenge* was imported from Indonesia via Holland, but today the most highly desired and expensive *kitenge* cloth is a "waxed" variety imported from the Congo. Especially popular in western Kenya, this bright, colorful, and attractive cloth is typically folded in half, leaving the large diamond pattern in the center to form a V shape along the fold. When a neck hole is cut at the center of this diamond and the sides are sewn shut, leaving armholes near the top to which sleeves are attached, the result is a quick and easily made pull-over shirt or dress. *Kitenge* cloth is often further decorated with sewing machine-produced embroidery along the neck and sleeves to make an attractive shirt or dress, reminiscent of finely embroidered clothes from West Africa.

In other parts of the country, what constitutes traditional dress is very much a matter of time period. Although some people in rural areas still wear what is often described as traditional dress, and on occasion a Maasai warrior can be seen in Nairobi wearing a red cloth tied around his body with another over his shoulder like a cape, such sights are rare. What once constituted traditional wear is nearly everywhere being replaced by readymade, off-the-rack Western-style clothing, with more-traditional dress reserved for and most appreciated on special ritual and ceremonial occasions.

Another development in clothing is the growing use of traditional cloth for making a fashion statement. The brightly colored *kikoi* is being made with colorfast dyes and marketed as "Kikoy" beachwear.[4] Even the red and red-patterned cloth or *shuka* worn by the Maasai wrapped around the waist or draped over the shoulder is now being commercially sold as "Warrior Wear" and marketed as "the fabric with a culture."

Clothing and Identity

In the nineteenth century clothing and sandals made of animal skins were worn nearly universally. Whereas the hides of cattle, camels, and some wild animals were used to make the sandals, goatskin, which is more pliable and could be made softer, was more commonly used for clothing. However, some groups, such as the Samburu and Maasai, wore skins of cowhide, which they beat to make it thin as cloth and then rubbed with fat to make it soft and pliable. Typically, men wore an animal skin as a cape over the shoulders or tied around their waists; women wore either two or three skin pieces depending on whether they were unmarried or married. Generally, the top of the body was bare, although the head and shoulders were often "painted" with red ochre or other colored clay substance. In this period around Mount Kenya, Kikuyu men wore goatskin, or *kizii,* over their right shoulders. Kikuyu women wore a kind of skirt, *musuru,* around the waist and extending nearly to the ground, with a small apron piece, *mwengo,* at the front under the *musuru.* Over all this married women wore a cloak of animal skin (*zetu*), which was tied around the shoulders and allowed to hang down, typically to below the waist. Such leather garments were sewn together with the sinew of an animal, using an iron awl or punch obtained from a blacksmith. That such animal-skin clothing was widely common can be seen in the clothing once worn by the nearby Kamba, as well as by the distant Turkana in the north and the Kavirondo and Luo in the west.

Regardless of what goatskin garment was being worn, people were distinguishable ethnically by the adornment that accompanied such garments, even if they wore them in the same manner. Sometimes beads, small cowrie shells, or pieces of metal were sewn along the edges of cloaks and skirts to make them more attractive or so that they would clink together when dancing. Again, these uses and styles were ethnically specific. The Kamba, for example, were known for the wide and beautifully patterned beaded belts that they strung together to secure the skins they wore around their waist. Younger women and men, especially those not yet married, wore strands of beads that would be progressively discarded as they grew older and women became mothers and men became elders. The Kamba once wore blue-and-white beads around the neck and smaller white beads around their waist and ankles. Here, too, the colors worn were often particular to certain times and eras since what was worn and fashionable was often related to what could be obtained from neighboring communities or to what traders brought to the region. Just as cloth would replace animal skins for clothing, so glass and plastic beads have replaced the seeds from plants and trees that were worn like beads.

Others groups, such as the Kikuyu, also wore beads as a form of adornment. They were especially known for wearing small hoops of red beads attached to the top of the ear. It was not uncommon for an ear to be pierced at four or five places along the top, and for the earlobe to be pierced at the base as well. In addition, coils of heavy brass wire and strands of thinner copper wire were worn about both the arms and legs. In the past the Kikuyu wore coils of brass and copper around their arms between the shoulder and elbow, around their wrists, between the knee and calf, and around their ankles as well. In addition finger rings were popular. Later, as other sources of metal, such as brass cartridge casings, found their way to the interior, these too were attached to a strip of leather and worn decoratively. Among the Turkana the color of the neck ring worn by a wife indicates to which of two tribal sections her husband belongs. A brass neck ring indicates that he is a Leopard (*ngeri-*

sai); a silver-colored one, which is today most commonly made from aluminum, indicates that he belongs to the Stones (*ngimur*).

The same traders who brought in metal wire and glass beads to the region introduced white cotton sheeting, known as *Americani,* and woolen blankets. Both of these were products of the newly mechanized industrial output coming from cities such as Birmingham and Leicester in the English Midlands. Generally, the elders preferred to wrap themselves in the blankets, whereas younger men and women were fond of cloth. A length of cloth was worn tied from under the armpits so that it fell straight to midcalf or knee length. With constant wear this white cloth soon took on the color of the local landscape, as well as the red ochre or clay and animal fat that was frequently used to add color to the shoulders, neck, and shaved head of a young person trying to attract a suitor.

Today among some peoples, the clothing is still a combination of animal skin and cloth. Among some of the Turkana and Dasenech around Lake Turkana in the extreme northwest of Kenya, women still wear two-piece leather aprons or skirts around their waists. In the front is a smaller triangular apron, while a much larger and longer one is wrapped around from the back. The Turkana have access to cloth and sometimes wear it in place of the animal skins, but it is not nearly sturdy enough to have sewn to it the distinctive and decorative rectangles of colorful beads usually found on their hide skirts. Unmarried girls also wear high collars of large multiple-coiled red beads around their necks. With their shaved heads covered in red ochre and with leather-backed beaded pendants hanging from the back of the coiled necklaces, these girls will likely not remain unmarried for long. At one time Turkana men proudly wore leopard skin as well as domesticated animal skins, along with decorative ostrich feathers in their hair. Today they still do so on special ritual occasions if they have them, but because the universal ban on hunting in Kenya prevents them from adding new leopard skins, cloth and shorts with a T-shirt are more common.

As already noted, occasions for which individuals genuinely want to wear traditional clothing are often those that celebrate particular transitions in life. Among many Kenyan peoples, weddings and circumcision rites, the latter marking the transition from adolescence to adulthood, are two of the most significant occasions. At circumcision the Maasai, who are known for the striking red-patterned cloths they wear, wear cloth of dark blue (shades can range from purple to charcoal gray), which is culturally appropriate for this occasion. For the closely related Samburu, this color shift is from red to black. Because the circumcision of males marks their transition from boys to warrior, and that of females from girls to being eligible for marriage, it is understood as a time of danger. The threshold between one social status and another marks the symbolic death of one stage in life and the rebirth into another. The space between is thus a time of separation when one is particularly vulnerable, and so Maasai boys will enter this time wearing the coiled brass pendants of their mothers as protection. Such transitions are also sometimes marked by lengthy periods of seclusion, as is the case with circumcision. The new warriors spend this time recovering from their ordeal and later hunting birds, which they stuff with ash and grass. These are then mounted on a circular frame and worn like a large crown extending over the neck in the back and up and forward in the front. In other ceremonies warriors wear different sorts of headdresses, from those made of lion mane that rise high from the top of the head to those of ostrich feathers worn tightly around the face. These "face ruffs," which are marks of masculinity and serve to extend a warriors height, are said to draw the eyes of girls to a boy's face. Additionally, these warriors almost always also decorate either their faces or torsos with white chalk markings.[5]

The Maasai warriors are not the only ones who wear such headdresses. Indeed, at one time they were common among different communities found across the country. Lion mane was always popular, in part because of the courage required to kill a lion. During the colonial period government-appointed chiefs among the Turkana were encouraged to wear manes as headdresses. Also widely worn among many warriors or individuals of special status were headdresses or cloaks made from the black-and-white skin of colobus (*guereza*) monkeys. These were popular with the Kamba, Kikuyu, Luo, and Meru, among others, but as an endangered species, they are today seldom seen.

Body Identity

Just as certain types of clothing and jewelry create a distinctive appearance that can identify the wearer as belonging to a particular ethnic group, a specific hairstyle or other form of ornamentation can also communicate identity. Some of these practices have a long history, some have long since been abandoned, and others continue to be practiced today. Some of the most distinctive hairstyles are found among the herding peoples of the north. For example, Dasenech, Pokot, and Turkana men cover their hair with clay in such a way as to make a kind of headdress or mudpack (more properly called a chignon). The hair is pulled from the center of the head forward toward the front and covered with a thin coating of mud. Similarly, hair is pulled from the back of the head upward and from the middle of the head backward and again coated in mud. Among the Turkana at least, this back portion is often painted blue. Set in the mud in the front will be a piece of leather with small holes, whereas in the back section four small wooden posts will be planted in the mud. When the occasion warrants, small white feathers can be affixed in the front piece, and large white or black ostrich plumes mounted in the back, making for a very impressive warrior or elder at ceremonial dances and rituals. Because so much time can be expended in preparing this ornate hairstyle, and the Dasenech, Pokot, and Turkana typically sleep on the ground in their homes, each man carries a wooden headrest or "pillow" to lay their head upon so as not to destroy it. By offsetting the hairstyle with other beaded and metal decorations around the head and neck, or worn in the ears, each community can create a distinctive style unique to them. Women among these same groups commonly wear the hair on the side of their heads shaved, leaving a smaller tuft of hair at the center or center-front of their head. From this they let the hair grow so it can be braided in thin strands that fall down their heads. When Turkana women wear high collars of red and blue beads or the Pokot and Dasenech women wear strands of large red and yellow beads, they make an impressive appearance every bit the equal of their husbands and sons.

The shaving of hair also typically marks a change in status. Among the Maasai and Samburu, it is part of the initiation ceremony that denotes the passage of a warrior to elderhood. Prior to this warriors not only wore their hair in long plaits down their back, but they often added strands of grass that they braided with their hair to make it appear even longer. With their hair and shoulders covered in red ochre, wearing long knives at their waist, carrying two spears in their hand, and taking on an attitude of aloofness, they make a striking appearance to all who encounter them.

For the Maasai and Samburu the use of red ochre, especially by young men and women following initiation, is nearly universal. Other locally found natural substances are also applied to the body. For example, the use of henna and kohl is critically important to Swahili identity. Kohl, a finely powdered substance, is used to blacken and accentuate the eyes and eyebrows much the way eyeliner and mascara is used elsewhere. Whereas kohl can be worn most anytime, henna is used only on special occasions. A kind of cosmetic stain or dye for use on the body, henna is made from the shoots and leaves of the Egyptian privet (*Lawsonia alcanna*). When made into a powder and mixed with water and the juice of unripe limes, it produces a darkish red paste that can be applied to the hands and feet in decorative patterns.

The use of white chalklike substances to paint faces, chests, and legs is another common feature of human adornment. Once it is applied to the body, a finger or fingers can be drawn through the paint to leave behind an intricate pattern where the underlying natural skin color has been exposed. At various times this practice has been used by the Kikuyu, Kipsigis, and Luo, among others. Because white is often as sign of death, it is commonly used at those rites of passage that mark a transition from one status to another, such as initiations, when a child is reborn as an adult. Scarification is another form of body decoration used to indicate distinctions between individuals and to mark specific accomplishments. Among many of the peoples of northern Kenya and the border area with Ethiopia and Sudan, such scars can indicate any number of things. For some, it may be the number of warriors killed; for others, success in a hunting certain animal, a hippo for example. To still others, it may indicate nothing more than someone who has been through a particular healing ritual, or may simply be part of a cultural aesthetic of what pleases the eye.

Contemporary Practice

Clothing, body decoration, and other forms of adornment have long served to identify publicly the wearer's status or to reflect the importance of a particular ritual occasion, such as a wedding. Sometimes the adornment can be elaborate and even ostentatious, but always it can be assumed to be culturally determined. Religion may also sometimes encourage a particular practice as illustrated by Muslim men wearing a white embroidered skullcap. However, just as they always have, patterns of clothing and adornment continue to change. For example, the once-common custom of enlarging holes in the earlobe has become much less common. At one time a warrior of the Maasai, Samburu, or Rendille wanted to be identified by wearing an ivory earplug made from the cross-section of an elephant tusk end and later, as an elder, by the small metal earring that hung from the bottom of this long extended earlobe. Today, however, for young men who go off to boarding school for their education and may end up working in a city instead of defending the family's animal herds, such permanent disfigurement holds less pride of place. Similarly, the wearing of long, braided, red-ochred hair is today less common than it once was.

When looking at an image of people wearing traditional clothing, it is important to remember that although it is still popular in many areas and among certain ethnic groups, such clothing is being worn less frequently. More often than not, it is being replaced by the same Western-style clothes being worn everywhere around the world. And on those occasions when individuals wear traditional clothing, they do so as a matter of pride and heritage for community and family rituals. This point is made quite poignantly in an article that appeared in 1991 in the Nairobi *Daily Nation*. It reported that when two young people from the Samburu were married in 1978, they wore customary clothing. A Roman Catholic priest from a nearby seminary came to the wedding and, unbeknownst to the bride, took her photograph at the event and later sold it to a local publisher. The publisher not only turned it into a postcard, labeled "Samburu Girl with the Fertility Necklace," but also sold the image for use in a tourist brochure. When the couple—she is now a teacher in a childcare program and he a primary school headmaster—accidentally discovered the picture being used this way, they were upset for a number of reasons. First, as modern Kenyans whose marriage was also blessed in a Catholic church where a commercial photographer took their wedding pictures, they found the use of a picture depicting her as backward and primitive to be degrading. Second, she was not wearing a fertility necklace, but an *mporro* necklace that denoted her status as a woman engaged to be married, much as an engagement ring communicates a similar status in the West. And third, many in their families accused the couple of being too Westernized and having made a profit by selling the picture. Eventually, they sued the publisher in the Kenyan courts and won a damage award.[6]

For a while in Kenya, there were highly charged debates over the wearing of Western-style clothes, cosmetics, and even hairstyles. Today, these are of little concern for most Kenyans, who often equate Western fashion and tastes with education, material possessions, and a decent standard of living—things that most Kenyans strive for. Although there is widespread recognition that there are appropriate times and places for wearing traditional clothing, some urban dwellers criticize their rural brothers and sisters who do not fully cover up their bodies. The equating of nakedness with primitiveness is not really new and is part of the seeking of a national identity in times of rapid change. So too is the consternation many feel over preserving traditional values associated with family, and especially women, at a time when outside Western and urban-based values are everywhere evident on television, in films, and in newspapers and magazines and are so readily assimilated as signs of success. For Kenyans the preserving of traditional cultures is just as important as making the statement that Kenya is a modern nation.[7]

NOTES

1. A number of recipes from Kenya and East Africa can be found at www.geocities.com/congocookbook/.

2. At least thirteen other countries in Africa are also significantly dependent on the export of coffee. Other cash crops in Africa subject to the same conditions include cocoa, cotton, groundnuts (peanuts), palm oil, and tobacco. As noted in chapter 1, cut flowers grown almost exclusively for sale in the West represent a new cash crop that has recently emerged in Kenya and other parts of Africa.

3. Paul Spencer, *The Maasai of Matapato* (Bloomington: Indiana University Press, 1988), 252–58. Also see Paul Spencer, *Nomads in Alliance* (London: Oxford University Press, 1973).

4. See, for example, the Kikoy Company Web site, www.kikoy.com.

5. More about Maasai use of adornment can be found in chapter 4, "Art, Architecture, and Housing." A number of photographs of Maasai wearing traditional dress in various ceremonies can be found in Carol Beckwith and Angela Fisher, *African Ceremonies,* 2 vols. (New York: Abrams, 1999).

6. Ngugi wa Mbugua, "Saga of Samburu Postcard," *Daily Nation,* 27 February 1991.

7. A consideration of these issues as they were being debated in the 1960s and 1970s can found in Audrey Wipper, "African Women, Fashion, and Scapegoating," *Canadian Journal of African Studies* 6, no. 2 (1972): 329–49.

6

Gender Roles, Marriage, and Family

Kenyan women provide the largest measure of labor at the village level. They are the backbone of the rural economy as well as of the urban economy. One of the factors helping to create this situation is that the gender division of labor (those tasks assigned culturally to women and those to men) assigns both productive and reproductive activities to women. At the household level women are responsible for collecting and carrying home water, fuel wood, and agricultural produce, in addition to caring for children's health and educational needs. This is not unique to Kenya. In Africa as a whole three-quarters of all food production is done by women. Another factor is that women find this situation acceptable. This is so because they receive directly the income that they earn, which they can then use as they choose, such as for their children's school fees and home improvements. Many women find they cannot rely on their husband, even if he is the principal income earner, because husbands do not put the family's needs first. Some women are going so far as to have children without bothering to get married because they do not want the burden of a husband. In the urban areas the same social stresses that exist in Europe and North America are confronting Kenyan women who now work outside the home but are still expected to do all the work inside the home—cooking, laundry, raising the children, and so on.

The most significant altering of traditional family life began early in the colonial period, when men were forced or drawn into the wage-earning economy. Various factors figured in this shift, including the need to pay "hut tax" (designed to have those with more than one wife pay more because each wife had her own house) and the attraction of trade goods that could only be obtained with cash. The result was always the same. Husbands and, later, eldest sons left their wives and families behind in the rural areas to move to cities and towns or to large white-owned farms, where they worked for cash. The colonial government actively discouraged or forbade these men to take their families along. As a result their wives and other female family members took on still more responsibility for producing the family's food and meeting the family's needs. That is not to say that the men did not want to send money home, but given the low wages they received plus the necessity of maintaining a place to live in the city, what they could afford to send home was generally very small.

In the rural areas women's many tasks were, and are, made more difficult by the poor quality of the roads and the limited and expensive public transportation they need to use to take their perishable crops to market. Failure to get them to market in a timely way results in significant financial losses for women, who are already limited by physical and cultural factors in their access to income. On a continent where today half the population lives on less than a dollar (U.S.) per day, development specialists often speak about a "feminization of poverty." Yet at the same time, women are a significant potential resource to be used in programs designed to reduce poverty, that is, if they are allowed to participate in the planning and design of such schemes.

Nevertheless, the role of women is changing, just as is the social, economic, and political fabric of society, and they are no longer as marginalized as they once were or were thought to be. In the cities and towns women are professionals of every sort, from doctors, lawyers, and police officers to shopkeepers, accountants, and university professors. Their homes, their families, and their desires and aspirations for their children are no different from those of women everywhere, and the same can be said about the challenges they face. Thus when the government puts forward legislation as they did in 2001 in the Affirmative Action Bill, which calls for 33 percent representation of women on city and town councils, many men are mystified. This is particularly true of men in the far reaches of the rural countryside, who complain that serious political functions are in danger of being hijacked by "a small minority of noisy women."[1]

EXTENDED FAMILIES AND KINSHIP

Only by understanding the extent of personal ties and relationships within and between communities can one fully appreciate the role and nature of the family in Kenyan society. Whereas people in the West generally think of a family as being a mother, father, and children, or what is known as a nuclear family, this is not the only form of family found in Kenya. For Kenyans a family can also consist of a number of such nuclear families that live together or very near each other. This form of family is called an extended family. Members of an extended family interact and share hospitality as a group during rituals, and they regularly give and receive mutual assistance. Frequently, the close ties that people in these families share are also reflected by children calling the "aunts" of their mother's family "mother," and the "uncles" on their father's side "father," and calling the children of these relatives "brother" and "sister." An extended family will also have at least one set of grandparents residing with the family. Typically, the grandparents in residence are on the husband's side of the family. Most Kenya ethnic groups are patrilineal, meaning that inheritance passes through the male line; as a result, at marriage a bride generally leaves her family and moves in with and becomes a part of her husband's family.[2]

In addition, extended family members recognize that they are related through a common ancestor, even though they cannot precisely trace their genealogy back to that ancestor. All those people who share this recognition of a common ancestor, although they come from a whole series of often widely separated extended families, make up a clan. As clan members, all these people are each other's relatives to whom they have certain social obligations. Even more important, members of the same clan may not intermarry. Additionally, because many Kenyans—not just Muslims, but a number of Christians, as well as practitioners of traditional religion—still practice polygyny (having more than one wife),[3] knowing who is related to whom is very important. Common expressions capture the significance of clan membership and its importance to the solidarity of the community. For example, it is often said that a clan never breaks even though people might separate, or that although the members of a clan leave one another, they always return to help one another. Again, the importance of these relatives to survival in an uncertain and ever-changing environment is obvious. As part of this recognition of clan membership, clans may have a recognized association with a particular animal, such as the crocodile or a certain antelope, for which they will share a taboo on eating it. In other instances they will be understood to have control over something in nature, such as the wind, or, as in the case especially among herding peoples, they will claim to share a particular cattle brand. The members of an individual's nuclear and extended family together with those people that constitute the clan make up the membership of an individual's kinship group.

In the life of any individual, a number of events are marked by particular rituals and symbolic acts that include ceremonial aspects. Events such as birth, initiation, marriage, and death are together called rites of passage. (In Western society, first communion, confirmation, bar mitzvah, graduations, and marriage are all rites of passage.) Since as an individual passes through the rite, they acquire a new and different social status, participation is often described in terms of an individual's symbolic death and rebirth. For example, in death an individual moves from the world of the living to that of the ancestors, and at initiation a boy or girl enters the ceremony as a child but emerges from it as an adult.[4] Yet while participation in an initiation ceremony confers adult status, it is through marriage and, most important, the birth of a first child that individuals prove their manhood or womanhood. Women who bear many children are considered particularly blessed and virtuous; those who are do not have children, even if through no fault of their own, are thought to be cursed and evil. Marriage is also the most important event in a Kenyan's life because it is through this event that an individual begins to establish his or her own kinship network, which can be critically important to the family's success in times of both plenty and want.

BRIDEWEALTH AND MARRIAGE CEREMONIES: OLD PRACTICES AND NEW

For a young man to ask a young lady to marry and then be joined as man and woman in a wedding ceremony does occur in Kenya today, but generally, this is a new phenomenon and confined to urban centers among children of well-educated professionals. In many more Kenyan communities, to enter into marriage requires a far more involved process. Critical to understanding the practice of marriage is the realization that it is not merely the joining together of a man and a woman but the linking of two families.

Marriage practice among the Kikuyu today, which is an interesting mix of tradition and customs adapted for use in contemporary society, can serve to illustrate the kinds of processes that are followed in many Kenyan communities. The first step in this process is to let it be known publicly that there is interest by a young man or his family in having him marry. This is known as "the asking" for the girl, *njurio,* and takes place at her home village. It is increasingly common for a young man to make it known to his family that he is interested in a particular young lady. In the past, however, it was more typical for his family, or more accurately, his father, to decide that it would be useful for their son to marry a girl from a particular family. A spokesman for the groom's family will lead a small delegation to the village of the girl who is being sought as the wife, taking with them a ewe, a he-goat, and a local brewed beer (*njohi*) to make clear the seriousness of their visit. As increasing numbers of people no longer live on farms but in the towns and cities, cash is sometimes substituted for the sheep and goat, and the beer comes in bottles from Kenya Breweries.

At this first gathering the spokesman for the bride's family stands up and asks, "There are strangers among us here; why are they here?" The groom's spokesman will then announce that there is interest by a boy of their family in a girl of the home being visited. Girls from the village are then brought out one by one, and the visitors are asked, "Is this the one?" "Is this the one?" and so on. When at last the prospective bride appears, and they respond "This is the one!" a family today will often ask the girl, "Do you know anyone here?" (i.e., Are you interested?). If she agrees, they can move to the next stage, which is that of negotiating the bridewealth. To be certain, the groom's spokesman will ask, "So now I can drink beer?" And if again the response is affirmative, the negotiation stage can begin. In theory it is possible for the girl to say no, which is supposed to be the end of it, and increasingly among educated families this is indeed the case. In practice, however, the reality is that a young girl comes under strong family and social pressure to accept and, if not exactly coerced into the marriage, may not have the strength to refuse.[5]

The negotiation stage is all about bridewealth. What bridewealth actually consists of varies from ethnic group to ethnic group. Generally, it involves the transfer of an agreed-upon number of animals, food, and *pombe*. Among herding groups, such as the Samburu and Rendille, the transfer usually includes a culturally prescribed number of cattle or camels and a negotiated number of sheep and goats, although many husbands argue that the requests for these small stock never end. Among other herding groups even the number of cattle is negotiated. Today, with people living and working in urban communities and the importance of money to even remote rural communities, cash has entered into the bridewealth equation, as have major commodities such as appliances and even cars.

The reason that bridewealth is such an important concept in traditional African society is because a woman's labor is so important to her family's existence and her departure is a significant loss to her family. In essence, the giving of bridewealth from the family of the groom (the wife receivers) recognizes this loss of labor by the family of the bride (the wife givers).[6] Further, bridewealth is not just a gift to the bride's father. Various parts of the negotiated total, whether cash or goods and livestock, are given to various members of the bride's family, including her uncles and brothers. Similarly, the gifts do not originate only with the groom's father or even immediate family, but uncles and brothers all contribute, again demonstrating that marriage is truly the forming of an alliance between two extended families and a whole range of members. To ensure that the relationship between these two families stays strong and active, a groom is really never finished paying bridewealth. Continuous gifts, even small ones, but especially small stock such as sheep and goats, are always being requested by the wife's family and given by the husband. For this reason husbands often refer to bridewealth as the "rubbish pile," since the payment of these gifts seems to be never ending.

Bridewealth is also a kind of "marriage insurance" since in a divorce the bride's family must return these gifts. Thus in any potential breakup considerable pressure will be exerted by the extended family for the couple to resolve their differences. If a bride feels that she is being treated poorly, she can even ask the elders to convene to hear her grievances against her husband. If the elders agree she should divorce, the husband's extended family will provide the wife with land to farm and help look after the welfare of the children, since with marriage she became part of her husband's family.

Among the Kikuyu the spokesmen for each family also negotiate the bridewealth that is to be transferred to the bride's family. Over food and *pombe,* the spokesman for the bride's family, who serves as the "master of ceremony," sets the stage for negotiation. This is supposed to be a fun time when the families enjoy themselves. The basis of this joking relationship is all about sending a signal to the groom's family that they expect their daughter, who at marriage will be incorporated into this new family, will be looked after and taken care of properly. This joking relationship may continue when the groom's family brings out the beer that they are expected to supply for this event. Today, this might more typically be cases of bottles taken out of a car, to which a woman on the bride's side might ask, "Did you bring a cloth to wipe the dust off the bottles?" And if they did not, the bride's family will make them pay to borrow one. Because the beer is considered to be especially for the men, the next question might be, "Did you bring soda for the women?" And if they did not, the bride's family will make them go and get some. Most important, however, the bride's spokesman will indicate the bridewealth that the groom's family will be expected to produce.

Increasingly today, these bridewealth occasions are being commercialized. A father might demand that a car or even two cars be parked in his driveway before proceeding with anything further, and such demands have on occasion led to the end of the relationship, with daughters becoming severely depressed over such breakups. More common today is a situation in which the bride's family demands an outrageous sum of money, for example, 1 million Kenya shillings (in 2001, this equaled roughly U.S.$17,000). The groom's family spokesman simply responds "no problem," but when the family later gathers to consider how much to really transfer, the discussion is over how not to give too much, yet not to give too little so as to be insulting. They might settle on 60,000 shillings, or $1,000. With this money in an envelope, they return to the bride's home to transfer the bridewealth, but say, "Yes, we agreed to 1 million shillings, which is not a problem, but we don't have all of it right now. But look at this strong young man (the groom, who might roll up his sleeves to show his muscles). When he marries your strong daughter— together they'll earn a lot of money and you will have your million shillings."

At this point the envelope of cash will be handed over. When asked how much it contains, the response is, "We never say—it is not our custom." And when someone in the bride's family says, "Let's count it," the response would be, "Not in front of us; that is insulting!" And so they leave with the envelope, and that is the last that is heard of the 1 million shillings.

After the negotiation stage the bride's family must pay a visit to the groom's family. They need to know where their daughter is going. This stage, which is referred to as *guthii kuona mucii* ("to go and see the home"), is like all the other occasions in this process, notable for more feasting and socializing. Only after these activities can the actual marriage ceremony, *kuguraria,* take place. The occasion is marked by the ritual slaughter of animals for feasting. As part of this the groom cuts a piece from the shoulder of the animal and feeds it to his bride in an event known as *gutinia kiande,* which literally translates as "to cut the shoulder." This public act seals this customary marriage practice, an act that is recognized as legal under the law.

The permanence of the move by the wife to her husband's family is made clear by the fashion in which the children born of this union are named. The firstborn is named after the husband's father's father or his father's mother, depending on whether the child is a boy or a girl. If the second child is the same gender as the first, it is named after the wife's mother's father or her mother's mother. If it is of the other gender, then whichever name was not used at the time of the first child's birth is given. If then three sons are born to the family, the third son is given the name of his father's eldest brother.

Public recognition that a wedding has occurred is characteristic of most societies. Among the Swahili it occurs in a mosque. Prior to the event a messenger, much like a town crier, goes through the streets of the town announcing the wedding. A traditional trumpet, or *siwa,* is then blown, and all those attending follow to the home of the bride, where celebrations of singing and dancing occur, although not for the bride. With her hands and feet painted with henna in elaborate patterns, she remains inside her room until the faithful are summoned to the mosque. Here, in front of a judge (*kadhi*) and before the community elders, the bride and groom take their wedding vows and sign the certificates legally marrying them. Only during this process will the bride see her husband for the first time. The keeping of the bride and groom apart until the wedding is understood to be a valuable custom that has served this community well for many generations.

Marriage Forms

The pattern of marriage in most societies in Kenya is very similar to that described for the Kikuyu. For example, among the Pokot a male and his friends take a gift of beer to the father of the girl he wants to marry. By accepting and drinking the beer, the father gives his approval. After this the negotiation stage is taken over by the male elders on both sides. On the man's side the girl's ancestry must be traced to be sure she is not a relative and that she comes from a family or clan of recognized strength. Elders on the girl's side also scrutinize the potential groom's family and heritage. When this is resolved to everyone's satisfaction, the bridewealth is negotiated and agreed to. As with so many other peoples in Africa, this is generally a matter of livestock, cash, or both, and the wedding ceremony can occur only after the bridewealth has been transferred. Pokot weddings take place in the compound of the man's family, where a leather wristband is placed on the girl's right arm. After prayers are said and blessings of the elders given, the entire community celebrates with singing, dancing, and drinking. The songs sung on these occasions are not simply joyous songs but remind the new bride and groom, and everyone present, of the expected behavior of a husband and wife and their responsibility toward each other and their families.

Similarly, in some herding societies the first approach to the bride's family is made directly by the suitor along with some of his age-mates. Among the Turkana, for example, marriage discussions are begun when a potential groom makes his intentions known with a gift of some chewing tobacco and a goat or two to the girl's father. If the father approves, the families enter into talk about the bridewealth. Among herding societies this is almost exclusively a matter of animals. Some societies like the Samburu and Rendille recognize that this transfer of stock should always be eight head of cattle or eight camels, respectively, with the number of sheep and goats open to negotiation. For the Turkana there is no fixed number, and the negotiated amount will include cattle, camel, sheep, goats, and even donkeys. In all these societies the groom is expected to provide a significant portion of these animals, but his extended family and age-mates will also assist him. On the day of a Turkana wedding, the groom, dressed in a leopard-skin cape and with ostrich feathers in his hair, takes a marriage ox to the home of the bride. Here, the women of the bride's family prepare a feast of roasted meat and ox blood for the consumption of the males of both families, who thus seal the marriage. When the groom's wedding party departs for home, the bride goes with them, as she is now a part of this new family. The next morning the mother of the groom and other wives of the household distribute the bride's girlhood clothes and adornment to the girls of the family and replace them with items worn by a married woman. When she is properly dressed, the women of the family then place a child on the bride's lap to make clear what her true responsibilities are to the family.

As with the transfer of bridewealth, various aspects of traditional weddings also demonstrate important linkages that bring the two extended families together. Among the Somali a wedding basket provides an important focus and message. The basket (*xeedho*) is covered in leather and decorated with cowrie shells by relatives of the bride, filled with food, including spices, dates, butter, and meat, sewn shut, and finally sent to the relatives of the groom. It is the groom's family's task, encouraged and teased by family and friends, to untie the elaborate stitching without spilling or spoiling the food inside. The message conveyed by the wedding basket is clear: the groom's family and kinsmen must take this same kind of care to look after and protect the bride and the new family she will help to create.

The importance of a traditional or customary wedding remains so crucial that even for Christians, this ritual will often precede a church wedding. Although this adherence to two seemingly separate and very different traditions may seem strange to some, it is quite common in Kenyan life, where the mix of traditional and modern patterns are an everyday reality. The logic of this dual approach to marriage is that it satisfies both the needs of those relatives who continue to live and follow a traditional way of life and those who see themselves as members of an emerging contemporary society. The most widely practiced form of marriage remains that of a negotiated one. Still, it is possible that in emphasizing negotiation, there is a sense that young couples do not engage in the same practices recognized in other parts of the world, such as flirting, making amorous advances, or actively courting a particular partner. In rural communities this occurs at traditional dances, while a young lady is performing daily chores such as collecting firewood or water, and increasingly, at church or school. Churches and schools are also used by urban youth to meet youth of their own age but of the opposite sex, but so is passing the time at neighborhood shops, the mall, discos, coffee shops, and most recently, Internet cafés.

In some societies, however, a young couple may choose to run away together and elope. A young couple who elopes may do so because of parental opposition on one side or the other to their marriage. In some communities there is even something of a tradition of young people doing so for the fun and excitement of it. However, even when a couple signals their marriage by running away, there will still be subsequent negotiations between the family that will result in the transfer of bridewealth. In still other societies opposition to a marriage from the bride's family may lead to the groom and his agemates capturing the girl and taking her back to his family's compound for the wedding ceremony. Among herders capturing a bride, and sometimes a child, was simply an added benefit that came with raiding neighboring communities for livestock. Historically, raiding was a sporadic activity of these communities, instigated by a broad range of causes, from environmental to ritual. Although generally described as incidental, the capture of a girl or woman could be quite significant. This was especially true in times of illness and disease, as was the case in the late nineteenth century when smallpox killed hundreds of people. This epidemic was particularly devastating to the youth population of these communities, which meant a shortage of labor to herd the animals, and was exacerbated by the spread of rinderpest, a disease that killed large numbers of cattle. The capture of women at such a time served two purposes, depending on their age. The capture of a woman of childbearing age meant the acquisition of a wife for which no bridewealth needed to be given. This was important since bridewealth at this time meant the transfer of cattle, which were in limited supply because of the rinderpest. The capture of a young female child was a kind of investment because it meant that one day soon bridewealth could be collected and thus help return a herd devastated by rinderpest back to a healthy size.

Traditionally, those men who could afford the bridewealth took a second, third, fourth, or even, as for example among the Luo, a fifth wife; similarly, Muslims may marry up to four wives. In households with more than one wife, a separate house is nearly always provided for each wife within a large family compound. When adapted to towns and cities, this may involve two houses that are not always next to each other and that are sometimes even in an entirely different neighborhood. In polygynous households the first wife always occupies a position of authority with respect to other wives, even though they are commonly referred to as cowives. Similarly, her children are always deemed to be socially older than those of a second or third wife, even if in biological age they are younger than the eldest child of a cowife.

The practice of polygyny is sometimes difficult for outsiders to comprehend, but life in such a household is believed to be made easier by the addition of a cowife or cowives; not only do they share a husband, but they also share household work. Some chores are so burdensome and difficult, such as collecting water from a distant communal waterhole or well, that sharing these and other domestic responsibilities makes life easier. Men often argue that the advantage of this marriage pattern is that they have more children to herd animals or to work their fields. Even though it is often necessary for a husband to ask his first wife's permission before taking another, in practice she has little power in the relationship, and so the consequence of permission may not be particularly significant.

Another reason for a husband taking a second wife may be the perceived failure of the first wife to bear children. Rarely spoken is that the man may be the cause of no children being born, but this reality is recognized in Kipsigis society. A man in a childless marriage is allowed to take another wife when the first wife becomes too old for childbearing. If this too fails to produce children, then it is turned around and the first wife will seek a younger man to help her younger cowife conceive. Among the Kipsigis such a marriage is recognized as being between the two women, as a result of which any children born are said to be of the original family. For the Kipsigis, like so many other peoples, the importance of children is related to their belief that the spirit of a past ancestor is carried in each newborn child and that an ancestor not reborn can cause considerable trouble for the living.[7]

In the past, some men also acquired an additional wife or wives upon the death of their brothers. Traditionally, family values did not allow a widow and her children to live alone. Instead, it was the obligation of one of the husband's brothers to maintain family solidarity by marrying his brother's widow and providing for her care and needs. In such cases it was understood that the brother adopted all the children of the marriage, inherited all the property including land and livestock, and would maintain the wife's house and assist in the cultivation of her fields. Which brother was to accept these obligations was usually dictated by cultural prescription. Sometimes it was the eldest, and at other times a junior brother nearest in age to the deceased. Almost always this also required the agreement of the woman, but given her options and the arduousness of life alone, it was a reasonable way of ensuring her well being and those of her children. Today, this practice is seldom employed, and if it is, it is often done in secret. More common today, as it is in much of Africa, is for the eldest son to inherit his father's wealth and provide for his mother and his brothers and sisters.

Today, the practice of a Christian marriage is widely followed in Kenya, where the vast majority of the population is in fact Christian. As such, a husband is permitted only one legal wife even if customary law allows more. Adherence to this rule is generally followed, although some men who live and work in a city or town have been known to marry one wife in the church and take another wife according to traditional custom. Thus one wife lives with him in the city while the other looks after his farmland in the countryside.

Although marriages are assumed to last a lifetime, there is in most traditional practices a means of recognizing divorce, and sadly, divorce is also becoming an increasingly common feature of modern society. Nevertheless, divorce is actively discouraged in Kenyan society as a whole, and considerable pressure is brought on a couple to resolve their differences. This pressure comes both from family members and the community. The family's interests are especially strongly exerted since in a divorce, as already noted, the bride's family will be expected to return all the bridewealth they received. The reasons a man might divorce his wife are familiar ones—unfaithfulness, incompatibility, laziness, or practicing sorcery or witchcraft. On rare occasions a woman might seek to divorce her husband. Cruelty is usually given as the principal reason. More rare are two instances that require divorce: if after marriage it is discovered that the two individuals are indeed from the same clan or clans that are not allowed to marry, or if there has been a murder that involves the husband's clan and that of the wife. Divorce between a Muslim husband and wife can occur when the man says the word *talaka* ("I divorce you") three times.

Nearly every Kenyan society is patrilineal (inheritance as well as succession to social position is transferred from father to son), and children are understood to belong to the man's family. Because this customary rule is also the case in Kenyan law, it serves to discourage women from seeking a divorce. Rather ironically, however, a man who deserts his family is under no obligation to support his children. Unfortunately, given the dominance of men in Kenya's patriarchal society, divorced women are looked down upon and face a difficult future. Those women who have a profession and live and work in an urban area have a considerably easier time than those in more traditional outlying communities. Still, marrying for a second time for a woman is more difficult than it is for a man.

Also difficult for women is old age. As a child, a female depends on her father; when an adult, she depends on her husband; and in old age, typically as a widow, she depends on her sons. In contemporary Kenya the limited welfare system leaves few other options, especially because so few women own any property, whether fields or livestock. Although in some rural locations missions have given a place for older individuals to stay and perhaps helped provide a small market for them to sell traditional crafts, older women are increasingly learning to master tasks formerly left to the men in their lives. This is especially the case in the town and cities.

Intermarriage across ethnic lines is neither unknown nor new among Kenyan societies. In the precolonial period such marriages were used to improve relationships between two potentially hostile communities and to facilitate trade in needed commodities. It was also a means of extending one's kinship ties beyond a particular environmental niche, which could serve a family, and even prove critical to survival, in times of need, such as when drought and famine struck or a herder's animals were stolen in a raid. Such ties could prove to be a source of food and, in truly disastrous times, a place of refuge. Further, a farmer might marry his daughter to the son of a herder as a way of adding, by way of the bridewealth he would receive, needed livestock to his holdings. The animals would not only provide fertilizer for his fields but could also assist him in meeting the bridewealth obligations of his sons. This union could also be advantageous to a herder in times of prosperity, when cattle were plentiful but labor was frequently in short supply. By adding a wife or wives from outside, and the subsequent children they produced, the herder added to the labor he needed for herding, while at the same time reducing a bit the size of his herd and thus preserving grazing for his remaining animals.

GENDER AND INITIATION

As with so many traditional societies, the community view is that the woman has the heaviest responsibility in the marriage for keeping the husband content. A stanza from a traditional Swahili poem, full of advice and instructions for young women for understanding their role in Swahili society, makes this obligation quite clear:

Enda naye kwa imani
Atakalo simkhini
We naye sikindaneni
Ukindani huumia.

Give him all your heart,
Do not refuse what he wants
Listen to each other
For obstinacy is hurtful.[8]

The traditional notion that the role of a woman in a relationship is always to acquiesce, as well as the notion that women are the source of many problems, is reinforced in a variety of ways, including poems and proverbs. Among Kikuyu proverbs, consider these examples:

Haro ni ya muka uri thiri.	A woman in debt is quarrelsome.
Mundu muka na iguru itimenyagirwio.	Woman and sky cannot be under stood, *or* Woman, wind, and fortune are ever changing.
Mundu muka ndatumagwo thiri-ini.	Let women spin and not preach.[9]

Despite the inequality that exists between the circumstances of women when compared with those of men, women are nevertheless accorded high status given their potential for bearing children, and motherhood is honored in traditional society.

The Kikuyu and Swahili are no different from other societies in Kenya in that responsibilities both inside and outside the home are divided according to gender and age. Referred to by anthropologists as the sexual division of labor, certain activities are culturally defined as those of women and others as those of men. For example, men commonly have responsibility for clearing fields, tending livestock, hunting, fighting, making utensils, community deci-

The tasks culturally designated as those of women include rearing children, planting, weeding, harvesting, grinding grain, collecting water, gathering firewood, and plastering the house.

sion making, and local governance. Women are responsible for planting seeds, weeding gardens, harvesting crops, storing food, grinding grain, making beer, and weaving baskets as well as collecting water, gathering firewood, plastering houses, thatching roofs, and caring for children. Equally common is for men to have responsibility for anything that has to do with livestock, and women with grain. Among the Dasenech, for example, a man can invite his age-mates home for roasted meat whenever he wishes because he has responsibility for the animals and their disposition. If, however, it is a season when grain is widely available, he must always first ask his wife's permission before bringing his age-mates home to eat porridge.

The way in which children take on these traditional male and female roles is through a process called socialization. Communities begin to emphasize these different roles soon after a child begins to walk. In the first months or years after birth, a child nearly always accompanies his or her mother strapped to her back. No matter what household tasks she is performing, whether planting or weeding, milking goats or cows, collecting water or firewood, cleaning the house, or sweeping the family compound, the child is there. However, once a child begins to walk and move about the family house picking up objects, it is not unusual to have items that are gender specific to a boy taken away from a girl and vice versa. For example, among herding people, should a baby girl grab a herding stick or headrest, it will be taken from her, but a baby boy will be allowed to hold and even play with them. Similarly, among agriculturists a baby boy who picks up a winnowing or food storage basket will have it taken away, but a baby girl will not. In other matters the differentiation comes somewhat later. For example, in communities where women make clay pots, it is not uncommon to see both two-, three-, and even four-year old girls and boys playing with clay and attempting to shape small pots alongside their mothers and older sisters. Soon after this time, however, the boys are diverted to tasks performed by men, such as herding livestock, and are no longer allowed to work with clay.

In addition to learning gender differences in the home and family compound, children in most Kenyan societies undergo an initiation that transforms their social status from child to adult. In addition to marking a time of both physical and psychological changes, initiations are designed as a time of learning, especially for acquiring the special knowledge and skills necessary to be an adult. What are these skills the initiates acquire during initiation? For young women the time immediately following initiation often sees their entry into marriage. Thus much of their instruction tends to focus on confining them to the domestic domain, being a good wife, and always using sound judgement. For example, when Swahili teenagers are gathered together, an older woman whom they call Senior Mother, *Ma Mkubwa,* gives their instruction. She begins every sentence to them by saying *Nisikize, mwanangu,* "Listen to me, my child," and gives instruction in norms and beliefs regarding appropriate gender rules for women and men, allowable conversation topics, and matters such as the correct practices related to serving food.

Stories are also told as part of the shared initiation experience. As well as being entertaining, they instruct and provide a commentary on both the desirable and the undesirable aspects of human behavior. For example, the Kikuyu tell the tale of an ogre who had assumed the appearance of a handsome fellow. Ogres are wild characters who eat anything and everything and are understood to be able to change themselves into anything they choose. This particular ogre, while appearing handsome, met a beautiful girl and fell in love with her. Determined to marry her, he took her home to meet his parents. But as they neared his parent's compound, they could see many white-colored objects brilliantly shining in the sun. The ogre told the beautiful girl that these were his family's sheep and goats, and he asked her to wait while he went ahead to herd them into their pen. All these white objects were in fact the bones of all those creatures that ogres eat, and he worked frantically to sweep them away. Today, people sometimes say, when they are cleaning and preparing their home for visitors, that they are "sweeping away the bones."[10]

Tales of animals are also popular. Stories of elephants, for example, typically emphasize the destruction that results from greed. Those of leopards and other spotted cats, whose skins are often worn as capes by traditional leaders and elders, emphasize the role of authority and leadership. And tales of dogs and monkeys are metaphors for the catastrophes that can result from lust and sexual promiscuity.

The conclusion of the initiation period, when young adults reemerge to begin the process of reintegration into the society, is typically a time for an elaborate and joyous celebration. Generally, male rituals tend to be more public, whereas female rituals are less dramatic and colorful. On this occasion it is usual for the new adults to demonstrate publicly the new knowledge they have acquired, which often takes the form of performing newly learned songs and dances. In addition to being a time of learning, the confinement of initiates for a period of time also allows any physical changes that may have been part of the ceremony, such as circumcision or body decoration, time to heal.

SOCIAL CHANGE

In many parts of East Africa, including a number of Kenyan communities, the ceremony that marks the passing of a girl to womanhood has included what is today recognized as female genital mutilation (FGM). Today, many Kenyans find this traditional practice, sometimes referred to as female circumcision (clitoridectomy), to be an outdated rite. This is a result of a number of factors. One of these is the postindependence conversion of many women to Christianity, especially in the highlands. Another is the impact that increased school attendance has and its more general role as a "modernizing agent." And more recently, there has been greater recognition that this practice has serious and far-reaching implications for a woman's reproductive health—it is medically risky, is painful, and can create serious problems in childbearing—as well as have serious psychological and social consequences. Nevertheless, each December stories and commentaries regarding FGM appear in the local press. The timing is predictable because December marks both the end of the school year and the beginning of the Christmas holiday. With so many children in school today, these long school vacations often provide the only lengthy period of time available for the initiation rite and the healing and instruction that must follow.

Rooted in long-standing tradition and custom, the issue of FGM is a complex one. For many villages the physical attributes associated with these ceremonies are considered vital to the well-being of their community and that of the girl and her future family. The practice is certainly not performed with the intention of harming a girl. Rather, it is seen as an accomplishment that protects the initiate and her family so that she can be properly married. Others adhere to the practice as a religious obligation. The Wardei, a people of the coast, and other people of the Muslim faith are said to believe that Islam sanctions FGM; others disagree. What is clear is that male and female circumcision have taken place for generations.

Trying to understand the place of FGM in traditional society has proven very difficult for Europeans and North Americans, where the issue, especially among feminist organizations, has become a cause célèbre. Condemned as child abuse, an act of oppression against women, or both, the practice has been removed from its cultural context and demonized. That there are contradictions involved in this custom is readily apparent even within Kenya. Consider the remarks made by a woman in northern Kenya where this practice is still followed, when a scholar explained to her that FGM is not practiced in the West: " 'It is bad that you don't circumcise women in your country. That child which is born to such a woman, is it human? We think it is bad to bear a child if the woman is not circumcised. But you know, the men like to see us circumcised. They think we won't see other men if we are circumcised. But they are wrong,' she laughed."[11]

The government has tried a number of responses, including arresting the parents of girls who undergo this rite. The impact, however, has not been particularly effective yet because the passing of laws that change cultural practices must go hand in hand with a change from within the communities and from the people themselves. Such change, however, is typically slow. In part this is because the peer pressure on young girls is enormous, especially in rural areas. Those not initiated "properly" find themselves shunned, taunted, and verbally abused. Some girls whose parents stop them from participating are so afraid of being ostracized that they have gone so far as to threaten suicide. Others, however, such as two teenagers in Rift Valley Province, went to court to get an injunction against their father to prevent him from forcing them to be initiated unless it was with their consent. Girls in urban areas have a distinct advantage. They and their parents are often better educated, they have many more options of associating with young people like themselves, and such customs are no longer considered central to marriage ceremonies.

The strongest and most effective support for changing this custom is coming from women themselves. A series of recorded life histories of Kikuyu women make it clear that they no longer deem initiation to be necessary to signal the change that a young woman goes through from being a child to an adult. "When you are a girl and then give birth, you find that you are changed. Your body features change ... and show that you are no longer a girl. And you change mentally, too, because you are always thinking of your children. So you have gone from girlhood to womanhood."[12] In bringing about this change, women are being supported by nongovernmental organizations that have taken to helping organize alternative rites of passage events for young women. This is proving effective because it recognizes that equally significant to those communities that emphasize the importance of initiation rites is the period of instruction that follows initiation. These teenage girls are still isolated as an initiation group, but today the emphasis is exclusively on their preparation for marriage. Similarly, the same elder women of the community provide their instruction in the manners and duties of a wife, including cooking and other domestic responsibilities, child cares and how to live a moral life. Also giving positive hope in this ongoing debate is the cultural change that has occurred over the past thirty or so years among those communities that have always initiated their young men to be warriors. Marked by changes in cultural practice in combination with legislation, warriors no longer launch raids for cattle against neighboring communities, and Maasai warriors, for example, no longer need to prove their manhood by killing a lion to wear its mane in initiation ceremonies. At one level this is because each act violates a law and a warrior would be arrested or even shot and killed by the police if they raided for cattle or killed a lion. However, equally important has been the role of communities in adjusting their cultural practice so that it no longer require warriors to demonstrate their manhood by performing such tasks.

Also changing is the place of women as second-class citizens. Increasingly, girls and women are challenging this notion, breaking away from the pattern of being educated only at home. Parents and children alike value education highly despite the expense of attending—required school fees and uniforms—and schools that are too often bookless, penless, and paperless. Nevertheless, across Kenya one sees girls in red gingham dresses with maroon sweaters, or green or khaki skirts with yellow or navy blouses and sweaters, walking along roadsides on their way to and from school. For boys the uniform consists of shorts or slacks, depending on whether they are in elementary or high school, with shirts or sweaters in similar color combinations to those of girls. Today, both girls and boys from rural areas are attending school in increasing numbers. Across Kenya there is gender equity in school attendance through ages 12 to 13. Attendance of boys, however, gradually begins to increase over that of girls at age 14–15 until 23 percent more boys are in school than girls at age 18–19.[13]

Many children are also leaving home for boarding schools, where they meet and become friends with children from other ethnic groups, including children from herding communities. As would be expected, the children of families in the urban areas are also attending in large numbers. But so too are young people sent from rural areas to their urban relatives who are then expected to support and educate them. This generosity is all part of the responsibility that comes with being part of an extended family and the widely understood sense that one person's success needs to be shared by the entire family. These children, who live and learn in the environment of a town or city, are far removed from those family members who live by traditional means and who insist upon strict rules of custom and tradition. Their hopes and ambitions are decidedly different from their cousins in the rural areas.

Traditional marriage patterns are also changing. Under considerable criticism are polygyny and early marriages, especially the pattern in which older men—elders—marry young girls as second, third, and even fourth wives. Such marriages, a tradition in many rural areas, have for a long time been taken for granted as the normal state of affairs. They are not based on any romantic notion of love, but rather are the result of family negotiations, with the soon-to-be-married girl usually the last to know. Why these marriages are favored at all is because of the benefits that are thought to accrue to the bride's family—stock, cash, and other goods.

The criticism being leveled at these marriages comes from both politicians and women activists. Politicians offer their usual quick fixes, such as public whippings for old men who marry schoolgirls. The more thoughtful critiques come from activists who point out that by marrying off these young brides, families are actually mortgaging their futures. Not only do many of these girls have no interest in leaving school to get married, worldwide evidence consistently demonstrates that girls who have completed their primary education are better mothers and wives. They care for their children and family's health and nutrition more effectively, and they take more seriously the next generation's need for more education. Generally, the family's standard of living is also higher, which in turn can add significantly to a higher quality of life for her children. And this is without even considering the fact that many of these young girls have the potential with further education to become brilliant professionals who will aid Kenya's badly needed economic and social development.

Two women who demonstrate the significant potential that women can bring to the development table are Wangari Mathai, the founder and coordinator of Kenya's Green Belt Movement, and Naomi Kipury, an anthropologist who also happens to be Maasai. Mathai was the first Kenyan woman to receive a doctorate degree, which she earned in veterinary medicine. The winner of many national and international awards, she is recognized worldwide as a women's rights advocate and has served as a member of United Nations Disarmament Council. When in 1992, at the height of the demands for multiparty elections in Kenya, she ran as an opposition party presidential candidate, the government arrested her on the flimsy charges of having published a "false document." Today, her Green Belt Movement operates more than 3,000 tree nurseries that raise millions of seedlings each year, which in turn are provided to rural farms, schools, and churches. Since its founding in 1977, the movement has assisted more than 50,000 Kenyan households in planting more than 20 million trees, while raising public awareness of the critically important relationship between the environment, trees, and firewood use. In the simple act of planting trees, Mathai has run into more government opposition. This is because it is government policy to resettle poor farmers on forest land even though Kenya has less than 2 percent forest cover (most scientists recommend a country maintain a minimum of 10 percent), which greatly increases the chances of drought and famine. Opposition to her activities has sometimes also emerged at the local level, where her work with women's groups provides opportunities for rural women to participate actively in decision making and the formulation of public policy. This has certainly been the case near Mombasa, where local women have organized to demand fair market value for land the government insists they must sell to a Canadian company that plans to mine titanium (a metal important to the air and spacecraft industry).

Kipury is another conservationist, whose insights into Maasai culture have made her a recognized spokesperson for the critical issues faced by the herders in both Kenya and Tanzania. The Maasai and other herders have lost much of their traditional grazing lands to national parks and reserves that attract the tourists who are so important to the Kenyan economy. With their movement severely restricted, they have been forced into smaller areas, where animal diseases tend to be more common. Yet Kipury points out that the Maasai are natural conservationists, who have generally avoided eating wild animals. Therefore, she argues, if they cannot have access to some of the grazing now held by the national parks, then they should at least receive more benefits from tourism. More and more, this is beginning to happen, with small tented camps owned and operated by local communities such as the Maasai and Samburu providing tourists with eco-sensitive wildlife safaris. These local community management schemes are pioneering new forms of conservation and, through ecotourism, are bringing valuable resources to the people whose lands these once were.

Similarly, women are also playing a significant role in monitoring wildlife populations, especially those that were decimated by poaching in the 1960s and 1970s and that are now endangered, such as the elephant and black rhinoceros. Today, for example, two Kenyan women near Amboseli National Park north of Kilimanjaro continue critically important research on elephant behavior and society begun by wildlife biologist Cynthia Moss.[14]

Whereas the contributions of individuals such as Mathai and Kipury are seen as extraordinarily positive, other changes in the way women are taking their place in global society are not always viewed in the same way. What can only be described as beauty contests—Miss Tourism Africa, Miss National Costume, and Miss India Kenya—have become a regular and popular part of Kenyan urban life. Pageants such as these often lead to participation in other contests at the world level, such as Miss Tourism Planet, staged in Athens, Greece, in 2001, and Miss India World in Los Angeles, also in 2001. With panels of dignitaries, movie stars, and fashion designers, these contests draw a huge audience on television and radio, both inside and outside the country. What the outsider may miss is the sense of pride that this brings to a country where publicity about Kenyan women is otherwise dominated by their winning of marathon races or tied up in television documentaries that focus on their traditional roles in rural communities.

Across Africa the spread of urbanization, Western education, and the expansion of modern economies are all leading to significant changes in the life of women. Whereas initially there were changes in bridewealth from patterns of livestock and other traditional gifts to cash, increasingly today there are women in rural and urban areas alike who are resisting any transfer of bridewealth at all. This opposition is especially strong in urban areas among educated women, where cash—the amount of which is often based on a woman's education, with the largest amounts being transferred for a university graduate—is seen as payment, thus making the woman nothing more than a commodity over which a husband has power. Along with changes in bridewealth traditions can be seen a decline in polygyny. In part this is based on the spread of Christian teaching, but it is also a matter of basic economics. Should a husband spend family resources, be they cash or livestock, on a second wife or buy a house or a car? And if the first wife is involved in the cash economy and earning income, will she want money she brings to the household spent on her husband acquiring another wife? The answer to both questions is increasingly a resounding "No!"

With the number of urban-based families increasing, the importance of the extended family is also in decline. When both husbands and wives work, old divisions of labor are breaking down. With many husbands working in towns and cities, women are resisting older patterns such as one that required a bride to work for her mother-in-law. Similarly, inheritance patterns are changing as parents want whatever they have earned in their lives, be it land, possessions or cash, to be shared equally by all their children. The size of families is also growing smaller as women opt to have fewer children. In the long run this can only be of benefit to a country whose population mean is 17.9 years of age. The spread of education has also led to many more children attending school, rather than working from a young age on the farm or herding animals. With more education, young people's horizons have been expanded and their expectations for the future are greater.

This has led to another notable change in Kenyan marriage practice. In many areas, both rural and urban, it is increasingly common for a woman to be pregnant when she gets married. Social scientists are uncertain as to whether this is related to the rise in marriage age, since this delay obviously lengthens the period of time for adolescents to have premarital sex. What is known is that there is a growing pattern of young women, when they discover that they are pregnant, moving into the boyfriend's home. Only later, when they have saved enough money for a ceremony, either church or civil, and the required feast will a couple actually marry. According to an anthropologist who has studied this phenomenon, the shame once attached to being pregnant and unmarried seems to be in decline. From the man's perspective, it is argued that this allows him to be sure his wife is fertile before he begins bridewealth payments. From the woman's perspective, the thought is that the man will be compelled to marry his pregnant girlfriend, although this does not always happen.[15]

Related to this is an increasing number of women who, if they are not actually the heads of household, certainly do not rely on their husbands to support them and their children. Women who work outside the home want to work only for themselves and their children. Even in rural areas women are supporting themselves and ensuring their children have food to eat, clothes to wear, and school fees to attend school. They accomplish this by making a living however they can. They sell food and vegetables in the market, work as artisans making crafts, and run their own shop or market stalls stocked with secondhand clothes and shoes. Similarly, their expectation is that their children, and not their spouses, will assist them in their old age.

The postindependence period has also seen a significant increase in the numbers of men and women taking jobs in parts of the country far from where they were born or even went to school. This has led to new levels of contact between men and women and to many more marriages across ethnic boundaries. Some of this has also been a result of education, not merely the amount of education young people receive but the fact that they are learning in boarding schools that, as noted earlier, are no longer the exclusive domain of one particular ethnic group. The overall impact of this change is leading to many more people who think of themselves as more "Kenyan" than anything else. This has also resulted in a shift of commitment away from kinship and ethnic groups and to the nuclear family. According to many Kenyans, however, the nature of Kenyan politics, which all too often continues to emphasize ethnicity, has prevented this feature of traditional society from being diluted even further.

Long-established traditions and customs remain strong, and so do people's commitments to them. This is especially true of the strong family values that have always been practiced in Kenya. Whether the family is described as traditional or modern, these values include an obligation to children, their well-being and future, respect for elders, and preference for a lifestyle that emphasizes kin and family over the needs of an individual. Yes, women usually work harder than men and have far to go to obtain equity in the home and workplace. Where once the boundaries between the sexes were fixed and unbending, women are today no longer confined to domestic tasks of child care and cooking, and those activities associated with farming or herding, and they regularly challenge the inequality that exists between their circumstances and those of men. They no longer accept that they can only be honored and held in high regard for their potential for bearing children and motherhood. Today, as well as being mothers and daughters, they are also artists and athletes, journalists and judges, members of parliament and musicians, scientists and scholars, soldiers and social workers, and writers and recording stars. Their voices are being heard, the injustices they suffer are being recognized, and they are increasingly setting their own agenda and taking the actions necessary to ensure their own futures.

NOTES

1. "Issues on Women Take Center Stage," *Daily Nation,* 5 November 2001.

2. In contrast to a patrilineal society is a matrilineal society, in which descent and inheritance pass through the female line.

3. Anthropologists make a distinction between having more than one wife, polygyny, and having more than one husband, polyandry. Both forms of marriage with multiple spouses are known more generally by the term *polygamy.* It has been estimated that more than 20 percent of Kenyan women are part of a polygynous marriage.

4. There is more information on rites of passage, especially as they relate to men and boy's initiation into warriorhood, in chapter 7, "Social Customs and Lifestyle."

5. Personal communication, Godfrey and Margaret Muriuki, November 2001.

6. The property that a bride brings with her to the marriage is called a dowry, and its intent is that it be used for her support.

7. Abdul Karim Bangura, *Kipsigis* (New York: Rosen, 1994).

8. Stanza 27 in Kitula King'ei, *Mwana Kupona, Poetess from Lamu* (Nairobi: Sasa Sema, 2000), 7.

9. G. Barra, *1000 Kikuyu Proverbs,* 2nd ed. (Nairobi: Kenya Literature Bureau, 1960), 20, 62.

10. Personal communication, Margaret Muriuki, November 2001.

11. Elliot Fratkin, *Surviving Drought and Development: Ariaal Pastoralists of Northern Kenya* (Boulder, Colorado: Westview Press, 1991) 70; see also Jean Davison, *Voices from Mutira: Lives of Gikuyu Women* (Boulder, Colorado: Lynne Reinner, 1989).

12. Nyambura, quoted in Davison, *Voices from Mutira,* 202.

13.   Barbara Mensch et al., "Premarital Sex, Schoolgirl Pregnancy, and School Quality in Rural Kenya," *Studies in Family Planning* 32, no. 4 (2001), 286.

14.   Research on elephant behavior and society can be found in Cynthia Moss, *Elephant Memory: Thirteen Years in the Life of an Elephant Family* (Chicago: University of Chicago Press, 2000).

15.   Davison, *Voices from Mutira,* 205–6.

7

Social Customs and Lifestyle

Daily life is dominated by the hard work of providing food and shelter for one's family. Yet, as difficult as life is for the vast majority of Kenyans, whose average annual income is under $400, life is not so brutal as to prevent people from having fun and enjoying themselves. Traditional ethnic rituals and national and religious holidays all provide an occasion for having a good time. Many traditional rituals and festivals center on events that have already been noted in other chapters. Rites of passage such as a wedding always provide such an occasion. Among those communities that initiate their youth, the shift from child to warriorhood provides another. So too do funerals.

TRADITIONAL LIFE

In childhood boys and girls live with their mothers. As babies they are found most often tightly wrapped and carried on their mothers' backs. When they are older and can walk they still accompany their mothers most everywhere but also begin to spend large amounts of time at play. This might be some type of ball game with a real ball or one made from wrapping strips of old cloth round and round each other. Traditional toys have also included dolls made from mud and clay and small bows and arrows used to hunt insects or small rodents. Today, children in urban areas are found using recycled tin cans and discarded wire creatively to make cars, trucks, bicycles, and airplanes to play with and even to sell to tourists. In rural areas attending school, which is required through primary grades, coexists with chores. In an agricultural setting such chores include assisting with planting, weeding, and harvesting, as well as feeding chickens. Among pastoralists chores include herding, often the youngest animals since this is done near to the main settlements, and assisting with milking and carrying milk between the herding camps and main settlement.

In adulthood, as noted in chapter 6, the emphasis is on finding a partner, raising a family, and providing for the children of that family through the many uncertainties of life. In an African context, the inability to do any one of these—marry, have many children, provide for the family—has historically been regarded as failure. These are the measures of a successful life. Two aspects of adulthood for men are the historically important role of warriorhood and, more relevant today, the later role of elderhood. Although it is commonly thought that African societies are all headed by chiefs or kings, that is the situation only for some. Many others are structured as a gerontocracy, in which the elders of the group exercise greater influence because of their age and accumulated knowledge, and thereby hold authority. This is a democratic system of governance and most commonly associated with the governance structure of those communities built around lineages and clans—groups of descendants of a common ancestor who is either known or not known but assumed to have existed. Elders in a gerontocracy cannot actually coerce people to behave in a particular way; rather, they are respected because it is they who will pass this knowledge on the next generation, who will thus profit by learning from it. That in many societies these elders also have an ability to curse helps since often only the threat of a curse will result in the desired appropriate behavior. The principal concern of the elders, depending on the particular society, is the well-being and health of the clan, lineage, or community.

Rites of Passage

In Kenya, as in much of Africa, people's social age is generally more important than their biological age. It may be nice to be twenty-one years old, but far more important in one's community is whether they have passed through the necessary rituals that transform them from being a child to an adult, or from being a girl to eligible for marriage, or from being a warrior to an elder. To achieve such a new status is not a matter of how old one is in years, but whether he or she has participated in the proper initiation rituals. It is not enough to be an adult physically; those who are uninitiated are treated socially as a child regardless of their age. The critical feature is whether the society to which an individual belongs recognizes that person's new role in the community. The number of these rituals, called rites of passage, varies from society to society.

Only by going through a rite of passage ceremony is the community able to acknowledge the change in an individual's status. Birth, puberty, marriage, and death are all rites of passage. Generally, each has a three-part structure. It begins with the symbolic death of the individual and that person's separation from a previous status, and it ends with "rebirth" or reintegration into the community with a new status. In between is a period of liminality when the individual is in neither one nor the other. Probably the easiest to understand is the rite of passage between childhood and adulthood. As one crosses the threshold between these two, boys are no longer children, but neither are they yet adults; the same is true of the transition from girlhood to womanhood (this initiation is examined in detail in chapter 6, "Gender Roles, Marriage, and Family").

Initiations are performed rituals with the explicit purpose of education; it is the transitory time that is generally used for this purpose. Because the rituals associated with initiation are all about being transformed from one status to another, they are typically conducted in a special location away from everyday community activities and other family children and playmates, physically separated from the rest of society. The construction of a temporary enclosure or small village some distance from the regular settlement also symbolically marks the separation of a child from its mother's home. Here, the initiates often wear distinctive clothing that emphasizes both their separateness and new status. Prior to their entry into this temporary enclosure, initiates will have given up all those possessions that are associated with their previous life as a child. These can include toys, as well as particular types of clothing and adornment. In this symbolic period of liminality, all initiates wear the same clothing. Among the Maasai and Samburu, for example, initiates wear a blue or black skin or cloth along with a crown of stuffed dead birds and their mother's earrings. They also paint their faces with chalk markings (see chapter 5, "Cuisine and Traditional Dress").

Guided by the elders and in many communities by the ancestors and spirits as well, initiates face physical and psychological challenges designed to prepare them to face the responsibilities that come with their new status. Circumcision is a common feature of the initiation associated with puberty, transforming a boy or girl from being a dependent to active participation in adult life. Through the various activities and trials that these initiates undergo as a group, suffering together and learning together, the importance of friendship, cooperation, mutual respect, and the allegiance they must have toward each other are all reinforced. From a community point of view, this is critically important because they not only learn how to act together for the common good but learn the necessity of doing so for the good of their entire society.

Included in the learning process is respect for their elders and ancestral spirits and, in those societies that have them, a high regard for the authority of a traditional chief. Often this is presented to the initiates in the form of folk-tales, proverbs, and songs through which they acquire knowledge, both practical and esoteric, that the community will require of them as adults. Today, as a result of urban life and school calendars, these initiations are taking place earlier, when children are younger, and the time of seclusion is often for shorter periods. However, they remain important to the construction of young people's cultural identity.

Historically, whereas in many ethnic communities females moved directly from being girls to wives, males first entered into warriorhood, a time of further preparation for moving from boys to elders. This remains the case even today among many of the herding peoples, including the Maasai, Rendille, and Samburu, and in the past was true for most societies. As warriors they were subject to the instructions of the elders, whose responsibility it was to manage community affairs. During this time of warriorhood, young men developed a strong sense of camaraderie and group cohesion. In part this came from the distinctive clothing, adornment, and hairstyles they wore, and which the warriors in some societies still wear. In addition, they lived with the herds in camps far away from the settlements and shared food and other daily activities, all while defending their family's and more generally, the community's herds, which provided the major source of nutrition and everything else that made them pastoralists. The lessons learned taught them to act in their common interest for a common good. Historically, they also used this time to demonstrate their prowess as warriors and their courage in the face of danger. Armed with shields, spears, and wooden clubs or throwing sticks, warriors conducted raids on neighboring societies to rustle cattle, learned the various tactics employed by their enemies against them, and killed wild predators such as lions. Their success in these tasks was always marked by village celebrations and, among the Maasai and Samburu, the wearing of a lion's mane headdress. Today, when raids occur between two peoples they are unfortunately more likely to be carrying automatic assault rifles rather than the spears and clubs of bygone days. In the contemporary world these cultural artifacts are mostly for effect.

Passage from the stage of childhood through warriorhood to elderhood is in many societies formally structured through an age-set system. An age-set is a social institution that groups together males who, after being initiated together, take a unique name to identify themselves. These male peers, who identify each other as age-mates, then pass together through the culturally defined stages of life, including warriorhood and elderhood. Each of these stages, which anthropologists call age-grades, confers on the males a status that has expected rules of behavior, privilege, and responsibility. An age-system can be thought of as a ladder in which each rung represents a different age-grade that needs to be passed through as one climbs higher and higher to advance from the status of child to senior elder. Another way to think of an age-set system is to compare it with the structure of a high school or college. Each named class (e.g., the class of 2005) represents a named age-set, and members of the Class of '05 proceed together through the various age-grades of first-year student, sophomore, and junior until they reach the high status of being a senior. Spreading these one-year periods out to a number of years gives you an idea of a basic age-set system. Similarly, age-mates from the same age-set carry their unique name for evermore, much as alumni do after they graduate. This is clearly seen when an alumni office contacts members of a named class to attend a reunion or to contribute to the alumni fund ("Dear Member of the Class of 2005, ... ").

The transition from being a warrior to being an elder is again marked by ritual and the same three stages of separation, liminality, and rebirth/reintegration. Warriors leave behind herding and protecting animals in the bush and emerge with responsibility for maintaining social harmony. And because they can now marry (part of the ritual that often marks this change in status), their new status brings with it responsibility for family affairs. Elders will continue to demonstrate the value of cooperation they learned as warriors, but instead of the excitability that often characterized their actions as warriors, elders are admired for their reserve and patient judgment. Instead of physical assertiveness and ostentatious displays, elders emphasize debate, peaceful compromise, and ritual control. Similarly, the way they dress, wear their hair, and adorn themselves (e.g., Maasai and Samburu earrings) reflects this change. After they have climbed to a new rung on the status ladder, by crossing the moral boundary to enter the age-grade of elderhood, there is the expectation that they will serve as models for community life.

Pastoralism and Social Relationships

Today, life among the herding, or pastoralist, people on the semiarid plains of the north and east is both the same and different. The principal reason this practice is so well adapted to these regions is that the land on which the people live and herd is often marginal for raising crops. The type of vegetation that grows directly determines what type of livestock can better be herded on it. For example, cattle and sheep need grass to eat, whereas camels and goats can survive quite nicely by browsing on thorny shrubs and bushes. However, no matter what the animals eat, a specialized pattern of herding is required that involves moving the livestock from place to place. Where each group of pastoralists herds their animals is also directly related to the condition of the vegetation, the quality of which determines whether the animals will grow and survive. The movement they follow when herding their animals is anything but random. Rather, it is quite sophisticated. In the past herders took their animals much greater distances than they do today. One major reason for their travelling shorter distances, if they move at all today, is the development of small towns. Here, people can buy the foodstuffs they need and the other commercial products they want at local shops. Another significant reason that herding societies have so severely limited their traditional patterns of moving livestock from place to place is the development of water projects, such as pumps, which have created permanent and readily available water supplies. As a result there is no longer any incentive for people to herd their animals to better-watered areas or to regions where newly fallen rain has renewed the grass. Staying near to permanent water and small shops that supply what were once scarce luxury products is the much easier option.[1]

Along with becoming more sedentary, another major change among herders is the new expectation that families be nearly self-sufficient. As a result, they increasingly turn to government, missions, and nongovernmental organizations for food security, medical care, and protection in times of civil unrest.[2] In the past, however, reliance exclusively on one's own skills or even those of one's immediate family was not nearly enough to survive. Extended family, friends, and community were critically important to the overall enterprise of existing as a herder. The most crucial element in this way of life was the animals the individual herded, and those he gave away. Why would a herder give away animals if the idea was to be sure the family had enough to survive drought, famine, disease, and the loss of stock to raiders? The reason is that animals also provide the key link in both making and maintaining friendships with people inside the herder's own community as well as within neighboring ones. Essentially, the maintenance of these relationships with friends and neighbors is like having a range of insurance policies. Herders give animals to each other to acknowledge that they have a special relationship, which often extends beyond the individuals directly involved to include their immediate and even extended families. Each relationship established and cemented by the gift of an animal represents a potential source of assistance in a time of need.

In the past, for example, if a herder's animals died during a drought, or were ravaged by a disease such as hoof and mouth, or captured in a raid and driven off by an enemy, he could turn to all those with whom he had a formal relationship and request their help. Through gifts of small stock, a cow from one friend, another from a second friend, and some oxen from other friends, a pastoralist could rebuild his herd. It is for the same reason that herders often break up their own herds and send animals to graze with those of their friend's herd. If disease strikes their own herd, it might not infect their friend's. If an enemy takes their animals in a raid, chances are good their friend's herd will not suffer this same disaster. By spreading some of their own livestock among those of their friends, they are betting that even given the worst-possible scenario, some of their animals will survive and thus be available to help rebuild a new herd to again provide milk and nourishment. Further, not all of these friends were necessarily within the herder's own ethnic group. Many ties of friendship were also made across ethnic borders. At one level this extended the range of those to be relied on in times of need, and at another level the establishment of such relationships took on the form of an alliance. Here was not only a neighbor that could be counted on but also an ally who might direct a stock raid to a different area or warn of an impending disaster entering the region.

The mutual aid system a herder enters into through the formation of formal relationships with friends is also at work within families where brothers and uncles rely on each other in the same sort of way. And this network is further expanded through marriage. Because marriage is actually the establishment of a formal social relationship between two families—not just immediate families, but extended families—every marriage provides a host of potentially new relationships that can be used in times of need. Similarly, by being in a position to call on a range of these in-laws when in need, the herder too is available to be called upon when they need help. Like a formal relationship with a friend, the ties established through marriage are also cemented with an exchange of animals. Typically, each marriage is affirmed with the gift of a culturally determined number of animals that will include both large stock and small stock. Called bridewealth, these animals are usually collected by the groom from members of both his immediate and extended family and given to his father-in-law and to various other members of the bride's family, including her bothers and uncles (see chapter 6, "Gender Roles, Marriage, and Family"). This mutual aid system was not limited to pastoralists or to members who shared the same ethnicity. The importance of the system in precolonial times was that it extended across ethnic boundaries and thus led to the formation of relationships between ethnic groups that served everyone well in times of need and distress.[3]

Agencies of Change: The *Harambee* Movement

The same traditional spirit of mutual aid that existed and functioned so effectively in precolonial times found new expression in the late 1960s when the word *harambee* came to epitomize a national self-help movement. Under President Jomo Kenyatta, the *harambee* movement became a major social and political force for both rural and national society. Derived from the Swahili *Aaaaa-mbee,* said to have been a work-gang cry that translates as "Ready— push!" its more usual translation today is "Let's pull together." In this form

Kenyatta turned *harambee* into a national motto and rallying cry with a central message: let's all work together to be self-reliant.[4] At *harambees*, individuals or groups of people gather and contribute money as they are willing or able to fund projects designed to fight illiteracy, disease, and poverty. Especially powerful in the countryside following the first few years of independence, the spirit of *harambee* resulted in the successful completion of a significant number of smaller development projects. Such projects included the building of hundreds of schools, health clinics and dispensaries, new bridges and access roads to rural communities, the capping of springs, and the drilling of wells, as well as the establishment of community halls, children's nurseries, and youth centers. At one level *harambee* projects began to provide rural communities with many of the benefits they expected from independence. At another level *harambee* projects allowed Kenyatta to consolidate his power as a national leader by avoiding some of the pitfalls that immediately befell many new governments that simply could not meet the level of expectation for education and the alleviation of poverty and disease that was anticipated by a newly independent citizenry.

More recently, *harambees* have added new dimensions. For example, when a student has been awarded admission and a scholarship to study at a college or university in the United States or England, a *harambee* will be organized to raise the necessary funds required for travel, room and board, or books. In parts of Kenya today, especially among the poor working class, a *harambee* will also be conducted to help offset the expenses of a wedding. There is always a master of ceremonies who resembles an auctioneer, announcing the amount already raised and imploring people to dig deeper and give still more. As individuals come forward to make promises to the engaged couple, family members, and even the bride and groom, move among those attending holding a plastic bag into which people put their 500 (U.S.$8) and 1,000 (U.S.$16) shilling denomination notes. What began with community members rolling up their sleeves to put bricks and mortar together for essential community building projects has increasingly become just another source of fund-raising for personal needs. Among many Kenyans there is a sense that the *harambee* is being abused and that the money collected is not always being spent for the purpose for which it is intended. Self-help can only carry a country so far for so long. In the end only a modern economy operating within the bounds of the new globalization will have a serious impact and result in the basic government services people need and expect.

Agencies of Change: The Economy

Kenya's involvement in a world economy is not new. In fact, some ocean-going sailing dhows (*madau*) reminiscent of this past still trade along the East

African coast. They carry products from Saudi Arabia, the Persian Gulf, and on occasion, Pakistan and India to exchange for local products just as they have for a thousand years. Today, there are only a few, and they have been fitted with motors, but not all that long ago the numbers of these dhows could be counted in the hundreds. Nevertheless, while the *madau* are disappearing, the coastal dhows (*jahazi*) still ply the Lamu archipelago. On the beaches of small villages such as Matondoni on the island of Lamu, shipbuilders and sail and rope makers continue to repair the dhows and occasionally make a new one, just as they have always done. Using tools that include an adze (a kind of hand ax) and rope-operated drills, these shipbuilders can construct a 50-foot-long *jahazi,* whose interior hull ribs resemble a whale's skeleton, and fill cracks in their planking with oil-soaked cotton strips. Others paint the hull with a pastelike substance made from beef or camel fat and lime (*shamamu*) to protect the vessel from wood worm, or rub the upper boards with fish oil that gives a dhow its distinctive reddish color. On the ocean, with its unfurled triangular sail billowing in the wind, its woven coconut mats protecting the interior from the splash of the sea, and the ornate carved boards on its prow announcing its presence, these dhows carry their cargo from island to island and island to coast.

Although there is still a very real demand in the Middle East for timber and poles from the mangrove swamps of the coast, few other natural products still have any market value there. Instead, cement, metal and plastic pipe, and finished commercial goods are in real demand in the communities that dot the islands, the coast, and the inland rivers. Imports that arrive by sea do so in large ocean-going freighters, including oil tankers. Today, it is these goods that are transported by coastal dhows or commercial trucking.

Often overloaded, trucks (lorries) and the trailers they pull move goods from point to point over road surfaces that are no longer in good repair. The wear and tear on vehicles and the high costs of repair have been enormously costly to the economy. Vehicles either are not repaired or are jerry rigged to keep them on the road. When this is coupled with the high speeds of drivers, especially the notorious taxi (*matatu*) drivers in their minivans adorned with names such as "Slum Princess," "Destiny," and "Play Hard," the roads are unsafe at any speed.

Once said to be a model of capitalism and entrepreneurial ventures, Kenya's economy was in the first fifteen years following independence the envy of many of its neighbors. Leading the way were industries that produced cement, milled flour, produced soft drinks and beer, assembled vehicles, especially trucks, manufactured plastics, and processed chemicals. Today, many of these industries still produce, but their growth has slowed considerably, and the country's long-term trade imbalance continues to grow. With its major exports of tea, coffee, and other horticultural products, all subject to world price fluctuations, these industries have been no help in bailing out the economy. With exploitation and corruption seemingly rampant, and individuals profiting enormously at the expense of both the economy and the general population, the undercurrent of resentment continues to grow, and it is increasingly more violent. As the rich get richer, they must build higher and higher walls around their homes and hire more and more guards to protect them in their gated communities. One growth industry that has captured the Kenyan entrepreneurial spirit is that of security companies, with more and more factories, businesses, and individual homes marked by signs that announce they are protected by Securicor, Wells Fargo, Ultimate Security, or Kali (Swahili for "fierce").

But today, the economic cushion that was once provided by the rural economy for the unemployed and underemployed, and to which children and wives could return, is a much less viable alternative. The country, once self-sufficient in food, today suffers from smuggling, corruption, and environmental problems and must periodically import maize, wheat, and powdered milk. Whereas agriculture was once the heart of the economy, today the service industry is dominant. With the past two decades dominated by periods of inflation, recession, and stagnation, investment by foreign corporations has become less attractive. The only ones to step in have been the multinational organizations such as the World Bank and the International Monetary Fund, and their terms and conditions have often been counter to those favored by the government. As a result one of the largest expanding areas of the economy, and playing an increasingly significant role in the lives of a many people, is the informal or underground sector of the economy. Legal and illegal, unregulated and untaxed, the informal sector includes everything from the manufacture and sale of furniture and tourist curios to the making and selling of food and homemade beer.[5]

Urban Living

With 42 percent of Kenyans living below the poverty line and only 24 percent of school-age children in secondary school, the city is the magnet that attracts people. Here street hawkers and makeshift kiosks dominate street corners and traffic roundabouts. It does not seem to matter that they all sell the same things. People have families to feed, clothe, and house and children to educate. And it is better to sell something than to turn to crime or waste away from drink. So some have constructed wooden frames with yellow plastic coverings or canvas. From these open-air kiosks, which require everything be set out daily and packed away each night, people sell everything from vegetables and fruits to basic electrical or plumbing fixtures to farm implements, cassette tapes, belts, and U.S. sports team hats. The more permanent ones are the used red or green cargo containers that have been converted into shops. The creativity and ingenuity used to attract a customer can astound. Those selling Coke, Sprite, and food may even have one or two plastic tables with a few chairs surrounded by a small picket fence. Recently, two sorts of kiosks have mushroomed in number. In Nairobi there are those that sell African curios and handicrafts. Outside the capital the sale of secondhand clothing and shoes has come to dominate, but these kiosks are now severely undermining the local textile industry, and manufacture of shoe and leather products and are hampering the ability of the economy to grow.

Along the roadside at roundabouts, hawkers announce what they have to sell, competing with traffic noises that include taxi and minivan drivers shouting out their destinations. The availability of two other items for sale along the roadsides—firewood and charcoal—is having a disastrous effect on the country. The vast majority of people cook and heat with one or the other of these fuels, and this use is causing severe deforestation. With more trees cut down than are planted, the environmental impact continues to spread. Those trees cleared from mountainsides increase erosion and cause valuable topsoil to be washed into nearby streams. The felling of trees in forests combined with the clearing of new farmland exposes soils to high winds that blows it away. Together with these activities, agricultural pesticides and industrial effluents have led to the contamination of Kenya's lakes and streams and thus, people's drinking water. Similarly, on the plains of the north and east, the growth of the desert is demonstrable and the impact on animal herds negative. Such environmental degradation not only limits the sustainability of natural resources but also contributes to the decline in agricultural productivity that has adversely affected the ability of Kenyans to feed themselves.

For many people eating two meals a day is considered a blessing; so too is not being tossed onto the streets by a landlord when the rent is due and money is short. For others sleeping inside or outside the house makes little difference since the rain leaks through in so many places. Some, out of desperation and with little to no hope of advancement, turn to drink, but not one of the many brands of beer produced by the Kenya Breweries or the recently arrived South African Breweries. These are too expensive for a worker or day laborer. Far more typical for these people is the consumption of a cheap and sweet fermented drink made from either maize or sorghum and called *chang'aa*. Brewed illegally, it is widely available in *chang'aa* "dens" that dot the slum neighborhoods surrounding Nairobi and the trading centers of other towns. *Chang'aa* is easy to make from a variety of grain crops and easy to sell; quality varies from poor to dangerous. A potent mix of whatever is available, it almost always begins with the heavily contaminated stream or runoff water found in the slums. With consumption comes drunkenness, a decline in labor productivity, and increases in crime and prostitution. Destitute young children in these neighborhoods, who see one or both parents drunk and passed out, can also be found drinking illegal brew in response to the seeming hopelessness of their condition. On the increase are sniffing glue and other toxic substances, as well as the use of hard drugs. Local newspapers frequently carry reports of what happens when a community, especially the women, become outraged at what is happening around them and to their drunken husbands. Not only do they regularly petition the government to outlaw illicit brewing, but they also move through their neighborhoods singing songs that declare war on the dealers of the brew. With fire and passion, they have even been known to stone vehicles suspected of carrying *chang'aa* and to tear down bars that serve it.

"Sometimes you might think you are on Mars or Venus but all the same you are still on earth. You can see so many houses squeezed and there is no space for young children to play. Very few children go to school because education fees are very expensive compared with the jobs that their parents are doing. But whatever you have, thank God." This description offered by one 13-year-old from Mathare Valley, a community on the edge of Nairobi that is said to be Africa's largest slum, points to a major impediment to Kenya's development dilemma—overpopulation.[6] With a birthrate that until recently hovered at more than 3 percent, among the highest in the world, it is nearly impossible even with the most effective economic system to grow at a level that keeps up with the population. When coupled with the fact that half the population is under the age of eighteen, the cost of educating all these children, much less providing needed health care and other social services, is impossible.

Nevertheless, for most parents education is seen as not only the best avenue to success but as the only one. Early in the morning, at midday, and again in the afternoon, along any road—paved or unpaved, rural or urban—the roadsides of Kenya are festooned with the colorful uniforms of kids going to and from their school. Green shorts or red gingham dresses with maroon sweaters, or red shorts with yellow shirts and green sweaters have broken with the more monotonous tradition of what was almost exclusively the white shirts, gray shorts or trousers, and navy blue sweaters that once dominated British-influenced school uniforms. Today, unfortunately, although thousands of children attend, their schools are all too often bookless, penless, and paperless.

For children who do well academically on the Kenya Certificate of Primary Education exams, acceptance into high school or even a scholarship to one of the prestigious high schools can become reality. Doing well in high school and achieving a high score on the Secondary Leaving Certificate can lead to acceptance into one of Kenya's growing number of universities. Yet the reality for most youth is far different. Even when the incentive for doing well in school exists, the large families that are all too common in Kenya cannot afford the school fees, mandatory uniforms, and increasingly, other fees imposed for desks, library, sports, and upkeep. In many neighborhoods completing high school is a rare accomplishment. Graduating from university (and Kenya's universities graduate hundreds each year) may lead to a job, but often it is not in the chosen field of study, and often not in desired white-collar jobs. The same is true for those graduating with professional degrees in law, medical sciences, and engineering. In fact, positions in these areas sometimes only open up when those holding them leave Kenya for another country, which has increasingly been the case with doctors emigrating to South Africa. Indeed, the kiosk owner from whom a family regularly buys their vegetables may in fact be an electrical engineering graduate whose younger brother is now refusing to attend high school, declaring that the spending of limited family funds on school fees is foolish. The good news is that in recent years there has been new emphasis on technical and vocational subjects, from agriculture and carpentry to metalwork and automotive training, each with a strong element of practical training.

Through such trials and tribulations, parents—or sometimes only a mother—somehow manage to hold their family together. Oftentimes a radiant smile and a strong religious faith provide the key ingredients as children assume that if their mother can still smile and read stories to them from the Bible, then life cannot be as bad as it seems. But life is complicated, and a smile only goes so far. For those who live and work in the urban areas, the assumption by rural relatives is that they have now "made it." From these rural families come cousins and other offspring with the expectation that the urban dwellers will shoulder their upkeep and education And the urban relatives will do so, not because they can afford to but because meeting these expectations is simply a part of being in an extended family. It is assumed and expected that one person's success will be shared as widely as possible.

However, there is often little to share, and even those with regular jobs are not immune from hardship. A Grade II teacher, who is one with four years of university education, earns less than 26,000 Kenya shillings a year, or just over U.S.$3,000. How, then, does an elementary school teacher survive given that they are among the lowest-paid civil servants in the country? Even a medical doctor with six years of university training and two additional years of specialization only earns about 50,000 Kenya shillings a year, or a bit more than U.S.$6,000. When compared, for example, with what a member of parliament earns each year—440,000 Kenya shillings or approximately U.S. $55,000—it becomes rather clear who is living in the gated communities in the suburbs of Nairobi and who has to dwell in what are everywhere else labeled slums.

Conflict, Order, and Political Change

Traditionally, decision-making processes have been based on consensus, which it was the responsibility of the communities' elders to build. Groups of men who could be found sitting around under a large tree were not being lazy, although it is true that they often left the vast majority of the agricultural and household tasks to the women. Instead, they were meeting in a kind of open forum to determine the course of action for whatever issues faced them and their community. Their method for reaching consensus was not characterized by fierce debate or the exchange of harsh words. Rather, it was a highly structured and controlled affair. Often holding a staff or club, symbolically giving the holder the right to speak, one elder after another would air their views until everyone who wanted to speak had done so. In such situations certain elders, who were looked up to either for their successful counsel in the past or because they were wealthy and held or had loaned to others large numbers of cattle, had more persuasive voices. Often, such individuals waited until nearly everyone else had spoken, and only after they had the sense of the majority would they weigh in with their view, summarizing a position that would move the group to consensus. Once a consensus was reached, it had the force of law and was binding on everyone.

Across the region traditional patterns of governance had many common features. For example, leadership among the Luo was traditionally undertaken not at the level of the ethnic group as a whole but rather at the clan level, which included people who are understood to be historically related through a commonly recognized ancestor. The leading elder in a Luo council of elders held the title of *ruoth,* and those men who attained the position of *ruoth* did so by virtue of their character and having demonstrated their ability to lead. One of the principal attributes of any good leader was the ability to speak well in public. Among the Meru, who were also governed by a council of elders, called the *kiama,* an elder who displayed an ability to speak well and offer wise counsel was said to have a quality called *ugambe.* It was these community-recognized qualities that allowed an elder's decision making to carry the recognized weight of law.

Despite the high regard and respect with which elders were held, they seldom had the ability to coerce a particular behavior from an individual or the power to enforce a specified judgment. Yet rarely did an individual risk disregarding an elder. Instead, elders brought their influence to bear through the moral force of persuasion coupled with emphasizing their ability to bless and

Often sitting under a large tree, the elders of a community regularly gather to make decisions by consensus. Both the earrings and fly whisk denote this man's status as an elder.

curse individuals and events. While in practice, it is a blessing that was nearly always offered, the potential for this to be replaced by a curse was well recognized. Because those individuals that elders have the most regular contact with were family and immediate neighbors, everyday reality was such that no elder wants to utter a curse and bring misfortune on those closest to him. Often well before a situation might bring forth a curse, others in the family or community used their powers of persuasion, even intimidation, to bring about more appropriate or correct behavior. People operating outside acceptable norms were ridiculed and ostracized. In small rural communities this was often enough to bring such behavior back in line. Yet, always in the background, underpinning the social order, was a recognition that an elder could indeed use his power to curse. This recognition—not the threat of a police force or militia taking someone to court or tossing them into jail—is what aided the maintenance of law and order in many traditional communities. When these social norms were not enough to limit particular behavior, other forms of punishment existed. A community, for example, might impose sanctions such as the payment of a fine in stock or cash on an individual. If this still proved inadequate, there are examples of banishment and, as a last resort, even the imposition of capital punishment.

Today, the force of law in Kenya is maintained through three different judicial systems. There is the just-described pattern of traditional law, which still carries the force of law in many rural communities although it does not play as marked a role as it had in the past. Second, in most cities and even many rural towns, there are courts of law, as established in the national constitution. Third, among Muslims and recognized in Kenya as a legitimate part of the judiciary, are Islamic courts. Based on religious law, *Shari'a* is a legal system derived from the Qur'an and the traditions and sayings of the prophet Muhammad that Muslims believe can govern every aspect of an individual's life.

Increasingly, with the growth of large urban areas and especially in the tightly packed living conditions of the poor neighborhoods and slums that surround Nairobi, mob justice has emerged as a fourth form of justice. Thieves in particular have been subjected to this collective punishment. Almost instantaneously with the first shout of "thief!" a horde of people with stones, sticks, and machetes, or pangas, takes chase. If a respected voice is able to intervene soon enough and persuade the crowd to back off, a thief may be taken away to jail. If not, those who escape with only a severe beating count themselves lucky. The unluckiest are those who when caught are beaten to death or once beaten bloody are given an old tire "bow tie" and burned to death, a form of punishment that gained worldwide attention in apartheid South Africa, where it was called "necklacing."

From time to time since independence, ethnic violence has flared in Kenya. This also occurred before independence, when the colonial government labeled a community as belonging to one or another ethnic group, delimited their boundaries, and then declared individuals to be members of this or that "tribe," thus preventing communities from peacefully interacting. For the colonial government, preventing tribal raiding and warfare was paramount, and yet without realizing it, they had eliminated those activities such as trade and marriage ties that had always existed to ameliorate such tensions. Certainly, interethnic conflict occurred in the precolonial era; however, the limiting of such interethnic strife was a major concern of the elders. Raiding severely limited opportunities for the trade that was often necessary for a community's economic well-being. It also prevented the contacts that might result in marriage ties across interethnic boundaries, which, as already noted concerning pastoralists, was another strategy communities used to make sure they got the help they needed to cope during times of hardship.

Patterns of intermarriage were widespread and found among the Kalenjin and Luhya, the Luo and Gussi, Samburu and Rendille, and Kikuyu and Maasai. The Kikuyu and Maasai and the Kikuyu and the Samburu also maintained traditions that allowed their women to trade peacefully even at times when their warriors were raiding each other. In times of drought and famine, depending on who was being adversely affected, families or larger groups from one community might take refuge among a neighboring community. Such occasions led to the adoption of children, marriage across ethnic lines, and others who stayed permanently among their neighbors and in the course of time took on a new ethnic identity. Such situations are recorded as having occurred widely among herders, as well as among people with ties to communities of nearby gatherer-hunters and fishermen.[7]

Thus, while recent interethnic tensions are not new, the roots of today's conflicts are to be found in issues that simply will not go away, such as land ownership, as well as more contemporary issues related to the economic realities of modern-day life and environmental concerns. According to some accusations, many of the recent outbursts attributed to ethnic issues are said to have been government instigated as part of its active discouragement of multiparty democracy. Following independence, regional rivalries between ethnic groups led to the formation of ethnically based political parties. Under President Kenyatta this system worked more or less well as long as the Kikuyu and Luo, the two largest ethnic groups, were able to dominate the political scene. However, soon after President Moi, a member of the much smaller Kalenjin community, came to power, he introduced a new constitution that made Kenya a one-party state. Ostensibly, the reason for this change was to avoid having political parties based exclusively on ethnicity. Thus, when KANU was declared the only legal political party, all opposition parties became illegal, and every candidate for office needed to register with KANU to be eligible to run. Nevertheless, often in Kenyan national elections, far more sitting legislators are defeated for reelection than occurs in most Western democracies.

In the late 1980s economic difficulties multiplied, and a prodemocracy movement gained momentum. Initially, the government resorted to arresting and detaining activists. Then human-rights violations and violent political unrest led to calls for reestablishing a multiparty system. In the end the government bowed to international pressure and the threatened cutoff of foreign aid. In December 1991 a multiparty system was introduced, ending nearly a decade of one-party rule. Dozens of opposition political parties were formed to contest the 1992 election. Despite being terribly divided ethnically and geographically, the opposition managed to gain a significant number of parliamentary seats. Nevertheless, KANU remained the majority, and President Moi won reelection with 37 percent of the vote. In 1997 more opposition parties were allowed to register, and again their formation was largely along ethnic and geographic lines. Just as occurred seven years earlier, their registration was preceded by demonstrations that all but shut down the commercial parts of Nairobi and Mombasa. The government tried to suppress dissent by banning public rallies. To do so they had to resort to tear-gassing protesters and worshipers, beating university students, and worse, but the deep divisions within the various opposition factions meant that the government realistically had little to fear. Once again international pressure was brought to bear, and a generally open and peaceful campaign followed, in which Moi was elected to his fifth term. Although, Moi had declared he would not remain the head of state for life, it was suspected he wanted to change the constitution to do so. In the event he did not, and his hand-picked successor was defeated in 2002.

History is not likely to be kind to Moi and many of his peers, who belong to the "second-generation leaders" of independent Africa. As described by one astute, longtime observer of the African political scene, these "kleptocratic, patrimonial leaders ... give Africa a bad name, plunge its people into poverty and despair, and incite civil wars and bitter ethnic conflict. They are the ones largely responsible for declining GDP levels, food scarcities, rising infant-mortality rates, soaring budget deficits, human rights abuses, breaches of the rule of law, prolonged serfdom for millions—even in Africa's nominal democracies."[8] Another compares their leadership by "murder, corruption, manipulation, deceit, extortion, intimidation, cunning, imprisonment of perceived opponents and a lust for power" to the treacherous and "diabolical natures of Shakespeare's characters Iago and King Richard III" transported to the twenty-first century.[9]

National and Religious Holidays

Kenya celebrates a number of holidays special to it, as well as others that are common to many parts of the world. Among the former, Madaraka Day marks the birth of the republic on June 1, and Jamhuri Day celebrates Kenya's independence on December 12. Two other days also recall important dates in Kenyan history—October 20, Kenyatta Day when in 1952 Mzee Jomo

Kenyatta was arrested for opposing British colonialism, and October 10, Moi Day, which celebrates Daniel arap Moi's becoming president. Among holidays celebrated elsewhere in the world, New Year's Day, a long Easter weekend (including Good Friday and Easter Monday), and in the British tradition, both Christmas and Boxing Day (December 26) are celebrated in Kenya.

Although not official national holidays, a number of Muslim festivals are also celebrated at the coast and increasingly in Nairobi and other up-country cities. One of the most significant is *Id al-Fitr,* which takes places on the first day of the month of Shawwal, the month that immediately follows Ramadan, or "the fasting month." During Ramadan, which is the ninth month in the Islamic calendar, Muslims do not eat or drink between sunrise and sunset, in order to purify their hearts and minds. Instead, believers only eat and drink after dark, often while visiting with family and friends. Traditionally, the distinction between day and night has been noted by a white thread, which, when no longer visible while held at arm's length, indicates that the day is over. In many respects the days and nights are inverted during Ramadan. The more pious typically spend large portions of each day reading extensive portions of the Qur'an, while nights are dominated by socializing, feasting, and various forms of entertainment.

On *Id al-Fitr* Muslims gather to pray by the hundreds and in some places by the thousands, often moving excitedly through city streets on their way to a large open space, where in a public display of community solidarity, they participate in a worship service. Not an especially long service, what most impresses is the thousands of men, women and children, all dressed in finest clothes, arranged with men in front, women and children behind, all facing Mecca. Led by an imam and other notables, these believers gather, as do Muslims throughout the world, to proclaim the goodness of Allah and to thank him for bringing them through the arduous month-long fast. *Id al-Fitr* is generally celebrated over three days, but in Kenya the first day of celebration is an official holiday. The next two days are celebrated unofficially.

On some of the islands off the coast, especially on Lamu, the festival of *Maulidi* is celebrated in commemoration of the Prophet Muhammad's birth. The dates for each of these Muslim festivals is fixed in the Islamic calendar, which is a lunar one and thus different from the Western calendar. As a result the days of Islamic celebrations change annually in much the same way as the date of Easter varies each year (The date for Easter in the Western calendar is fixed on the first Sunday following the first full moon after the spring equinox.)

Another celebration of considerable importance at the coast is the Swahili New Year (*Siku ya Mwaka*). This is thought to be an indigenous pre-Islamic ritual onto which have been grafted various Islamic practices. Designed to help ensure the well-being of a town in the new year, it contains rituals that cleanse and protect the community from evil spirits. These rituals have included people bathing in the ocean and the ritual slaughter of a bull, whose bones were then placed in its skin and sunk in the ocean. Singing and dancing brought the day to a close.[10] Similarly, each November the Hindu communities in Kenya celebrate their New Year, *Diwali,* the eve of which marks the end of the financial year for those merchants who follow the Hindu calendar. The days preceding *Diwali* are marked by the exploding of fireworks as part of the ritual of making loud noises to chase away the evil spirits of darkness that might otherwise dwell in one's home. New Year's Day itself is dedicated to Laxmi, the goddess of wealth, and marked by believers who throng to the main temples. Following prayers for peace and prosperity, there is feasting, visiting friends and neighbors, and always trays of sweets for visitors to homes and shops.

Gift giving and visiting with family and friends are the primary activities associated with most holidays, On these days arriving unannounced at a friend's or neighbor's home is acceptable. For example, Christmas is often a day to present small gifts to service workers, tradespeople, and servants. Urban visitors often arrive with flowers or tea leaves; rural visitors may bring instant coffee, sugar, or even flour. Such gifts have traditionally been presented in a woven bag (Gikuyu: *kiondo*), which the host then returns to a departing guest with a small gift inside since it is impolite to return a *kiondo* empty. Invariably, tea will be served to guests, who can stay as long as they wish since it is impolite to ask a guest to leave. When they do depart, a host will not just see them to the door but often walk some distance with them before returning home. Special parades, speeches, meals, such as Christmas lunch, and church services are all a part of celebrating many of these national holidays.

On most any given holiday the grass of Uhuru Park in Nairobi is filled with families playing, relaxing or picnicking. Another favorite place for urban Kenyans to go on holidays and especially weekends is Bomas of Kenya, which is essentially an ethnic theme park and performance center. At the outdoor auditorium, which seats 3,500 and is complete with stage and bar, a national folklore troupe of government employees regularly performs traditional dances and songs as a way of preserving the cultural heritage of Kenya's many ethnic groups. In the same way the nearby "village" of houses built in the traditional architectural styles of many of Kenya's ethnic groups ("as built by the ancestors") addresses directly both the change to modernity occurring in Kenya and the sense of Kenyan nationalism. In the village, in which no one actually lives, citizens can visit and take their children to see the sort of house in which their grandparents may have grown up. They can purchase handi-

This woman is weaving a bag called a *kiondo,* which is used for shopping and for taking small gifts of food such as tea or sugar to friends, especially when visiting on holidays. Working on it in the market, she can readily sell the bags she makes.

crafts that preserve the simplicity of past lifestyles. And they can watch dances and songs of many of these same ethnic groups, but performed by a troupe of artists whose make up consists of representatives of from different ethnicities. Essentially, Bomas is a place for urban Kenyans to honor the heritage with which they are increasingly less familiar with each passing year.[11]

Film is another form of popular entertainment in Kenya, whether seen in a cinema or on video or DVD. Popular international films quickly find their way to the local screens, which are found in most urban areas. Nairobi and

Mombasa each still have a drive-in cinema. Newly released videos are also easily found in rental shops. A recent development in rural areas and in poorer urban locations has been the growth of living room or kiosk "movie houses," where for a small fee people watch a video. Action films and Indian films attract the largest audiences.

Sports and Games

Kenyans are avid sports fans, and the back pages of all the daily newspapers provide detailed coverage from football (American soccer) and cricket to track and motorsports. Outside of Africa, Kenya's best-known athletes are their middle-distance, steeplechase, and marathon runners. They have been winning medals and setting records at every Olympic game since 1964 (except the two boycott years of 1976 and 1980) and regularly win or place high in nearly every major city marathon from Boston and New York to London and Venice. For example, Kenyans dominated the New York Marathon in 2001, with Margaret Okayo winning in record time (2:24:21) and other Kenyan women placing second, fourth, and fifth. On the men's side in the same race, Kenyan runners took second and third, as well as seventh, eighth, and tenth, or half of the top ten places. Among Kenyan's many fine runners, one of the best was Henry Rono, who in the 1970s held as many as four world records at the same time. Unfortunately, he never earned Olympic gold since he was at the top of his form when the political boycotts kept Kenya out of the competitions in Montreal and Moscow.

Many ask why Kenyans have such great success in these distance races. Part of the answer has to do with the higher altitudes that are common across Kenya (the plains around Nairobi are more than 1,600 meters [5,250 feet] above sea level compared with Chicago, for example, at 180 meters [590 feet]). At higher altitudes the air is thinner, which means that there is less oxygen available to breathe. The bodies of first-time visitors adapt to this—you increase your rate and depth of breathing, your heart rate increases, and eventually you produce more oxygen-carrying red blood cells. Normally, a visitor acclimatizes in a few days, but not fully for about three weeks. Kenyans, however, born and raised at these altitudes, have the instant advantage of having greater lung capacity, which increases even more with training. Further, a runner does not lose this expanded lung capacity when competing at lower altitudes (and most marathons outside of Kenya are at lower altitudes). This is one of the reasons the U.S. Olympic training facilities are in the higher elevations in the mountains of Colorado.

Altitude is also a major factor in trekking and mountain climbing, and Kenya is a great place for both. The lack of oxygen that trekkers and climbers face can begin to appear at 2,500 meters (8,200 feet) and it is said that about 50 percent of trekkers experience mild altitude sickness at 3,500 meters (11,480 feet). The symptoms—headache, nausea, and loss of appetite, tiredness and irritability—disappear after a few days as long as one does not try to go higher. Still, Kenya regularly attracts people who attempt to scale Mount Kenya, which at 5,199 meters (17,058 feet) is only 200 meters (656 feet) less than the base camps on Mount Everest in the Himalayas. Kilimanjaro, just across the border in Tanzania, is the highest point on the continent and East Africa's only other snow-covered peak. Whereas those who are fit can reach Kilimanjaro's 5,895-meter (19,340-foot) summit in four days of hiking, to reach Mount Kenya's two highest peaks of Batian and Nelion requires the technical skills of a mountaineer. Nevertheless, to hike across the glaciers of a mountain only sixteen kilometers (ten miles) south of the equator, and settle for reaching Lenana, the third-highest point on Mount Kenya, is many a trekker's goal.

Although Kenya is known worldwide as a nation of runners, the sport of choice at home, as it is in much of the world, is soccer, called football in Kenya. Two teams in particular, Gor Mahia and AFC Leopards, have tended to dominate the Premier League and have won international football competitions including the Africa Cup and the Mandela Cup. Kenyan players also play on international teams, including in Belgium and Sweden. Many Kenyan teams have an ethnic root; for example, Gor Mahia is a Luo team, AFC Leopards is Luhya, and Shabana is Kisii. But many other nonethnic groups also have football teams with notable followings. One such team is the powerful Mathare United whose players are drawn from the Nairobi slum of Mathare Valley. Other teams are drawn from various branches of the armed forces and police,, as well as corporations and government groups such as Kenya Breweries, Kenya Commercial Bank, Kenya Posts and Telecommunications, and the Kenya Port Authority. Across Kenya youth sport associations run football programs that ensure the sport's popularity.

Boxing is another competitive sport with a considerable following and also one in which Kenya competes in the Olympics. Increasing in popularity, both as a men's and women's sport, is basketball. Rugby, although not nearly as popular as football, has a growing and enthusiastic following. Rugby is played at the high school level and nationally through organized clubs whose membership is often made up of alumni from particular high schools. Two of the rugby giants are the popular "Nondies," whose official name is the Nondescripts, and the University of Nairobi Mean Machine. Some teams, such as the popular Watembezi Pacesetters, have managed to compete well internationally. They do so, however, by finding their own sponsorship or by footing much of the bill themselves.[12] Also played seriously in Kenya are fierce brands of field hockey and cricket, both of which are dominated by communities of East Asia origin. With these latter two sports played outdoors, Kenya's year-round mild climate makes it an attractive venue for national and club teams from around the world who come seeking skillful competition and excellent facilities.

Another sport that attracts both local and worldwide competitors is the Kenya Safari Rally. This bone-shaking auto race, which was originally run with only standard showroom cars, began in 1953 to celebrate the coronation of Britain's Queen Elizabeth II. When it began the race was run over a course that included parts of Uganda and Tanzania. With political changes in the region, the rally is today run entirely in Kenya. As part of the World Rally Championship series, run under regulations from the sport's international headquarters in Paris, the Kenya Safari Rally is the series' only African venue. Today, teams sponsored by auto international manufacturers Ford, Mitsubishi, Peugeot, Skoda, and Subaru regularly compete. Many pairs of drivers are international superstars, but many teams are also local, and only recently have the international teams begun to win over the local drivers. Given Kenya's local conditions and rough terrain—on some "roads" cars go airborne for fifty to sixty feet—international competitors often find it an advantage to have a local Kenyan driver on their team. Although the rally itself is run over three days, teams practice on the route for days and even weeks in advance. During this time the driver and codriver make the detailed notes that the codriver will read out to the driver during the actual race. Today's competition cars, supported by teams of mechanics, engineers, and technicians, are especially designed to win rallies. Some teams even include helicopters that shadow the race to radio warnings of coming hazards and facilitate communication between the drivers and their crews.

Outside of sports, a game called *mbao* (or *bao* or *ajua*) is played across the country and throughout many parts of Africa. More generally known by the generic term *mancala,* and in West Africa as *awari,* this is a "count-and-capture" game, which as a result of slavery and the African diaspora, has also spread to the Caribbean, North America, and Europe. Part of its popularity is that so little is needed to play. *Mbao* is played on a wooden board of shallow cuplike holes arranged in two, three, or four rows into which counters are placed. *Mbao* can just as easily be played on a "board" of holes scooped out of the sand or chipped from a piece of pavement on a street corner. Counters are also easily obtained—stones, seeds, and shells are all acceptable. The rules of *mbao* are also quickly learned. Each person plays in turn, taking all the counters in one hole and moving clockwise around the board dropping a counter one by one into each successive hole. If the first player's last counter lands on the opponent's side of the board, the first player captures and removes from

The widely popular game known in Kenya as *mbao* or *bao,* and in other parts of the world as *mancala,* can be played on a board carved from wood. Almost any surface can become a "board," with the holes or cups scooped from the sand or chipped out of the pavement.

play all the counters in that hole. Next, the second player does the same, and so on, until one or the other player can no longer play because no counters are left on their side of the board. The smooth surface and patina found on many old playing boards, as well as favorite smooth stone counters, is an indicator of the thousands of times a board has been lovingly used.

SAFARI

Finally, no book on Kenya would be complete without mentioning safaris. For as long as there have been people in this region, they have shared it with the wildlife that has also called this place home. The people who have occupied these lands have always hunted, not for sport but for the food and numerous other by-products such as clothing and shelter that the animals and their skins provide. People used wisely the resources these plains, deserts, and mountains provided. The early travelers known to us as explorers also hunted and generally used only those resources they and the people in their caravans needed. Even the safaris that these European and Americans mounted were not really new, for Africans had never been without contact with the surrounding peoples, and in some cases caravans moved across major stretches of the land trading goods from one region for those of another. The Kamba and Swahili are particularly well known for having done so. Initially, when European hunters arrived, it was these caravan leaders they hired to lead them into the interior, especially to hunt elephant.

At the end of the nineteenth century, hunting was still free and wide open to those who ventured forth. It did not take long after big-game hunting became popular for at least some of the wildlife to come under threat of extinction. Even early colonial administrators commented on the devastation being caused by these sportsmen. There were many well-known hunters, each of whom wrote at least one book of their adventures. One of the better known was "Karamoja" Bell, a Scotsman who acquired his name from one of his favorite hunting grounds (now in northeastern Uganda), which he described as a "country where a man could still slit a throat or grab a native girl without being badgered by alien law."[13] It was said of Bell that he personally killed over a thousand elephants in his twenty years of hunting in Africa, and he was but one of many such hunters.

Only two months after leaving office, President Theodore Roosevelt went on safari in Kenya. A preeminent conservationist who greatly expanded the United States National Forest system and created many wildlife refuges, "Bwana Tumbo" or Mr. Stomach, as he was known in Kenya, was also a prolific hunter. The safari he mounted in 1909 was at the time the largest in scale and cost ever seen. It was financed by industrialist Andrew Carnegie, Roosevelt's proposed writings,[14] and the Smithsonian Museum, for whom he shot specimens for their collection and that of the American Museum of Natural History in New York. With hundreds of porters, gun bearers, cooks, and tent men, Roosevelt's safari traversed across Kenya, during which time he collected and shipped back to the museums specimens of nearly 5,000 mammals, 4,000 birds, 2,000 reptiles, and 500 fish, some of which are still on display. Roosevelt the hunter not only shot randomly at animals that he wounded and never finished, but in one location he killed nine white rhinos that included four females and a calf at a time when they were already extinct in southern Africa and nearly so in East Africa.[15]

The crisis that emerged from the overzealous hunting of the most popular trophy animals known together as the "big five"—the buffalo, elephant, leopard, lion, and rhinoceros—is thus not a new issue at all but one of considerable history. Kenya's response beyond early game licensing fees did not begin in earnest until 1946, when the Nairobi National Park, Kenya's first game park, was established on the edge of the city. Today, it is still possible to go game watching there with the nearby skyline of Nairobi clearly visible in the background. At independence in 1963 there were a dozen parks; today, there are more than fifty parks and reserves.

While hunting at this time was forbidden in the parks and reserves, it was legal on the adjoining privately owned lands. But of course the animals in the parks were the same ones that often crossed the privately held lands. With great wildlife viewing at so many destinations in such a wonderfully temperate climate, tourists flocked to Kenya. In the 1960s and 1970s the poaching of animals overshadowed the issue of hunting and conservation. The threat posed to the wildlife was the trophies they carried. The poachers sought the tusks of elephants and the horns of rhinos, and soon both animals were placed on the list of endangered species. In 1977 Kenya banned all hunting, and in 1989 it joined with the rest of the world to ban the trade in dead or living endangered animals. Although such conservation measures are applauded by much of the world, it comes with a heavy cost to Kenyans, among whom the demand for land by the country's ever-increasing population is beyond the ability of the government to provide. And elephants in particular, while greatly admired in the Western world, are in fact among Kenyan farmers' worst nightmares. As they move across the land in search of food, they also eat planted crops, destroy trees, demolish water lines and dams, and sometimes even destroy homes.

Today, Kenya struggles to find a balance between protecting animals, which is a policy much favored by Western countries and their donor agencies, and the growing demand locally for a policy of "utilization." The protection policy is proving very expensive and is one that the Kenyan government cannot continue to afford. With a utilization policy, the wildlife is said to belong to the people among whom the animals live, and they would be allowed to make limited and conservationally appropriate use of them. For example, when the number of animals exceeds what the land can support, selected animals could be killed and the profits would go back to the local community. Similarly, ivory confiscated from poachers would be sold and the money used locally, including the protection of endangered species. With such a policy communities would have a greater vested interest in protecting the animals, and the tourists who come to see the animals would spend more money that could again circle back into the local economy. The foundations for this policy are already taking root with some local communities and the Kenya Wildlife Service, who are working more closely together to run small safari camps. With safari prices running more than $250 per person per night and the annual income of a Kenyan under $400 per year, these pioneering efforts, based on profit-sharing principles, are cause for optimism.

NOTES

1. Neal W. Sobania, "Pastoralist Migration and Colonial Policy: A Case Study from Northern Kenya," in *The Ecology of Survival: Case Studies from Northeast African History,* ed. Douglas Johnson and David Anderson (London: Lester Crook; Boulder, Colorado: Westview Press, 1988), 219–39.

2. Recent changes among Kenya's pastoralist communities are well documented in Elliot M. Fratkin, "Two Lives for the Ariaal," *Natural History* (May 1989), 39–49, and his *Surviving Drought and Development: Ariaal Pastoralists of Northern Kenya* (Boulder, Colorado: Westview Press, 1991).

3. Neal Sobania, "Feasts, Famines, and Friends: Nineteenth Century Exchange and Ethnicity in the Eastern Lake Turkana Region," in *Herders, Warriors, and Traders: Pastoralism in Africa,* ed. John G. Gallaty and Pierre Bonte (Boulder, Colorado: Westview Press, 1991), 118–42.

4. Martin J. D. Hill, *The Harambee Movement in Kenya: Self-Help, Development, and Education among the Kamba of Kitui District* (London: Althone Press, 1991).

5. See, for example, Norman N. Miller, *Kenya: The Quest for Prosperity* (Boulder, Colorado: Westview Press, 1984), 59–60.

6. "A Slum Eye View," in *Shootback: Photos by Kids from the Nairobi Slums,* ed. Lana Wong (London: Booth-Clibborn Editions, 1999).

7. Neal Sobania, "Fishermen Herders: Subsistence, Survival, and Cultural Change in Northern Kenya." *Journal of African History* 29 (1988): 41–56.

8. Robert T. Rotberg, "Africa's Mess, Mugabe's Mayhem," *Foreign Affairs,* September/October 2000, 80, quoted in Peter Schwab, *Africa: A Continent Self-Destructs* (New York: Palgrave, 2001), 167.

9. Schwab, *Africa: A Continent Self-Destructs,* 167.

10. Margaret Strobel, *Muslim Women in Mombasa, 1890–1975* (New Haven, Connecticut: Yale University Press, 1979), 81–84.

11. Bomas of Kenya Limited, http://www.africaonline.co.ke/bomaskenya/rofile.html.

12. The local rugby union Web site is http://www.kenyarugby.com.

13. Quoted in Bartle Bull, *Safari: A Chronicle of Adventure* (London: Viking, 1988), 149.

14. Theodore Roosevelt, *African Game Trails* (New York: Scribner, 1910).

15. Bull, *Safari,* 157–83.

8

Music and Dance

Music and dancing play important roles in all parts of Kenya. Often found together in traditional, religious, and popular settings, music and dance serve ritual and ceremonial functions and provide entertainment. Some songs and dances are said to have originated long ago with founding ancestors. Others are said to have come with immigrant communities. The influences can and do come from every part of the world to be modified, adapted, copied, and re-created by Kenyan musicians and dancers who make the sounds and dance steps their own.

Today, music can be heard coming from village centers and marketplaces, from schools and religious centers, and of course from the radio, television, and cassette and compact disc players. It is traditional and contemporary, and influenced by music from other parts of Africa, especially the Congo, as well as from Europe, North America, and Asia. Even when travelling from place to place, one hears music. Buses blast music from their speaker systems from the moment they pull out of the bus station and often before they depart. *Matatu* taxis, so named because a ride used to cost only three (*tatu*) shillings, compete for riders using the music they play as an attraction. Whether an old Peugeot station wagon with nine passengers squeezed in or a minivan with eighteen to twenty tightly packed passengers, these public transports have become what one source calls "the common man's disco." As buses and *matatus* traverse the countryside moving from town to town, the roads too become a battle of the bands.[1]

Trying to find a single word in an African language that encompasses all the meanings found in the English word "music" is an impossible task. There are words for drumming, words for singing, and words for playing instruments fashioned from animal horns or brass, but no overarching word includes all these things, unless one considers the imported word *musika*. The Swahili word *ngoma* comes close. When used at the coast its meaning includes the music, song, and dance that characterized traditional festivals, but outside the Swahili community its use is limited to either dancing or drumming. Nevertheless, music plays an important part in the social, ritual and ceremonial life of African people everywhere, and this certainly holds true throughout Kenya. It is used by the Swahili to symbolize leadership, among the Kamba to accompany dancing, among the Kipsigis to enhance the meaning of ritual performance, and among the northern herders to celebrate a favorite ox. And in all these societies it remains a form of entertainment.

TRADITIONAL MUSIC

Critics have often lamented that popular music sounds the death knell of traditional music and culture, but as many times as this is stated, it has yet to happen. People take this view in part because contemporary music has some-times condemned the backwardness of tribal society or sung of the exploita-tion and oppression found on small rural farms or in commercial agriculture. At the same time it both glorifies life in the city over the farm and criticizes the degradation of life found in the cities and towns. Yet traditional music is celebratory and tied directly to important social values, community obser-vances, and religious rituals and celebrations. The preparation of fields for planting is often accompanied by song. Weddings almost always include song and dance, as do festivities that include processions. This is also true for reli-gious occasions, including Islamic ones when the Prophet is praised and Allah's blessings sought.

President Kenyatta did a great deal to preserve traditional music and dance. Soon after independence and until his death in 1978, he actively encouraged communities to organize groups among themselves and send delegates to visit him to sing and dance the traditional music of their area or ethnic group. As he once commented, "Dance is the mirror of our life and beyond. It reflects our links to the spirits. Our dialogue with the past and our present feelings and thoughts."[2] In urban areas this led to the formation of ethnically based groups that kept the traditional music and dance of their home area alive. Political rallies and other public events and holiday celebrations provided important performance opportunities in venues that included sports stadi-ums and social halls. Another important venue was the airport tarmac, where such dance groups were always present when the president left the country and were there to welcome him home upon his return. These occasions also received national television coverage on what at the time was Kenya's only television station, the Voice of Kenya, when during the Kenyatta years this coming and going always led the reading of the national news.

All children learn to sing songs. They learn songs for harvesting, for herding cattle, and for entertainment, as well as songs to accompany specific ceremonies. More recently, music and dance have also been actively promoted in schools. High schools hold concerts in school halls, including Christmas carol sings, and participate in "Battle of the Choirs" competitions. The annual "Kenyan Music Festival" competition takes place each August between the country's secondary schools. The competition begins at the regional level, where students compete in a variety of performance categories, ranging from drama and poetry readings to traditional and Western dance. The top three competitors in each area then move on to the nationals at the Kenyatta Conference Center in Nairobi, where winners are named in each division, and the top schools are awarded prizes.

Similarly, the adaptation of traditional music and drumming by Roman Catholic churches has helped preserve important musical traditions in many regions. Vatican II declared that because people in certain missionary lands had their own music and instruments, it was acceptable for these to have a continuing role in the religious and social life of the community. Protestant churches were not so forthcoming, especially the African Inland Church, which continued instead to promote Western-based musical traditions sung in African languages. In the past decade or so, however, both Protestant denominations such as the Baptists, and Roman Catholics can be found with praise bands and singers who use music to create an upbeat atmosphere in the sanctuary before the pastor or priest introduce a service of praying and sermonizing. With electric guitars, drum sets with bass, snares, and cymbals, and well-amplified singers, these ensembles perform and lead the congregants in song. Much of this music uses the same interplay of guitars and singers that has long characterized the popular music of Africa, thus providing a welcoming atmosphere especially for the teenage and young adults the churches are trying to reach.

For the Kamba people Vatican II signaled that the drumming for which they are well known would continue to have a place in their lives. The Kamba play their drums both singly and in four- to six-drum sets, using them to accompany important religious festivals and dances. This association with dance is so close that a dance is often named after the type of drum used to accompany it. Kamba work groups, *mwethya,* can also be accompanied by dance. In fact, the word *kwina* means both "to sing" and "to dance."

Drums are any group of instruments covered by a skin or membrane that is beaten or played with the hand or a wooden stick. The variation and complexity of sound that a drum can produce is almost endless. Tightening the

skin or loosening it, stretching it across a frame that is wider or thinner, narrower or longer, that is open or closed at the other end, or made of different
materials all create different sounds. Add to this mix the variations in playing
patterns that the drummer uses, and the sounds elicited are even more
numerous.

Whether played alone or with other instruments, individually or in combination with other drums, drums are used to accompany dance, songs, ceremonies, and rituals, to announce the presence of a leader, a triumphant
victory, or hunt, and to enhance a religious celebration, be it Christian,
Islamic, or traditional. Drums in Kenya are typically made of wood that has
been hollowed with an adze, a kind of ax or hatchet with the iron blade
secured perpendicular to the handle. The thickness of the drum wall is also
directly related to the desired sound to be achieved. Smaller drumheads are
most often made from goatskin, with a more durable cow skin used on the
larger ones. The skin of a snake or lizard can also be used but is less common.

Among wind instruments, side-blown horns are known across Africa from
Liberia to Kenya. They can be fashioned from the horns of animals, such as
the greater kudu, oryx, and antelope, and have also been made from ivory,
copper, and brass. Among the most famous are two magnificent hundred-
year-old ivory traditional horns, *siwa,* from Pate, a small island off the coast
north of Lamu. Made from an elephant tusk, one is more than six feet long
(2.15 meters), and the other is about two-and-a-half feet long (.75 meters).
Undecorated but for cross-hatching lines at the mouthpiece, these horns were
part of the regalia and symbols of the aristocratic Swahili leaders who ruled
the coast in the seventeenth and eighteenth centuries. Historically, they were
used to announce weddings, circumcisions, and religious events.

Many of the herding peoples including the Maasai, the Samburu, and the
Rendille also use the curved horns of the greater kudu and the straight ones
of the oryx. Like the horns of the coast, these are side-blown instruments with
a mouthpiece cut into the outer wall of the horn's narrower end. When
blown, these bugle-like horns announce ceremonies and rituals or summon
communities at particular times to return the stock from a nearby herding
camp or for defense. Historically, there was a clear separation between horns
used in times of war and those used to announce a communal activity. Today,
horns are more commonly used in combination with other instruments for
the musical accompaniment of dances.

Other wind instruments include horns made from large gourds and flutes
or pipes made from bamboo and various grasses. The Luo of southwestern
Kenya (who also have one of the widest range of musical instruments) use
large gourds to fabricate a five- to six-foot-long horn called a *bu.* A large gourd
is also used as the sound box of stringed instruments, including the eight-

A lyre-like stringed instrument popular in traditional music from western Kenya.

stringed, lyre-like *nyatiti*. These instruments were traditionally strummed and plucked by orator-singers, professional musicians making their living singing the praises of community leaders who, along with others enjoying the performance, then paid the singers for their music. A singer would also wear a bell on his ankle. By stamping his foot, he could thus rhythmically enhance the overall effect of the music. Today, some performers, such as recording star Ayub Ogada, have combined the playing of the *nyatiti* with both traditional and modern instruments to create a sound that has crossed over into the realm of popular music. Another stringed instrument played by the Luo is the one-stringed *orutu,* a kind of fiddle played with a single string bow. Unlike the *nyatiti,* which still employs a large gourd for resonance, the *orutu* is today being made using a tin can, although the strings of each are still made of animal tendons.

The peoples of Kenya are as rich in the diversity of their singing styles as they are in their stringed and wind instruments. Songs are required on numerous occasions from weddings to lion hunts; often the name of the song is the same as the dance that goes with it. Singing is typically done in unison or in octaves, with the women and children singing one octave above the men. A common form of song is made up of a soloist and chorus, whereby the soloist sings a particular phrase and everyone else responds. Across the country there are of course regional differences.

At the coast, for example, the songs associated with weddings are called *taarab,* a word derived from the Arabic verb *tariba,* to be related to music. However, the lyrics, which are often accompanied by an unfretted lute (*'ud*) and a drum, are derived directly from classical Swahili poetry, with fixed numbers of syllables per line. This music is especially linked to the festive celebrations that follow a wedding ceremony. "Maneno Tisiya" is one such example, taken from a traditional wedding song:

> I've got nine arguments, if you like agree with me. If you object, tell me.
> First, think, don't worry, don't make fun of me. Neither for a price or a fee.
> Second, it would be luck if you accepted me, if I had not uttered a word which
>   would have angered you.
> And third, I thought to explain my desolation which has made me to become so
>   intimate.
> Fourth, I have no alternative but you, I don't want another.
> Offer me a taste, so that I may be calm.[3]

Among the Kamba traditional vocal music accompanies nearly every form of activity. There are songs just for the pleasure of listening, songs for dancing, and motivating songs that accompany work parties. When groups of Kamba construct a house, dig a well, grind grain, or work in their fields, for example, they sing songs called *mwethya.* Songs for pleasure range from those that record historical events to those that comment on, joke about, or protest current events, including local and national politics.

Of the three types of Kamba songs, the *mwethya* songs are among the most interesting. The work the group is doing determines who the singers are. For example, women and girls sing songs associated with threshing and grinding grain because they are the ones who perform these tasks. Men dig wells and so they are the performers of songs associated with this task, and so on.

Mwethya groups typically include a song leader, who may in fact compose a new song while singing, and a song-group, the chorus, to whom the song leader teaches the song. Since independence, such songs have moved beyond accompanying traditional everyday tasks to become a mainstay of self-help groups working on larger community projects, such as building a school or health clinic. These projects often bring together similar groups from neighboring villages who all work together.

The lyrics of *mwethya* songs cover a broad range of subject matters. They can praise a particular individual, such as a local chief or the member of parliament, or comment on local moral issues including greed, jealousy, love, and marriage. The songs have also taken on a life outside the work-group environment and are today sung at parades on national holidays or as part of the *harambee* self-help movement (see chapter 7, "Social Customs and Lifestyle"). On these occasions the *mwethya* song-groups, now accompanied by dancing rather than work, provide the major entertainment. In a *harambee* meeting the singing is used to raise money for new community projects. When the praises of an individual or special guest are sung or "called" (*kwitita*), there is the clear expectation that the person will respond by making a significant donation to the project. Such occasions also allow singers not only to praise a just-completed or newly begun project but to critique their current living conditions and set the stage for future projects. For example one scholar recorded the following:

Yes, Kenya's problems are many.
Kenya's problems are many.
How many are they?
Pasture for cattle,
Dams,
And rich men's shops.
Who was calling?
It was Mr. Kenyatta.
We even went there to visit him,
To greet Chief Mr. Kenyatta.[4]

The song recalls the visit of the song-group to President Kenyatta's home but also recounts the serious problems in their particular area: the need for pasture for their livestock, a dam to provide water, and the high cost of goods in the local shops. Through such singing the feelings of the community were expressed to national politicians, and a type of grassroots lobbying took place. Any contributions those present wished to make toward more self-help projects in the Kamba area were received gratefully. Also in the song can be seen the solo lines of the song leader and responses of the song-group chorus.

Praise Songs and Herders

Among herding societies that keep livestock as the basis of their existence, cattle are considered beautiful. Over the course of growing up, the men of these groups often come to identify a favorite color of ox or steer as their own, and a certain animal as a favorite. This is somewhat like combining a favorite pet with identifying a particular color or number as one's lucky color or number. As a favorite animal grows old, it is more common for it to be given away to a friend, to reinforce a particularly close relationship, than to slaughter it. Such an ox is usually given a special name, often associated with its color, and a song of praise will be composed about it. This name often carries over to the owner and is adopted by close age-mates as a kind of nickname. In the past a warrior might go into battle singing his "ox song."

One group of people who typify singers of ox songs are the Dasenech, who live along the north and northeastern shores of Lake Turkana in Kenya's extreme north. Similar songs are found among the neighboring Turkana and Pokot, both of whom have historical ties to the Dasenech. In fact, the Dasenech actually sing their ox songs in a language they claim is Turkana, even though most Turkana cannot understand it. The Dasenech say that every ox song must include three pieces of information: the color of the ox, which as already noted is also the name by which its owner will be known, the name of the cow that gave birth to the ox, and the man who gave the ox to its owner. Additionally, an ox song may also include words or phrases that describe particular features of the animal, such as the tilt of its head, the shape of its horns, the places the ox has been, or the name of the man who gave the owner the bell the ox wears. An owner always sings his ox song as a solo, called *foriti*, but others may shout out phrases, called *yer*, during its singing. *Yer* are described as "phrases without meaning that sound nice."

To give a detailed example, one ox song is about a blue gray ox named Lakoribuis, whose horns are bent tight over its ears (horns are purposely shaped by an animal's owner to meet his sense of what is attractive). The song also recalls the name of the owner's father, Lahur, who gave him the bell the ox wears, and the location on the eastern shore of Lake Turkana, called Alia Bay, where Lahur killed two men during a time of fighting with the colonial authorities.

Ox songs are but one variety among the many vocal compositions that herders sing. Some are about daily life; others provide entertainment during the drudgery and uneventful days that dominate the herding of animals away from the settlement. Some are about hunting wild animals. Although hunting in Kenya is now illegal, songs that recall the hunting of lions, warthogs, elephants, buffalo, and even hippos and crocodiles are remembered fondly.

With their accompanying dances, they provide great entertainment. Still others sung by children are merely comments about animals they regularly see while out collecting water or herding. These include a song about the white-and-black bird with a white head that can be seen sitting on the back of a donkey, or a topi, a type of large antelope with a white underbelly but that is otherwise red and brown. Another song is about a female goat that is red with hair on its chin, possibly a song used to practice pieces that may later take shape as an ox song when the child becomes a warrior.

Other songs may be satirical and used to remind the community of the moral code. Such songs may be about greed or ill-tempered individuals. Others are soft and calming lullabies sung to babies and small children. Still others are sung by children, who in any society can be among the cruelest to each other, teasing, insulting, and sometimes abusing. Warriors, for example, will sometimes sing songs about the younger boys who assist them in herding the animals. Later, the same boys may continue to sing one of these songs if for whatever reason it seems to catch on. In another example from the Dasenech, a particular song commented on a certain child with an especially prominent and round buttocks, the chorus of which suggested it was like a Landrover. In another song the solo child asks the question over and over, "What is smelling?" and the chorus responds with a variety of answers, from that of wood fire or rotten meat to a number that do not need to be spelled out.

Typically, religious songs ask for blessings on the community. These songs often take a call-and-response pattern with a senior elder speaking or calling a specific line followed by all those assembled responding in unison as a chorus. The following is one such an example. Note that a call is sometimes stated more than once for emphasis.

Solo call:	The river of my father is good.
Response:	It is good.
Solo call:	The river of my grandfather [ancestors] is good.
Response:	It is good.
Solo call:	It rains; it is good.
Response:	It is good.
Solo call:	Let my animals sleep in a good place.
Response:	Let them sleep.
Solo call:	All those bad things let God refuse.
Response:	Let God refuse.
Solo call:	All those bad things let God refuse.
Response:	Let God refuse.
Solo call:	All those bad things let God refuse.
Response:	Let God refuse.
Solo call:	Let me bring good things here.

Response:	Bring it.
Solo call:	Let me bring good things here.
Response:	Bring it.
Solo call:	The place of my father is good.
Response:	It is good.

The songs of girls and boys, each of whom have their own songs, often take on this same pattern of call and response. One girl sings of the shade found along the river, and the chorus of her friends responds, "The river with the shade." Another may focus on the long white ostrich feathers worn by young men to the dance. Such songs are always danced. And although most herding societies do not have musical instruments as such, they still can create a complex rhythmic sound. The singing that accompanies dancing usually includes the clapping of hands and the pounding of the feet on the ground. Additionally, unmarried girls wear heavy metal anklets, *mule,* that ride up and down on the leg to produce a most amazing clanking when the dancers rhythmically jump in place. In another girl's song the soloist sings of the bracelets and anklets the girls wear, and the chorus responds, "Blacksmiths made our anklets" and "Our anklets have become many."[5]

POPULAR AND WORLD MUSIC

Music in Kenya is even more diverse than the many ethnic groups found in the country. This is in large measure a result of the way Kenyans have taken and adapted the music from other parts of the continent and beyond. There are many groups representing particular locales producing records and recording cassettes and compact discs, but the more popular sounds are those drawn from the Congo and Tanzania. Concern about this invasion actually led the Kenyan government in the early 1980s to set a 75 percent Kenyan content standard for music being played on the radio. The standard was noticeably unsuccessful and soon disappeared.[6]

Fadhili William, who was called Fundi Gita, the "guitar craftsman," was one of Kenya's earliest popular musicians. Performing with two friends, Nashil Pilchen from the Congo and Peter Tsotso from Zambia, together they produced in the mid-1960s what was probably one of Kenya's first unique popular musical sounds. Theirs was a blend of music, including *kwela* from southern Africa, Latin American *rumba* rhythms made popular in the Congo, and traditional instrumental sounds from the Luo and Luhya from western Kenya. Later this swinging "new" sound came to be identified with artists such as Samba Mapangalal and bands like The Equator Boys and the Original Kilimambogo Stars. The original bands began with a couple of guitars, with or without drums, and were known for their heavy rhythm lines and flashy guitar licks. Today's bands can include electric and acoustic guitars, bass guitar, double bass, piano, Hammond organ, horn sections, saxophones, flutes, and assorted percussion.

Still, Kenya has never really developed what might be called an enduring, nationally recognized "Kenyan sound." Instead, it has a number of regionally recognized sounds in which the rhythm is distinctive and the voice unmistakable. The language in which a song's lyric is sung is clearly a factor. Nevertheless, even when sung in Swahili, a particular song can be quickly identified with a specific region by the style of playing and singing, the instruments used, and the rhythms and harmonies generated. One common feature in the music's structure, which typically begins and ends with singing, is the instrumental bridge called *katikati*. Literally "the middle," *katikati* often has a more catchy, upbeat sound with a series of musical bars played first by the guitars, then trumpets and saxophones, and finally returning to the horns or guitars. The purpose of this often-lengthy interlude is to give those dancing an opportunity to show off.

Each of Kenya's major ethnic groups has its own recording stars. It is not uncommon for people to identify certain bands as Kamba, Kikuyu, Luhya, Luo, or Swahili. Women singers, for example, are especially linked with Kamba and Kikuyu bands, while the style known as *benga,* with its pulsating guitar beat, although once the contemporary dance music of Kenya, is closely identified with Luo bands of the 1970s and 1980s. Its origins, however, are even earlier, beginning when some Luo musicians began to adapt the traditional sounds of their stringed instruments for the acoustic guitar and, later, electric instruments. With its strong guitar melodies and harmonies backed by a hard-driving bass line drawn from traditional drum rhythms, *benga* spread quickly across Kenya to bands from other ethnic areas and then to other parts of Africa as well.

Today, Kenyan popular music is sung in any and all languages. Sometimes one language will dominate, such as Luo, but it is often interspersed with phrases and words in Swahili or English. In other cases large ethnic groups such as the Kikuyu and Kamba, two of Kenya's most populous groups, have a built-in audience and thus have no need to sing in other languages. Other Kenyan singers and bands have cut across these regional lines and achieved something close to a national following simply because people like the musical sound even if they cannot understand all the lyrics. Still others gained national popularity singing in Swahili, which most everyone can understand and which in Kenya is understood to be essentially ethnically neutral. One of the most famous early popular singers to achieve this type of success was Joseph Kamaru. Kamaru, a Kikuyu, often used the words of his songs to criticize policies of the Kenyatta government. This sometimes led to his music being banned, which in practical terms is nearly impossible given the ease with which cassettes are copied and shared. One of his most famous songs commemorated the death of J. M. Kariuki, a prominent member of parliament and ex-Mau Mau detainee who was assassinated in 1975. An outspoken MP who fearlessly voiced the concerns of ordinary people, Kariuki had an immense following. Kamaru's song was part of the hue and cry from Nairobi and the central highlands following Kariuki's murder. In 1993 Kamaru became a Christian and today is a leader of the thriving gospel music genre. Another popular singer was the late Professor Naaman of Nine Stars, who sang in Swahili but always from a chair due to his large, rotund size.

Songs sung in Swahili have always had a strong national appeal. In part this is because Swahili is the country's national language and the one taught in all the schools. These songs have also attracted an audience because Swahili is the language in which the classical poetry of the coast has been written, and as poetry it has made an easy transition to song. As arguably the oldest regional music, the contemporary form of this coastal sound is popular throughout the country. Known at the coast as *taarab* music, it is derived from the wedding music of the Swahili people. Today, *taarab* songs address issues of real life. These can be songs of love and happiness or about grieving for someone who has died. They can be reassuring, reminding listeners that they are not the only ones who have to confront troubling situations or that everything in life is part of God's plan for them. And some are humorous to cheer people up.

Among the musicians who have made the transition from the local coastal scene to the national one are Zein l'Abdin and Zuhura Swahleh. Zein, who is an 'ud player, first came to prominence in 1960 regularly playing and singing at local weddings. In his popular identity, even though his music was based on the melodies and rhythms of *ngoma*, a traditional music of Lamu Island, his bands came to include bass guitar, violins, accordion, electronic keyboards, and full percussion section. Today, he is returning to what some think of as a more pure sound of only 'ud and drum. Zuhara made her singing start in Nairobi. Interestingly, for someone now known as a *taarab* singer, she initially sang pop songs with artists such as Fadhili Williams and Nashil Pichen. However, as her reputation as a singer of *taarab* spread, and invitations to sing at the coast grew in number, she moved there to establish her own identity and sound. Here, she was introduced to and in 1970 recorded with Zein and his group, the Zein Musical Party. Today, with the resurgence of *taarab* as a form of popular music on the contemporary scene, both Zein and Zuhara, as well as new and younger stars, are enjoying renewed popularity.

It was once said that if there is a true national sound in Kenya it is ironically not a Kenyan sound at all, but one adopted from the Congo. This

Congo sound has endured since the 1960s and early 1970s played by Congo musicians resident in Kenya and by many Kenyan bands as well. In many ways it is this that has provided a unifying sound cutting across Kenya's multi-ethnic communities. The Congo bands also bring to Kenya the most innovative and up-to-date sounds of their homeland. They sing in both Lingala, a national language of the Congo, and in Swahili, which is widely spoken especially in the eastern parts of Congo. Although critics have commented that few guitarists of this sound play anything more than three notes—and there is an element of truth to this—it is nevertheless a sound and rhythm that cannot be listened to for very long without moving your feet. Not surprisingly, this sound has managed to capture and enthrall much of the African continent for almost forty years.

One of the earliest to play this role was the late Franco Luambo Makiadi, a singer whose music was widely known and appreciated across Kenya. Today, one of the most popular Congolese in Kenya and elsewhere is Koffi Olomide, a singer-showman who is supported in his stage appearances by a score of dancers and musicians. When he was arrested in the Congo for strutting to the music in a way thought to be disrespectful of Laurent Kabila, the late former Congolese president, the outcry was as strong from outside the Congo as inside, including from Kenya. The music many young Kenyans listen and dance to remains that from the Congo, one of that country's most glorious exports.

In the 1970s, however, a new and exciting group of homegrown recording stars emerged in Kenyan popular music. Among the most prominent of this new generation of musicians was Them Mushrooms. A band made up of guitars, horns, and drums with lead and back-up singers, Them Mushrooms quickly came to national prominence as a reggae band. Later, under their leader Teddy Kalanda Harrison, they became identified with what became the hottest rhythm for dancing, *ndombolo* style (another Congo import). They have recorded more than fifteen albums. One of their earliest songs, "Jambo Bwana," with its "no problem" refrain (*hakuna matata*) is both a trademark song of the group and a kind of reference point for Kenya's entry into the international pop music market, as reggae stars such as Boney M and others have recorded it.

Today, Them Mushrooms' place is being taken by the next generation of bands, literally in one case, with two of Kalanda's sons and a nephew making up the core of musicians in Big Matata. With Teddy Kalanda producing their albums in his Nairobi studio, they are one of Kenya's hottest new bands. Like so many Kenyan groups, Big Matata began by playing to well-heeled European tourists at the hotels on the Indian Ocean coast. From the pop music of Africa and the West, they moved on to reggae, first backing Kenyan and now international reggae stars. Another hot contemporary band is Gidi Gidi Maji Maji, whose style of music blends African song and contemporary rap performed in Luo, the band members' first language. As others before them, these groups hope to move on to international venues, perhaps playing clubs in the Persian Gulf where East African bands with their driving guitars, keyboards, percussion, and saxophones are very popular.

Arguably the most significant development in Kenyan pop music has been the rise of female vocalists. The singer Mercy Myra, who has opened for a number of international stars appearing in Kenya, and Suzanne Kibukosya, the lead singer of the group Zannaziki, are examples of this phenomenon. Singing in English and Swahili, Lingala, and local Kenyan languages, these performers who relate the trials of love and marriage, money and survival, and friendship and lies are attracting major followings. Finding this popularity was not any easier in Kenya than it is for those elsewhere in the world trying to make it in music. Mercy Myra, for example, like so many Kenyan bands, has tried numerous styles. In 1994 while a college student studying computer science, she began to sing gospel. She then moved on to rhythm and blues and toured Kenya with a couple of groups. Finally, in 1997 a local producer heard her and recorded her first album of what she has called "contemporary with an ethnic fuse."[7] It includes cuts from rhythm and blues and Lingala songs to reggae and rap. Another singer is Nazizi, a female rapper who fronts the band Necessary Noize. Their music blends hip-hop and reggae with rhythm and blues. Other female singers are making a name in gospel. Although singers like Mercy Myra left this musical form, it is one that is increasing in popularity not just in Kenya but all across the continent. One of Kenya's best-known gospel singers, Esther Wahome, has recently had her song "Furahia" included in a new compilation album in "The Best of Afropop" series. The popular Christian revivals that have made Kenya one of their main international stops have also given added popularity to gospel singing.

Where are such sounds to be heard? All the major towns have clubs where musicians perform regularly. Still, the most lucrative venues remain those in the large hotels in Nairobi and on the coast. Gaining in popularity are the outdoor spaces associated with popular restaurants such as the Carnivore on the outskirts of Nairobi. There are also numerous recording studios in Nairobi, Mombasa, and even smaller towns such as Kericho that are anxious to meet the demand in changing tastes and encourage the rise of popular new stars. Unfortunately, the vast majority of Kenyans cannot afford to see their favorite musicians or up-and-coming stars perform or to buy their cassettes or compact discs. Nairobi does not even have a record store. There is only one store that sells cassettes and compact discs, but this is but a small part of their operation, which is dominated by the sale of radios, televisions, and other electronic appliances. Seldom does it even have multiple copies of any one album. Still, for individuals who want to listen to a favorite song or band, the cassette and more recently the compact disc are the preferred media. With the local labels producing and selling at what are essentially U.S. and European prices, it is the cassette-duplicating shops of cities and towns that are doing the greatest business by simply ignoring the intellectual property rights of the musicians and bands and pirating their work.

Artists and studios also lay part of the blame on local radio stations. They assert that the industry's biggest problem today is the lack of support given them by the radio stations who do far too little to promote Kenyan music. Some suggest that often as much as 75 percent or more of the play time goes to foreign bands, with Congolese music still dominant. Such accusations and the resulting controversies are frequently grist for the local papers and magazines, but there are signs that things are changing. Growing competition among an increasing number of FM radio stations finds more programmers willing to play local music. Similarly, the ever-increasing sophistication of the studios in Kenya, many with full digital production facilities, means that to stay in business, these producers and their investors will have to sort out the problem of distribution and sales that have until now plagued them. The irony of all this is that some of Kenya's best-known artists have entered and become known in the "world music" scene. As a result, it is sometimes even possible to find a separate section labeled "Kenya" within the "International" category in some of the largest record retailers in Canada, Germany, the United States, and the United Kingdom. Here are found the works of various regional musicians and bands popular in Kenya in the 1990s. One can find the *taarab* music of Zuhura Swaleh and Zein l'Abdin, or Ayub Ogada singing and playing the traditional stringed *nyatiti* of western Kenya. The opportunities given to these artists have frequently been born of concert tours to Europe that then lead to studio time in Berlin, Brussels, London, Paris, and more recently, New York. There are even two U.S.-based bands, Jabali Afrika and Milele Africa, giving live concerts across the United States. Jabali Afrika's concerts are performances in the fullest sense of the word, complete with their unique fusion of African instrumental music and rhythms accompanying their singing and choreographed dancing.[8]

TRADITIONAL DANCE

All that is associated with dance in the West—pleasure, entertainment, spectacle, eroticism—is also found in African dance. One distinct difference is that while African dance brings entertainment and pleasure to those participating and watching, on many occasions it also plays a vital role in religious ritual and ceremony. Another difference is that there are really no traditional African dances in which male and female partners hold each other. There are occasions when a girl may choose a male dance partner, but generally speaking, dances are strictly single-gender affairs.

For example, Swahili custom does not allow women or girls to participate in public dances, but men can and do, often to entertain guests. In the *kirumbizi* dance, the men, each armed with a walking stick or staff, form a large circle. As the music plays, they enter the circle in pairs and with threatening gestures perform a kind of mock combat. Swahili women and girls also dance, but they do so in the private interior courtyards of a home. Here, for example, they gather before a wedding ceremony to dance *chakacha.* This is exclusively a female time, and the songs and dance are filled with sexual overtones. During the dance they suggestively roll their hips in unison, while ululating and singing lyrics about the events that will follow the wedding ceremony. Today, the catchy *chakacha* rhythm has spread into music popular throughout much of Kenya, although the tendency remains even in the local clubs for the accompanying dance to be done primarily by women, with an emphasis on movements using their hips.

The warriors of the Maasai and Samburu are surely Kenya's best-known traditional dancers. Tourists visit Samburu and Maasai settlements (*manyattas*) at the entrances to game parks, and dance performances are sponsored at hotel and game park lodges and at certain Rift Valley farms. The greatest notoriety of this dancing tradition is probably as a result of scenes in two recent films, *The Ghost and the Darkness* and *The Air Up There.* In the first film, Michael Douglas leads a group of Maasai warriors on a lion hunt, prior to which they engage in some pseudoritual of dancing and drinking cow's blood. The dancing is authentic, but the ceremony of drinking blood is not. Nor did Maasai warriors ever need a white man, *muzungu,* to lead them on a lion hunt. In *The Air Up There,* a film about basketball that has an African backdrop, the Samburu are given the fictitious tribal name Winnabi, but the warriors' dancing is real enough. Also increasing recognition, *Sports Illustrated* (February 1998) in a recent swimsuit issue posed their models among Maasai warriors, and the Maasai are prominent in the recent photograph collections found in the coffee-table books *African Ceremonies* and *Passages.*[9]

One of the reasons people take note of Maasai and Samburu dancing is undoubtedly because of the easily recognizable performances of their warriors. With their rigid, upright bodies draped in picturesque red cloth, they leap high in the air without the benefit of a running jump. These on-the-spot leaps send their long, braided, red ochre-colored hair flying into the air. Further, each performance has a genuine sense of authenticity, even when spears are replaced by long sticks, and rubber sandals or athletic running shoes are worn instead of the hide sandals of days gone by.

The Maasai and Samburu distinguish distinct types of dances. The Samburu use the word "play" (*enkiguran*) as a metaphor for both dancing and singing. At the center of nearly all their dances are the warriors. Some include unmarried girls, but never married women, who have their own dances, and of course the elders see themselves as being above such frivolity. Characteristically, a dance can go on for an hour or more. In the first phase, *nbarinkoi*, the warriors form a tight group that moves as a single body. With their heads thrust forward, they move rhythmically around the dance clearing, bending their knees and rising off their heels. At the same time one warrior sings of the group's achievements, while the others chant in a wordless chorus. As if on cue, one warrior will then break away from the group, hopping forward and leaping into the air, accompanied by enthusiastic shouts of encouragement from the others. This entire sequence is repeated over and over with different warriors taking center stage. The audible exhaling sound made by members of the group, a kind of grunting sound, lends immeasurably to their aggressive, warlike appearance. Not surprisingly, one scholar, a specialist on the Samburu and Maasai, calls these "dances of display."[10]

Sometimes during these dances, young children, both male and female, can be seen around the edges mimicking the movement of the dancers. It is, however, in a second stage of these dances that girls will form a parallel group to face the warriors and dance rhythmically in a similar fashion. These dances provide a legitimate time for flirting between the warriors, who are typically in their twenties, and the unmarried girls, who are barely in their teens but who will later become their wives. At this time each group will tease the other in sung riddles. For example, the translation of one that the warriors sing is "Who is descended from monkeys?" the answer to which is Europeans because they are hairy all over. Similarly, the girls may taunt the warriors, singing, "If you're a coward who goes out to steal stock and returns with nothing, then you may as well go and sing from settlement to settlement [do not return for the girls will not be impressed]."[11] It is also during these dances that a warrior may break away from the group, not to leap high in the air as in the earlier dance, but to go up to one of the girls, flick his hair over her face, and then return to his group.

Finally, in the third stage, the warriors return to performing dances and songs they learned in their youth. These dances are performed in a circle, with the dancers holding hands and jumping in time to the songs. In these dances the girls are often mixed in among the warriors, providing ample opportunity for couples to arrange to meet later when fewer people are around. This sort of dancing is usually expected on the afternoon of weddings, but they can also

In traditional dancing it is rare for male and female partners to hold each other; dances are generally gendered affairs. However, when being on the dance floor together is permitted, each group uses the occasion to check out the other gender and do a little flirting.

occur spontaneously. The spontaneous dances tend to take place in the evening and are much more informal affairs.

When the various stages of such a warrior's dance are considered in total, one can clearly see how the transitions correspond with the social structure. The first stage, with the warriors' distinctive thrusting of their heads coupled with grunting and vertical leaping into the air, is a competitive all-male affair. As they move toward the second stage, when they will be joined by the girls, their leaping begins to occur in unison to reflect their unity. After all, they are all members of the same age-set, and it is through acting with each other in concert that they have established their reputation as warriors. Now, acting as a single group, they face off with the group of girls that enters the dance space. Each group, following the heavy rhythm of the dance, thrusts their heads toward the other group. Only in the third stage do the two groups break up into the more informal hand-in-hand dancing that immediately precedes the end of the performance.[12]

Weddings are also the occasion for women's dances. Because weddings among the Samburu take place in the *manyatta* of the bride, many people must travel to the settlement site of the ceremony. Women do so in small groups. As they process to the wedding they perform *ntorosi,* a women's song beseeching God for strong, healthy children. Although sometimes the verses contain obscene references aimed at the elders, this does not detract from the song's main theme, which is an issue they take most seriously. By taking advantage of the wedding ceremony as an occasion to sing together, they are also able to stake out a space that is the exclusive domain of women. Here they are freed from the drudgery of their everyday chores and the demands of their husbands, and while being serious, they can also have great fun directing remarks and jibes at the men in their lives. Parallel dances associated with female fertility also occur among Maasai women.[13]

One other traditional warrior's dance worthy of note is that performed by Maasai warriors following a successful lion hunt (*a-gilaki*). Lions are the most dangerous and notorious of the predators of herders' livestock. Therefore killing them, which is both a dangerous and an arduous task, has always been a principal symbol of a warrior's duty to protect the herds. Not all hunts are successful. When they are not, the warriors quietly return to the village, and no celebration takes place. However, when they are successful, they mark their return with the lion dance. With specific movements and great enthusiasm, they dance in celebration from village to village. The women of the village acknowledge the warrior-hero who successfully speared the lion by hanging beads around his neck. If the lion was a male, girls will later make the lion's mane into a particular headdress for the warrior to wear as a continuing mark of his triumph.[14] Today there are few occasions to perform this dance for its original purpose since all hunting in Kenya is illegal. However, the dance remains a part of the repertoire performed for tourists.

Like songs, dances change over time, and a song and dance once linked to particular occasions of work today may be almost exclusively performed as entertainment. Other ethnic groups have dances that seem to have always been performed as entertainment. Among the Luhya, the *sukuti* is such a dance and is named after the particular drum—the mother drum, or *isikut*—that features in the musical ensemble that plays it. Its popularity was such that it was performed for weddings, funerals, and other important community events. Interestingly, the community would extend an invitation to the music ensemble, not the dancers, who would then arrive for the performance with the dancers. Possibly, the musicians were invited because they were typically much older and therefore better known than the more youthful dancers. As the musicians and dancers traveled to the event, it was common for individuals and groups form neighboring communities to join them, resulting in an ever-larger audience. Two special features of such performance groups can be noted. First, performers were never paid with money for their efforts. Rather, they would be invited for food and drink by those who extended the original invitation to them. Second, these dance occasions were opportunities for the dancers to travel with a legitimate purpose to neighboring villages and clans that contained potential marriage partners. With admiration for their dancing prowess often came recognition by individuals of the opposite sex.[15]

Another Luhya dance, the *amabeka,* is not named for the instruments that accompany it but for the body movement that features in the dance. In the *amabeka* the shoulders, *mabeka,* are shaken vigorously in quick movements by dancers whose arms reach outward, but whose feet often stay in one place. Typically a women's dance, the *amabeka* is performed in villages as a public entertainment on occasions that range from beer parties to funerals.

In the past the Luo have performed a particular dance, *tero buru,* reserved exclusively for funerals. The greater the status of the departed individual the more extravagant was the funeral ritual and the size of the crowd gathered to mourn. Drums summoned the mourners to the homestead of the deceased; they would then symbolically take the dust of the individual (who in fact would have already been buried just outside the entrance to the main house of the homestead) to the forest or river that marked the clan's boundary. Once at their destination, those assembled would put on red ochre and add leaves and twigs to their clothing. Music and dancing would then occur until everyone was satisfied that their obligations to the deceased had been met. On the way back to the homestead the pace of the music and dancing would speed up, building to a frenzy of activity as those assembled chased Death and other unseen enemies from the area.

The Mijikenda wedding dance, *sengenya,* is also noteworthy because of the particular function it serves of introducing a new bride to the immediate and extended members of her new family. Moving in a procession of both males and females, with the bride at the front and the groom at the back, the entourage dances from house to house. Along the way the bride meets the relatives of the groom—his grandmothers, aunts, uncles, cousins, brothers-in-law. Only at the actual wedding ceremony does the bride take up her place at the side of the groom. The entire procession also includes instrumentalists, typically various drummers, flute, and double-reed players.

Still other dances have dual purposes, which can include entertainment but also a much more serious purpose. Such a dance is the *mwazindika,* performed at the coast both for entertainment and to appease the spirits to bring about healing. With dancing, drumming, and singing that can go on for hours, dancers become "possessed" to better communicate with a spirit. Possession by an evil spirit, *pepo,* is signaled by the dancer's uncontrolled shaking, which is visible to everyone present. In this as in many such dances, the rhythm of the dance and the speed of the steps are dictated by the drum or drum ensembles that accompany it.

All of these dances could still be found being performed to some extent in the more traditional communities of rural Kenya in the 1990s. Some dances that have traditionally been an essential part of ritual or ceremonial performance in local homesteads and rural communities are also being preserved in the urban area in organized companies such as the National Theatre Dance Troupe and at the Bomas of Kenya. They are also being preserved among ethnically based dance groups that have taken to dancing as a form of recreation. Groups of Kamba, Kikuyu, Luhya, and Luo, among others, in Nairobi and at the coast are keeping these traditions alive. When accompanied by local music and traditional dress, the entertainment value is indeed great.

POPULAR DANCE

There are many contemporary dance styles popular among young Kenyans. The *ndombolo* style, with its popular rhythm, remains one that many young people, as well as adults, continue to enjoy. Dancing to a particular rhythm is often associated with general "rules" of movement that are to be followed, but there is also an overriding sense of personal style. Some dance styles involve moving as little as possible—just enough to show off the clothes the dancer is wearing, which one would not want to get damp with sweat. For *ndombolo* the positioning of the feet, the body, and the hands is critically important if one is to be recognized as a good *ndombolo* dancer. In the original dance, which began in the streets of Kinshasa, the dancers' legs were spread far apart and bent at the knees, with their backsides prominently stuck in the air. Banned as obscene in the Cameroon and elsewhere, the dance has been somewhat tempered as *ndombolo* has spread well beyond Africa. Kenyans, other East Africans, and Congolese in the United States and Europe all know it and can be found dancing to it at weekend parties.

Both private parties and commercial venues are places where people go to dance and listen to music. In Nairobi, as in most urban cities and towns, there are clubs and discotheques. The Florida 2000, the Klubhouse, and the Carnivore are among today's most popular Nairobi clubs, providing both recorded music and live entertainment by popular bands from outside Kenya and from within. The New Florida and quieter Toyz Disco are venues for live music in Mombasa, as is the Mnarani in Malindi. One of the newer trends is the spread of these venues to the smaller cities of the country, such as Kisumu with the Octopus and the Kimwa Grand. Clubs cater to a wide range of clientele and in some cases those looking for more than music. Popular at one end of the social scale in lower-income areas of Nairobi are the more "hardcore" clubs that feature reggae music—hardcore because they are rough and a fight or thrown bottle is reputed to be not all that unusual. For those under eighteen the party scene is much as it might be anywhere else in the world among teenagers, except that they tend to be daytime affairs, with Sunday afternoons the most popular. Trendy teenagers wearing what they call their best "labels" head off in groups to clubs that host what are popularly called "jam sessions." Slipping away after church, when these clubs open, or citing a purported Bible study session as an excuse to disappear after Sunday lunch, the teenagers listen to tunes and dance the afternoon away. These jam sessions give new bands an opportunity to be heard, but there is a downside, socially. To pay the bands the clubs need to make money, and that money is often made from selling beer and other commercially produced alcohol-laden drinks, with names that include "Ice" on the label. That drinking and smoking are problems among Kenya's urban youth only serves to illustrate that such social ills are a part of youth culture everywhere and not a feature exclusive to a developed or developing country. Interviews with Kenyan youth also confirm that they are like youth everywhere, including their knowing how to say "no" to these hazards.[16]

The rich tradition of music and dance remains popular in Kenya alongside its contemporary counterpart, with which it is increasingly blended. For example, the fast-paced acrobatic dance style of the Kamba, accompanied by the rhythmic use of drums and whistles, has also found popularity and expression in urban dance clubs. Another dance style in which pairs of men and women move close to each other in a sexually suggestive fashion is said to be so provocative that it "could provoke a saint." Whatever form this new dance synthesis takes, it still has roots that are in the rural areas and is often based on songs whose melodies come from the same place. The artists who create these new blends are immensely proud of the rich cultural heritage that has produced the music and dance that are their specialty. Today, bands openly speak of striving to find what they hope will become an identifiable Kenyan sound. A recent Gidi Gidi Maji Maji album titled *Ismaarwa*, which is Swahili for "It's ours," pays homage to both the tradition that has shaped them (and other contemporary Kenyan musicians) and their desire to create from these cultural roots their own international, urban music sound.

NOTES

1. Simon Broughton, Mark Ellingham, and Richard Trillo, eds., *World Music: The Rough Guide—Africa, Europe, and the Middle East,* vol. 1 (London: Rough Guides, 1999), 509.

2. Quoted in Esther A. Dagan, ed., *The Spirit's Dance in Africa: Evolution, Transformation and Continuity in Sub-Sahara* (Westmount, Quebec: Galerie Amrad African Arts Publications, 1997), 5.

3. Quoted in *Zain l'Abdin, The Swahili Song Book* (Todtnauberg, Germany: Dizim Records, 1999).

4. Quoted in Martin J. D. Hill, *The Harambee Movement in Kenya Self-Help, Development, and Education among the Kamba of Kitui District* (London: Althone Press, 1991), 204.

5. Sobania, unpublished music recordings from the Dasenech with field notes, 1976.

6. Information in this section is mainly derived from articles in the Kenyan press, personal interviews and observations made in Kenya in 2001, and *World Music,* 509–22.

7. Moira Tremaine, "Making Waves, the Kenyan Music Scene," *Msafiri Magazine* 37 (2001): 63.

8. Kenya's independently produced magazine *Phat!* is a superb source of information on the contemporary African music scene. Published quarterly and distributed in eastern and southern Africa and Europe, it is available on the Web at www.Phatafrica.com.

9. Carol Beckwith and Angela Fisher, *African Ceremonies,* 2 vols. (New York: Abrams, 2000), and *Passages* (New York: Abrams, 2000).

10. See Paul Spencer, "Dance as Antithesis in the Samburu Discourse," in *Society and the Dance,* ed. Paul Spencer (Cambridge, England: Cambridge University Press, 1985), 145.

11. Ibid., 148–49.

12. Ibid., 140–64.

13. Ibid., 157–61.

14. See Paul Spencer, *The Maasai of Matapato* (Bloomington: Indiana University Press, 1988), 116.

15. See Charles Nyakiti, "Seven Traditional Dances of Selected Groups in Kenya," in *The Spirit's Dance in Africa: Evolution, Transformation and Continuity in Sub-Sahara,* ed. Esther A. Dagan (Westmount, Quebec: Galerie Amrad African Arts Publications, 1997), 290–91.

16. Articles in Kenya newspapers such as the "Young Nation" section of the *Sunday Nation* cover this and similar topics related to contemporary youth. See, for example, "Big Clash: To Jam or Not to Jam?" in the 16 December 2001 issue of *Sunday Nation*. Available at www.nationaudio.com/News/DailyNation/Supplement/ynation/16122001/index.htm.

Glossary

Aakuj   The Turkana name for God.

adze   A hand tool similar to an ax with the blade mounted at a right angle to the handle; used to cut or carve wood.

aesthetic   Concerning appreciation for beauty and good taste.

age-grade   A set of social categories that individuals pass through during their lifetime, for example, warrior and elder, each of which confers a particular status as well as specific responsibilities and privileges.

age-mates   Those men who are initiated together and become members of the same **age-set**.

age-set   A group of individuals, usually male, who have been initiated together as **age-mates**, take an identifying group name, and move during their lives through various **age-grades**.

a-gilaki   A traditional dance performed by Maasai warriors following a successful lion hunt.

ahoi   Kikuyu term for those forced off their own land by colonial policy, who then had to live as **squatters** on land now owned by white settlers.

AIC   African Inland Church, the strong and vigorous Kenyan-led church movement, that grew out of AIM.

AIM   African Inland Mission, a nondenominational Protestant evangelical mission group that seeks to establish self-sufficient communities; they first began work in Kenya in 1901.

amabeka   A Luhya dance whose name is derived from the vigorous shaking of the shoulders that is a familiar feature of the dance.

aregi   "Those who refused"—a Kikuyu name for individuals who refused to sign a loyalty oath, when in 1928, the **AIM** church imposed a particular doctrinal interpretation on who was a Christian.

Asis   A name for the Supreme Being recognized by the Kipsigis people.

athomi   The term given to the first Kikuyu catechists.

ayaana   An Oromo concept that explains the world in which the Oromo live, including the relationship among the creator, the created, and time.

benga   A pulsating musical style associated with Luo bands of the 1960s and 1970s that was once the rage of contemporary Kenyan dance music.

Boyot ab Tumba   The Kipsigis principal religious leaders.

bridewealth   Goods given by the groom's family to the bride's family in exchange for their loss of a daughter.

bu   A large five- to six-foot-long horn made in part from a large gourd and used as a musical instrument by the Luo.

bui-bui   A black covering worn by some devout Muslim women when outdoors, often so that only the eyes are uncovered.

catechist   In the Christian faith, one who gives religious instruction.

chang'aa   An illegally brewed alcoholic beverage made from maize or sorghum.

chebsogeyot   Female healers among the Kipsigis.

clan   A group of people related through blood who trace their relationship to a founding ancestor but do not know the exact links to that ancestor.

colonial   Relating to the process by which one country maintains or extends its control over another country or territory.

cowrie shell   A small mollusk shell found in the Indian Ocean. When polished it is used widely as an ornament and, in the past, as money.

dhow   A variety of ships with triangular (lanteen) sails used on the Indian Ocean and along its shores for carrying cargo and fishing.

divination   A ritual that uses secret knowledge to contact the supernatural in order to foretell the future or determine the source of illness or other trouble.

diviner   A person who practices **divination.**

dowry   The property that a woman brings to her marriage that is normally intended for her use.

elder   A senior male who with other senior males generally has influence and authority over most matters related to his community.

enculturation   The process by which people learn their culture.

Engai   The name for God used by the Maasai, Kikuyu, and others.

evangelist   One who goes from place to place preaching the Christian Gospel.

exogamy   The custom of marrying from outside one's family, clan, or other social group.

fora   Mobile herding camps, used by pastoralists to keep their animals closer to better grazing, without moving their settlements.

gada   The **age-grade** system followed by the Borana people.

gerontocracy   An egalitarian system of government in which **elders** rule by consensus.

gourd   The hard-skinned fruit of a plant that when dried is used to make an array of containers that are used for a multitude of purposes including storage, serving and drinking; also sometimes called a calabash.

hajj   The pilgrimage to Mecca; one of the five pillars of Islam. Hajji is a title of respect used for a person who had made the hajj.

harambee   A self-help movement popularized by Kenya's first president, Jomo Kenyatta, the translation of which is "let's pull together."

henna   A mixture of plant-based substances, but especially *Lawsonia inermis L.*, that when made into a darkish red paste is used to create decorative patterns on women's hands and feet.

hut tax   A tax imposed by the colonial authorities on every dwelling, which since it had to be paid in cash, forced men, especially, to seek wage employment to earn the money needed to pay it.

Id al-Fitr   In Islam, the celebration that marks the first day after the fasting month of **Ramadan.**

imam   In Islam, a leader of prayers.

imuron Aakuj   Turkana diviners, literally "diviners of God," who are understood to be the earthly representatives of **Aakuj**.

imuron ekitoit   Traditional healers among the Turkana who are less important diviners than the **imuron Aakuj**.

jumba   Stately multistory houses built of coral and limestone in the towns on the Swahili coast.

KANU   Kenya African National Union, the ruling party from 1960 to 2002.

Kanzu   The Swahili version of a plain white, long-sleeved, ankle-length gown worn worldwide by Muslim men.

kasha la mfuto   Sometimes called a scribe's box because it can be used to store writing implements, the Swahili also use it to hold money and jewelry.

katikati   An instrumental bridge between singing found in much of Kenya's popular music.

KAU   Up until the state of emergency was declared in 1952 during **Mau Mau**, the Kenya African Union was a militant political association for African expressions of nationalism. Kenyatta became its president in 1947.

khanga   A brightly colored rectangular piece of cotton cloth that comes in matched pairs with a Swahili proverb printed on it; can be tied and used as a skirt, blouse or head scarf.

kiama   The name for the council of elders found among the Meru people.

kigango   A memorial plank (pl. *vigango*) erected by the Mijikenda to honor their dead.

kikoi   A plain or patterned piece of cotton worn around the waist, especially at the coast.

kiondo   Among the Kikuyu, a popular woven bag used for carrying shopping and other goods.

kipande   During the colonial period, an identity document that every African was required to carry as the government tried to control African labor and population movement.

kirore   The small percentage of **AIM** parishioners who stayed within the **AIM** church during the controversy over the church's insistance that Christians sign a doctrinal loyalty oath (see **aregi**).

kiti cha enzi   This "chair of power," made of ebony wood with an elaborately caned back and seat, and often decorated with inlaid ivory and bone, is used by the

Swahili during formal gatherings of **elders** and to present a bride and groom at their wedding.

kofia   An embroidered cotton skullcap, usually white, that identifies the wearer as a Muslim.

kohl   Finely powdered antimony sulfide used to accentuate the eyes and blacken eyebrows.

kokwotinwekor   Village-level mediators or judges among the Kipsigis.

KPU   A socialist opposition party formed in 1966 when Oginga Odinga broke away from the ruling KANU party led by President Kenyatta.

kraal   An enclosure used for domestic animals, used with reference to herding peoples in Africa (related to "corral").

laibon   Maasai prophets and ritual specialists.

liminality   A transition state between two well-defined categories such that this time is neither one nor the other as in an initiation ritual, for example, when an initiate is no longer a child but not yet a warrior or man.

Local Native Councils (LNSs)   Organized in 1925 among different ethnic groups and chaired by the local district commissioner as part of a colonial policy of divide and rule.

luba   A generation in Oromo society consisting of five eight-year **gada** groups (a total of forty years), and through which political power successively passes.

manyatta   The settlement in which Maasai and Samburu live; frequently used more generally as a name for the settlement of any herding group.

marufad   A Swahili stand used for holding a Qur'an, similar to ones found throughout the Islamic world.

matatu   Taxi vans used by the public to travel between cities and towns; the name is derived from the original fare of three, *tatu,* shillings.

Maulidi   This festival celebrates the Prophet Muhammed's birthday.

Mau Mau   An organized, violent, armed resistance in the mid-1950s, when especially the Kikuyu and other Mount Kenya peoples fought against the British colonial authorities and the white settler population.

mbao   A count-and-capture strategy game more generally known in Africa by the generic term *mancala.*

methali   Swahili proverbs that are also found on **khanga** cloth.

mihrab   The place in a mosque, generally a niche, that indicates the direction of Mecca, to which Muslims turn when they pray.

monotheism   The belief that there is only one God.

monsoon   A large-scale wind system that blows seasonally in opposite directions across the Indian Ocean.

mutai   Samburu word for the period of time in the late nineteenth century when rinderpest killed thousands of cattle and disastrously disrupted their lives.

muzungu   A term commonly used to depict an outsider who is not Kenyan.

mwazindika   A dance performed at the coast both as entertainment and to appease the spirits and bring about healing.

mwethya   A type of song sung among the Kamba people when communally constructing a house, digging a well, or working in the field.

myth of genesis   A sacred narrative about the origins of an ethnic group or subgroup, believed to be true by the people who tell it.

naabo   A small stone enclosure found at the center of a Rendille settlement, where a fire is kept permanently burning and the elders regularly meet to manage the settlement's affairs.

ndombolo   Imported from the Congo, this is often considered the hottest rhythm for popular dancing.

ngoma   A Swahili word whose meaning includes the music, song, and dance that characterize traditional festivals.

ntorosi   A traditional wedding dance and song performed by Samburu women, calling on God for strong, healthy children.

nyama choma   Roasted meat that is a favorite food of those who can afford it, available at roadside food kiosks and in local restaurants.

nyatiti   Among the Luo, an eight-stringed lyre-like instrument traditionally strummed or plucked by an orator-singer.

nyayo   Literally translated as "footsteps," it was used by President Daniel arap Moi to characterize the way his presidency would follow that of President Jomo Kenyatta, whom he succeeded in 1975.

ochre   Usually an earthy red pigment from iron ore and clay used to decorate the body and hair.

orutu   Among the Luo, a one-stringed instrument played with a bow.

panga   A long-blade knife, also known as a machete, used for clearing fields, harvesting crops, and cutting wood.

pastoralism   A subsistence pattern associated with the herding of animals.

patina   The surface appearance of an object that has grown beautiful with age.

patrilineal   Descended through the male line.

polygamy   A pattern of marriage in which a person of either sex may have more than one mate at the same time.

polygyny   A pattern of polygamous marriage in which the husband may have two or more wives at the same time.

polytheism   The worship of several gods.

pombe   Locally brewed beer or other alcoholic drink.

posho   Maize meal, the staple foodstuff of many Kenyan families that can be made into a thin porridge, *ujii*, for breakfast, or into a heavy mixture, *ugali*, for the main meal.

qaalluu   Ritual specialists of the Borana people.

Qur'an   The sacred text of Islam revealed to the Prophet Muhammad.

Ramadan   In Islam, a month long fast, the timing of which is fixed according to the Islamic calendar.

rites of passage   Rituals held at particular points in people's lives that mark a change from one social status to another.

ruoth   A title held by the leading elders who make up the council of elders among the Luo people. The title indicates strength of character and is attained by demonstrated leadership.

Sabaki   The common ancestral language of Swahili and other languages spoken by neighboring peoples; together they are all part of the Bantu language family.

scarification   Decorative scars purposefully made on the body in specific cultural patterns to indicate social status or particular achievements.

sengenya   A Mejikenda wedding dance that serves to introduce the new bride to the immediate and extended members of her new family.

shamba   The farms on which the majority of Kenyans live and work.

Shari'a   Islamic law held by Muslims to be a complete legal system derived directly from the **Qur'an** and the traditions and sayings of the Prophet Muhammad.

siwa   Traditional horns from the coast used to announce weddings and other ritual celebrations; the most famous are made of ivory.

squatter   A person who settles on land without a right or title to it.

subsistence   The adaptation followed by a human culture that converts an environment's resources into what it needs to sustain its way of life; for example, **pastoralism.**

sufuria   Aluminum cooking pans that come in a wide variety of sizes from small to very large.

taarab   Songs from the Swahili coast associated with weddings, the lyrics of which come from classical Swahili poetry.

'ud   An unfretted lute or guitar.

ugambe   The quality among Meru elders of being able to speak well and offer wise counsel.

uhuru   Independence.

ululation   A loud protracted sound made with the tongue; used by women to demonstrate either excitement or mourning at public events.

ushairi   Poetry written in the Swahili language.

utendi   A traditional form of writing Swahili poetry of four lines of eight syllables in each line, in which the last sound of the first three lines in each stanza end in the same sound, and the fourth rhymes with the fourth lines of all the other stanzas in the poem.

vigango   Memorial planks erected by the Mijikenda people to honor their dead.

voodoo   An African-based religion practiced in the Caribbean and especially Haiti in which spirits are said to possess people.

Waq   The name for God among many Eastern Cushitic-speaking peoples of East Africa.

zikakasi   A small cylindrical box used by the Swahili to hold spices or cosmetics.

Bibliographic Essay

Much has been written about Kenya and still is being written, in large part because the government of Kenya has so generously allowed researchers and scholars to continue to work there. As a result, in addition to what is published in the United States and Europe, in certain subject areas there is considerable material published in Kenya, where many older titles continue to be reprinted. And while some of these publications can be found in university libraries, some of it is less accessible and even out of print. Nevertheless, because it is important bibliographically, it has been included in this essay. In addition, because so much of Kenya's earliest history and immediate postindependence history is tied to the surrounding region, some of the sources listed here also include material on Uganda and Tanzania.

GENERAL

Discussions of the customs and traditions of Kenya's many and varied peoples are found throughout many of the volumes listed in the sections that follow. A few, however, specifically address this topic. For the Swahili, see Mtoro bin Mwinyi Bakari, *The Customs of the Swahili People: The Desturi za Waswahili of Mtoro bin Mwinyi Bakari and Other Swahili Persons* (Berkeley: University of California Press, 1981); John Middleton, *The World of the Swahili: An African Mercantile Civilization* (New Haven, Connecticut: Yale University Press, 1992); and A. I. Salim, *Swahili Speaking-Peoples of Kenya's Coast 1895–1965* (Nairobi: East African Publishing House, 1973). Two that examine Kikuyu traditions are Jomo Kenyatta, *Facing Mount Kenya: The Tribal Life of the Kikuyu* (London: Secker and Warburg, 1953) and E. N.

Mugo, *Kikuyu People: A Brief Outline of Their Customs and Traditions* (Nairobi: Kenya Literature Bureau, 1982).

Introduction

There are a number of volumes that introduce the general history of Kenya, including B. A. Ogot, *Zamani: A Survey of East African History* (Nairobi: Longman, 1973); W. R. Ochieng', *A History of Kenya* (London: Macmillan, 1985); W. R. Ochieng', ed., *A Modern History of Kenya 1895–1980* (Nairobi: Evans Brothers, 1989); Thomas Spear, *Kenya's Past: An Introduction to Historical Method in Africa* (Harlow, U.K.: Longman, 1981); and Gideon S. Were and Derek A. Wilson, *East Africa through a Thousand Years,* 3rd ed. (New York: African Publishing, 1984). Norman N. Miller, *Kenya: The Quest for Prosperity* (Boulder, Colorado: Westview Press, 1984) is an interesting but dated political history.

On the early history of the Indian Ocean rim, see Philip Snow, *The Star Raft: China's Encounter with Africa* (London: Weidenfeld and Nicolson, 1988) and Samuel M. Wilson, *The Emperor's Giraffe and Other Stories of Cultures in Contact* (Boulder, Colorado: Westview Press, 1999). Other histories of the coast include Derek Nurse and Thomas Spear, *The Swahili: Reconstructing the History and Language of an African Society, 800–1500* (Philadelphia: University of Pennsylvania, 1985), and Justin Willis, *Mombasa, the Swahili, and the Making of the Mijikenda* (Oxford: Clarendon Press, 1993). Other sources on the precolonial history of Kenya's various peoples include reconstructions from historical texts. Particularly useful are John Berntsen, "Maasai Age-Sets and Prophetic Leadership, 1850–1912," *Africa* 49 (1979): 134–46; Jeffrey A. Fadiman's *An Oral History of Tribal Warfare: The Meru of Mt. Kenya* (Athens: Ohio University Press, 1982) and *When We Began There Were Witchmen: An Oral History from Mount Kenya* (Berkeley: University of California Press, 1993); Godfrey Muriuki, *A History of the Kikuyu, 1500–1900* (Nairobi: Oxford University Press, 1974); Neal Sobania, "Feasts, Famines, and Friends: Nineteenth Century Exchange and Ethnicity in the Eastern Lake Turkana Region," in *Herders, Warriors and Traders: Pastoralism in Africa,* eds. John G. Gallaty and Pierre Bonte (Boulder, Colorado: Westview Press, 1991), 118–42; and Richard Waller, "Ecology, Migration, and Expansion in East Africa," *African Affairs* 84 (1985): 347–70.

Overlapping the precolonial and colonial period are studies such as Charles Ambler, *Kenyan Communities in the Age of Imperialism: The Central Region in the Late Nineteenth Century* (New Haven, Connecticut: Yale University Press, 1988); Cynthia Brantley, *The Giriama and Colonial Resistance in Kenya,*

1800–1920 (Berkeley: University of California Press, 1981); Bill Bravman, *Making Ethnic Ways: Communities and Their Transformations in Taita, Kenya 1800–1950* (Portsmouth, New Hampshire: Heinemann, 1998); Neal Sobania, "Fishermen Herders: Subsistence, Survival, and Cultural Change in Northern Kenya," *Journal of African History* 29 (1988): 41–56; John Lamphear, *The Scattering Time: Turkana Responses to Colonial Rule* (Oxford: Clarendon Press, 1992); Robert L. Tignor, *The Colonial Transformation of Kenya: The Kamba, Kikuyu, and Maasai from 1900–1939* (Princeton, New Jersey: Princeton University Press, 1976); and Richard Waller, "The Maasai and the British, 1895–1905: The Origins of an Alliance," *Journal of African History* 17 (1976): 529–53. Also see the various essays in Douglas Johnson and David Anderson, eds., *The Ecology of Survival: Case Studies from Northeast African History* (London: Lester Crook; Boulder, Colorado: Westview Press, 1988) and Thomas Spear and Richard Waller, eds., *Being Maasai: Ethnicity and Identity in East Africa* (London: James Currey; Athens: Ohio University Press, 1993).

Histories of the early travelers or "explorers" to Kenya are found in Monty Brown, *Where Giants Trod* (London: Quiller, 1989) and Pascal James Imperato, *Quest for the Jade Sea: Colonial Competition around an East African Lake* (Boulder, Colorado: Westview Press, 1998). The role of labor during the colonial period is the subject of Frederick Cooper, *On the African Waterfront: Urban Disorder and the Transformation of Work in Colonial Mombasa* (New Haven, Connecticut: Yale University Press, 1987). An approach to the history of the twentieth century through the life of Jomo Kenyatta is found in Jeremy Murray-Brown, *Kenyatta* (New York: E. P. Dutton, 1973). Also useful for this period is Tom Mboya, *The Challenge of Nationhood* (London: Heinemann, 1970) and Oginga Odinga, *Not Yet Uhuru: An Autobiography* (New York: Hill and Wang, 1967). Particularly useful on Mau Mau are recent publications such as John Lonsdale, "Mau Maus of the Mind: Making Mau Mau and Remaking Kenya," *Journal of African History* 31 (1990): 393–421; Greet Kershaw, *Mau Mau from Below* (London: James Currey; Athens: Ohio University Press, 1997); and Marshall S. Clough, *Mau Mau Memoirs: History, Memory, and Politics* (Boulder, Colorado: Lynne Reinner, 1998). Also useful are the reprinted articles in Jim Bailey, ed., *Kenya: The National Epic From the Pages of Drum Magazine* (Nairobi: Kenway, 1993) that trace Kenya's history, highlighting many of the issues and personalities that were part of it. Contemporary issues regarding Africa are addressed in volumes such as Peter Schwab, *Africa: A Continent Self-Destructs* (New York: Palgrave, 2001). Kenya is addressed directly in Africa Watch, *Divide and Rule: State Sponsored Ethnic Violence in Kenya* (New York: Human Rights Watch, 1993). Better is Angelique Haugerud, *The Culture and Politics of Modern Kenya* (Cambridge: University of Cambridge Press, 1995), and Joel D. Barkan, "The Rise and Fall of a Governance Realm in Kenya" in *Governance and Politics in Africa,* eds. Goran Hyden and Michael Bratton (Boulder: Lynne Rienner, 1992), 167–92. Some useful websites provide good introductory *material* on Kenya. These include: www.sas. upenn.edu/African_Studies/Country_Specific/Kenya.htm, www.sul.stanford. edu/depts/ssrg/africa/kenya.html, www.embassyofkenya.com, and www. museums.or.ke/. Three other sites worth consulting are a Norwegian on line site www.africaindex.africainfo.no/africaindexl/countries/kenya.html, one on human rights, www.derechos.org/human-rights/afr/kenya-l.html, and the CIA's factbook on Kenya at www.odci.gov/cia/publications/Factbook/ke/html.

RELIGION AND WORLDVIEW

A number of volumes are helpful in understanding the place of religion in Kenyan society. These include David M. Anderson and Douglas H. Johnson, eds., *Revealing Prophets: Prophecy in Eastern African History* (London: James Currey; Athens: Ohio University Press, 1995) and Thomas Spear and Isaria N. Kimambo, eds., *East African Expressions of Christianity* (Oxford: James Currey; Athens: Ohio University Press, 1999) and Cynthia Hoehler-Fatton, *Women of Fire and Spirit: History, Faith, and Gender in Roho Religion in Western Kenya* (New York and Oxford: Oxford University Press, 1996). A discussion of the place of religion in the Mau Mau rebellion can be found in the "Religion and Rebellion" chapter of Benjamin S. Ray, *African Religions: Symbol, Ritual, and Community* (Englewood Cliffs, New Jersey: Prentice-Hall, 1976), 165–71. Good starting points on Islam include Rene Bravmann, *African Islam* (Washington, D.C.: Smithsonian Institution Press, 1983); Azim Nanji, "Beginnings and Encounters: Islam in East African Contexts," in *Religion in Africa,* eds. Thomas D. Blakely, Walter E. A. van Beck, and Dennis L. Thomson (London: James Currey; Portsmouth, New Hampshire: Heinemann 1994), 46–55; and books and articles on the Swahili identified under this bibliography's "General" section. On the place of Asian religions in Kenya, see Cynthia Salvadori, *Through Open Doors: A View of Asian Cultures in Kenya,* rev. ed. (Nairobi: Kenway Publications, 1989).

LITERATURE, FILM, AND MEDIA

The origins of the Swahili are the subject of Derek Nurse and Thomas Spear, *The Swahili: Reconstructing the History and Language of an African Society, 800–1500* (Philadelphia: University of Pennsylvania, 1985). Particularly useful on constructing history from oral traditions is Thomas Spear's "Tales of Origin: the Traditional Record," (chapter 3) in his *Kenya's Past: An Introduction to Historical Method in Africa* (Harlow, U.K.: Longman, 1981). William David Cohen and E.S. Atieno Odhiambo's, *Siaya: The Historical Anthropology of an African Landscape* (London: James Currey; Athens: Ohio University Press: 1989), on the Luo, provides a thorough and thought-provoking analysis of how the origin traditions of an ethnic community can be used to write history. Equally influential on the issue of constructing history from oral material is John Lonsdale, "When Did the Gusii (Or Any Other Group) Become a 'Tribe,'" *Kenya Historical Review* 5, no. 1 (1977): 123–33.

The history of the earliest writing in Kenya is found in Jan Knappert, *Four Centuries of Swahili Verse: A Literary History and Anthology* (London: Heinemann Educational Books, 1979). Anthologies of oral literature, folktales, and proverbs are widely available, although mostly in Kenya, where many continue to be reprinted. They include G. Barra, *1000 Kikuyu Proverbs*, 2nd ed. (Nairobi: Kenya Literature Bureau, 1960); Naomi Kipury, *Oral Literature of the Maasai* (Nairobi: East African Educational Publishers, 1983); and B. Onyango-Ogutu and A.A. Roscoe, *Keep My Words: Luo Oral Literature* (Nairobi: East African Publishing House, 1974). A good collection of Kamba folktales is found in Vincent Muli wa Kituku, *East African Folktales* (Little Rock: August House, 1997).

The writings of many Kenyan authors are widely available. Novels and plays by Ngugi wa Thiong'o include *Grain of Wheat* (Portsmouth, New Hampshire: Heinemann, 1968); *Matigari* (Portsmouth, New Hampshire: Heinemann, 1987); *Petals of Blood* (Portsmouth, New Hampshire: Heinemann, 1977); *The River Between* (Portsmouth, New Hampshire: Heinemann, 1965); *Weep Not Child* (Portsmouth, New Hampshire: Heinemann, 1964); and Nugu wa Thiong'o and Ngugi wa Mirii, *I Will Marry When I Want* (Portsmouth, New Hampshire: Heinemann, 1982). Works by Meja Mwangi include *Carcase for Hounds* (Portsmouth, New Hampshire: Heinemann, 1974); *Going Down River Road* (Portsmouth, New Hampshire: Heinemann, 1976); and *Kill Me Quick* (Portsmouth, New Hampshire: Heinemann, 1973). Popular authors published in Kenya include Mwangi Gicheru, *The Ivory Merchant* (Nairobi: Spear Books, 1976); Francis Imbuga, *Aminata* (East African Educational Publishers, 1988); Marjorie Oludhe Macgoye, *The Present Moment* (Nairobi: Heinemann, 1987); Charles Mangua, *Son of Woman* (Nairobi: Spear Books, 1988); Stella Kahari Njuguna, *Labyrinth* (Nairobi: 2000); and Margaret A. Ogola, *The River and the Source* (Nairobi: Focus Books, 1994). A new set of books from Nairobi publisher Sesa Sema, whose subjects are traditional literature or cultural and national heroes, target younger readers and include Ezekiel Alembi, *Elijah Masinde: Rebel with a Cause* (Nairobi: Sesa Sema, 2000), Kitula King'ei, *Mwana Kupona, Poetess from Lamu* (Nairobi: Sesa Sema, 2000), and Elizabeth Mugi-Ndua, *Mekatilli Was Menza: Woman Warrior* (Nairobi: Sesa Sema, 2000).

Discussions of film in Africa with a focus on Kenya can be found in Manthia Diawara, *African Cinema: Politics and Culture* (Bloomington: Indiana University Press, 1992) and Kenneth M. Cameron, *Africa on Film: Beyond Black and White* (New York: Continuum, 1994). Films about Kenya and their place in popular culture are the subject of Sidney Kasfir, "Slam-Dunking and the Last Noble Savage," *Visual Anthropology* 15, no. 3 and 4 (2002), 369–85. Some Kenya newspapers can be accessed on line. The best of these sites is that of *The Daily Nation* at www.nationaudio.com/News/DailyNation/Today. Also, the site www.africanews.org/kenya/ compiles news from regional news sources.

ART, ARCHITECTURE, AND HOUSING

The art of Kenya has not received the same wide attention as has that of West Africa. Nevertheless, material on Kenya can be found in a number of publications that consider aspects of African art. For example, household objects made from clay, wood, grass, and gourds are detailed in Roy Sieber, *African Furniture and Household Objects* (Bloomington: Indiana University Press, 1980). Also valuable is Philip Ravenhill, *The Art of the Personal Object* (Washington, D.C.: Smithsonian Institution Press, 1991). Headrests are the focus of William J. Dewey's *Sleeping Beauties* (Los Angeles: Fowler Museum of Cultural History, 1993). Similar objects specific to parts of Kenya are discussed in two older articles: Harold K. Schneider, "The Interpretation of Pakot Visual Art," *Man* 56 (August 1956) and Herbert Cole, "Vital Arts of Northern Kenya," *African Arts* 7, no. 2 (1974): 12–23. Issues of personal adornment and identity are addressed in Donna Klump and Corinne Kratz, "Aesthetics, Expertise, and Ethnicity: Okiek and Maasai Perspectives on Personal Adornment," in *Being Maasai: Ethnicity and Identity in East Africa*, ed. Thomas Spear and Richard Waller (London: James Curry; Athens: Ohio University Press, 1993), 195–221; see also Donna K. Pido, "Art among the Maasai of Kenya," *Art and Life in Africa* (Iowa City: University of Iowa, 1998), CD-ROM.

A number of recent publications that seriously consider contemporary art in Africa and contain sections on Kenya art and artists include Sidney Littlefield Kasfir, *Contemporary African Art* (London: Thames and Hudson, 1999); Andre Magnin and Jacques Soulillou, *Contemporary Art of Africa* (New York:

Abrams, 1996); and the exhibition catalog *Seven Stories about Modern Art in Africa* (Paris: Flammarion, 1995). Bernd Kleine-Gunk, *Kunst aus Kenya: Sieben Ostafriaknische Maler* (Essen: Graphium Press, 1994) is well illustrated with the work of prominent contemporary Kenyan artists, and a children's book, *Nyalgondho wuod-Ombare and the Lost Woman from Lake Victoria* (Nairobi: Jacaranda Designs, 1991) was illustrated by Joel Oswaggo. Also valuable is Marla C. Berns, *Ceramic Gestures, New Vessels by Magdalen Odundo* (Santa Barbara: University of California, 1995). Two particularly useful Web sites on contemporary art are "Contemporary Art of Kenya" at http://prometheus.cc.emory.edu/PS/1999/Ernst-Luseno/web_pages/index.htm and http://www.gallerywatatu.com.

Excellent material on the art and architecture of the Swahili coast is found in the publications of Usam Ghaidan, including, "Swahili Art of Lamu," *African Arts* 5, no. 1 (1971): 54–57, 84, "Swahili Plasterwork," *African Arts* 6, no. 2 (1973): 46–49, and *Lamu A Study of the Swahili Town* (Nairobi: Kenya Literature Bureau, 1992), as well as Jean Lucas Brown, "Miji Kenda Grave and Memorial Sculptures," *African Arts* 13, no. 4 (1980): 36–39, 88; James de Vere Allen, "The Kiti Cha Enzi and Other Swahili Chairs," *African Arts* 22, no. 3 (1989): 54–63, 88; and Nancy Ingram Nooter, "Zanzibar Doors," *African Arts* 17, no. 4 (August 1984): 34–39, 96. Anders C. Grum, "Rendille Habitation," in *African Nomadic Architecture: Space, Place, and Gender,* ed. Labelle Prussin (Washington, D.C.: Smithsonian Institution Press, 1995), 150–69, discusses the housing inhabited by the herding peoples of Kenya's north.

Cuisine and Traditional Dress

A number of recipes from Kenya and East Africa, "translated" so they can be prepared in the West, can be found at www.geocities.com/congocook book/. Other Kenyan and East African recipes can be found in *The Kenya Cookery Book and Household Guide* (1928; reprint, Nairobi: Heinemann Educational Books, 1970) and Tami Hultman, ed., *The Africa News Cookbook* (Durham: Africa News Service, 1985). Information on traditional dress can be found in Neal Sobania, *"The Khanga," Faces* 14, no. 4 (1997): 18–21, as well as on the Web site www.kikoy.com. Aspects of traditional dress are found in the paintings created in the middle of the twentieth century by and recorded in Joy Adamson, *The Peoples of Kenya* (New York: Harcourt, Brace, 1967). Recently, a number of "coffee-table" books that beautifully illustrate aspects of traditional dress and adornment have proven especially popular. Unfortunately, their exclusive emphasis on "disappearing Africa" and "warrior peoples," without any hint of modern, contemporary Africa, reinforces and supports the many stereotypes of Africa that already abound. They need to be considered carefully when thinking about contemporary Kenya. These include the various photographic books and *National Geographic* articles by Carol Beckwith and Angela Fisher, such as *African Ceremonies,* 2 vols. (New York: Abrams, 1999) and Carol Beckwith and Tepilit Ole Saitoti, *Maasai* (New York: Abrams, 1980). Also of this variety are Ettagale Blauer, *African Elegance* (New York: Rizzoli, 1999); Nigel Pavitt's books *Samburu* (New York: Henry Holt, 1992) and *Turkana, Nomads of the Jade Sea* (New York: Henry N. Abrams, 1997); and Yasuo Konishi, *Vanishing Africa: The Samburu of Kenya* (New York: Abbeville Press, 2003).

Gender Roles, Marriage, and Family

A number of valuable studies address the role of women in traditional societies and the issue of social change. Especially useful for the clear voices of African women speaking for themselves is Jean Davison with the women of Mutira, *Voices from Mutira: Lives of Rural Gikuyu Women* (Boulder, Colorado: Lynne Reiner, 1989) and Berida Ndambuki and Claire C. Robertson, *We Only Come Here to Struggle: Stories from Berida's Life* (Bloomington: Indiana University Press, 2000), which addresses contemporary urban life. Also focused on women are Margaret Strobel, *Muslim Women in Mombasa, 1890–1975* (New Haven, Connecticut: Yale University Press, 1979); Luise White, *The Comforts of Home: Prostitution in Colonial Nairobi* (Chicago: University of Chicago, 1990); and Cora Ann Presley, *Kikuyu Women, the Mau Mau Rebellion, and Social Change in Kenya* (Boulder, Colorado: Westview Press, 1992). Women and initiation is the subject of Corinne A. Kratz, *Affecting Performance, Meaning, Movement, and Experience in Okiek Women's Initiation* (Washington: Smithsonian Institution Press, 1994). Alice Walker and Pratibha Parmar, *Warrior Marks: Female Genital Mutilation and Sexual Blinding of Women* (New York: Harcourt Brace, 1993) is a good introduction to this topic.

Gender issues in herding societies are discussed in Naomi Kipury, "Engagement and Marriage among the Maasai," *Kenya Past and Present* 9 (1978): 38–42; Paul Spencer, *The Maasai of Matapato* (Bloomington: Indiana University Press, 1988); Jon Holtzman, "The Food of Elders, the 'Ration' of Women: Brewing, Gender, and Domestic Process among the Samburu of Northern Kenya," *American Anthropologist* 103, no. 4 (2001): 1041–58; and Belinda Straight, "Gender, Work and Change among Samburu Pastoralists in Northern Kenya," *Research in Economic Anthropology* 18 (1977): 65–92. See also the writings of Elliot Fratkin listed in the next section, "Social Customs and Lifestyle."

Social Customs and Lifestyle

Contemporary issues in Kenya are the subject of Mary Ann Watson, ed., *Modern Kenya: Social Issues and Perspectives* (Lanham, Maryland: University Press of America, 2000), as are many of the chapters in Judith Mbula Bahemuka and Joseph L. Brockington, eds., *East Africa in Transition: Communities, Cultures, and Change* (Nairobi: Action, 2001). Less has been written that focuses on the lives of children, but Lana Wong, ed., *Shootback: Photos by Kids from the Nairobi Slums* (London: Booth-Clibborn Editions, 1999) documents well what it is like living in the slums of Nairobi. Recent change in herding societies is the subject of a number of publications by Elliot Fratkin, including *Surviving Drought and Development: Ariaal Pastoralists of Northern Kenya* (Boulder, Colorado: Westview Press, 1991), "East African Pastoralism in Transition: Maasai, Boran, and Rendille Cases," *African Studies Review* 44, no. 3 (2001): 1–25, and "Two Lives for the Ariaal," *Natural History* (May 1989): 38–49.

The *harambee* movement is considered in Philip M. Mbithi, *Self-Reliance in Kenya: The Case of Harambee* (Uppsala, Sweden: Scandinavian Institute of African Studies, 1977) and Martin J. D. Hill, *The Harmbee Movement in Kenya: Self-Help, Development, and Education among the Kamba of Kitui District* (London: Althone Press, 1991). Information on the Bomas of Kenya is found at www.africaonline.co.ke/bomaskenya/rofile.html, while Kenyan sports can be followed in the on-line versions of local Kenya papers. Some sports have their own sites, including the local rugby union at www.kenyarugby.com. A detailed introduction to the history of safaris in Africa is Bartle Bull, *Safari: A Chronicle of Adventure* (London: Viking, 1988), while Theodore Roosevelt's safari is chronicled in his *African Game Trails* (New York: Schribner, 1910).

Music and Dance

There are a limited number of publications on traditional music. Useful is George Senoga-Zake, *Folk Music of Kenya* (Nairobi: Uzima Press, 1986). Those that address instruments include P.N. Kavyu, *Traditional Musical Instruments of Kenya* (Nairobi: Kenya Literature Bureau, 1991); Graham Hyslop, "Some Musical Instruments of Kenya," *African Arts* 5, no. 4 (1972): 48–55; Alan Boyd, "The Musical Instruments of Lamu," *Kenya Past and Present* 9 (1978): 3–7; and Hamo Sassoon, *The Siwas of Lamu* (Nairobi: The Lamu Society, 1975). More accessible is information on contemporary music. See for example, the section on Kenya in Simon Broughton, Mark Ellingham, and Richard Trillo, eds., *World Music: The Rough Guide—Africa,*

Europe and the Middle East, vol. 1 (London: Rough Guides, 1999), 508–22, and the following Web sites: www.Phatafrica.com for *Phat!* an independent quarterly magazine on the music of Africa and other entertainment, and www.jabaliafrika.com for this particular group.

An early article on dance at the coast is found in R. Skene, "Arab and Swahili Dances and Ceremonies," *Journal of the Royal Anthropological Society of Great Britain and Northern Ireland* 47 (1917): 413–34. Aspects of traditional dance in Kenya can be found in the section on Kenya in Esther A. Dagan, ed., *The Spirit's Dance in Africa: Evolution, Transformation, and Continuity in Sub-Sahara* (Westmount, Quebec: Galerie Amrad African Arts Publications, 1997), 278–91. On dance in traditional herding societies, see Paul Spencer, "Dance as Antithesis in the Samburu Discourse," in *Society and the Dance: The Social Anthropology of Process and Performance,* ed. Paul Spencer (Cambridge, England: Cambridge University Press, 1985), 140–64.

Index

About the Author

NEAL SOBANIA is Professor of History and Director of International Education at Hope College, Holland, Michigan. He has written widely on Kenyan and Ethiopian history and expressive culture, and photographs as historical sources.